USING STATISTICAL
METHODS IN SOCIAL
WORK PRACTICE

D1373909

Also Available from Lyceum Books, Inc.

Advisory Editor:
Thomas M. Meenaghan,
New York University

EVIDENCE-BASED PRACTICE FOR SOCIAL WORKERS:
AN INTERDISCIPLINARY APPROACH,
by Thomas O'Hare

MENTAL HEALTH IN LITERATURE,
edited by Glenn Rohrer

USING EVIDENCE IN SOCIAL WORK PRACTICE:
BEHAVIORAL PERSPECTIVES,
by Harold E. Briggs and Tina L. Rzepnicki

MODERN SOCIAL WORK THEORY: A CRITICAL INTRODUCTION, 3E,
by Malcolm Payne, foreword by Stephen C. Anderson

ENDINGS IN CLINICAL PRACTICE:
EFFECTIVE CLOSURE IN DIVERSE SETTINGS,
by Joseph Walsh

CLINICAL ASSESSMENT FOR SOCIAL WORKERS:
QUALITATIVE AND QUANTITATIVE METHODS, 2E,
edited by Catheleen Jordan and Cynthia Franklin

A PRACTICAL GUIDE TO SOCIAL SERVICE EVALUATION,
by Carl F. Brun

ADVOCACY PRACTICE FOR SOCIAL JUSTICE,
by Richard Hoefer

ETHICS IN END-OF-LIFE DECISIONS FOR SOCIAL WORK PRACTICE,
by Ellen Csikai and Elizabeth Chaitin

USING STATISTICAL METHODS IN SOCIAL WORK PRACTICE

A COMPLETE SPSS GUIDE

Soleman Hassan Abu-Bader
Howard University

LYCEUM
BOOKS, INC.

Chicago, Illinois

© Lyceum Books, Inc., 2006

Published by

LYCEUM BOOKS, INC.
5758 S. Blackstone Ave.
Chicago, Illinois 60637
773+643-1903 (Fax)
773+643-1902 (Phone)
lyceum@lyceumbooks.com
http://www.lyceumbooks.com

All rights reserved under International and Pan-American Copyright Conventions. No part of the publication may be reproduced, stored in a retrieval system, copied, or transmitted in any form or by any means without written permission from the publisher.

SPSS is a registered trademark of SPSS, Inc.
233 South Wacker Drive, 11th Floor
Chicago, Illinois 60606
www.spss.com

10 9 8 7 6 5 4 3 2

ISBN 0-925065-90-0

Library of Congress Cataloging-in-Publication Data

Abu-Bader, Soleman H., 1965–
    Using statistical methods in social work practice: a complete SPSS guide / Soleman H.
Abu-Bader.
        p. cm.
    ISBN 0-925065-90-0
    1. Social service—Statistical methods. 2. SPSS (Computer file) I. Title.
HV29.A28 2005
361'.0072'7—dc22
                                                                                2005009045

To my lifetime wife, Buthaina,
and my children, Nagham, Layanne, and Samer
with all my love and appreciation

Contents

Preface

Consider the following research questions:

1. Does the physical health of elderly people significantly affect their levels of depression?

2. Are there significant differences between the levels of anxiety of parents who have an autistic child and parents who do not have an autistic child?

3. Are there significant differences between BSW, MSW, and PhD child welfare workers with regard to their levels of burnout?

4. Do battered women who participate in stress management skills therapy significantly decrease their levels of stress after they complete the therapy?

5. Are people of color more likely to seek mental health services than White people?

6. Which set of factors best predicts self-esteem among welfare recipients: gender, race, marital status, age, education, physical health, mental health, or social support?

These are examples of the many questions that face social work researchers, administrators, and practitioners every day. The purpose of these questions is twofold: (1) to find whether a relationship exists among the variables under study, and (2) to better plan and develop a treatment therapy or intervention that helps social work clients to improve their day-to-day life.

For example, if statistical analysis shows that physical health significantly affects levels of depression among elderly people, this could help gerontological social workers to plan their treatments with elderly accordingly. Moreover, if social work practitioners were able to predict the levels of self-esteem among welfare recipients based on multiple conditions such as recipients' gender, race, marital status, or other factors, they could select and provide appropriate treatment to consumers who are predicted to be at greater risk of low self-esteem.

How do social workers statistically examine these questions? The answer lies herein. This is a book on data analysis for social work practitioners. There are already many outstanding data analysis and statistical textbooks and this book is not intended to compete with them. *Using Statistical Methods in Social Work Practice: A Complete SPSS Guide* is a comprehensive book that provides step-by-step description of the processes social workers will need to organize, summarize, analyze, interpret, and make sense of their data.

My intention is to provide a work that is academically sound but written for social work students with no statistical background. During my seven years of teaching research methods and data analysis for diverse graduate social work students in Utah, Kansas, and Washington, D.C., I have become aware that most social work students fear statistics, formulas, and numbers. My impression is that there is a growing need among social work students for a statistical book that helps them evaluate their practice, while refraining from applying major mathematical formulas and calculations.

Using Statistical Methods in Social Work Practice: A Complete SPSS Guide is the answer for this growing need. This book targets undergraduate and graduate social work students. The book can be used as a main textbook for statistics and data analysis courses, or as a supplement text for research methods or program evaluation courses that cover statistical methods.

The book is organized in twelve chapters. Each chapter is divided into two main parts: The first part discusses the theoretical background of the topic under discussion and the second part presents social work practice examples with step-by-step examination of a specific problem, how to analyze it, and how to interpret and write the results. Each chapter also includes a detailed discussion of the use of SPSS in computing appropriate statistics.

Chapter 1 reviews major methodological terms, specifically, terms related to data analysis. These terms include variables, levels of measurement, hypotheses, reliability, validity, descriptive and inferential statistics, and types of relationships between variables.

Chapter 2 introduces the Statistical Package for the Social Sciences (SPSS) and SPSS syntax file. The chapter discusses how to start SPSS, create variable names, labels, value categories, and SPSS templates. The chapter also discusses how to enter data in SPSS, clean, recode variables, and compute total scores for a scale.

Chapter 3 and Chapter 4 discuss descriptive statistics. Chapter 3 discusses the frequency distribution table, including absolute frequency, cumulative frequency, absolute percentage, and cumulative percentage. The chapter then presents three different graphs: bar graphs, histogram, and stem-and-leaf plot. Chapter 4 discusses measures of central tendency, measures of variability, percentiles, and presents the boxplot chart.

Chapter 5 discusses various types of distributions. The chapter discusses the properties of normal distributions and skewed distributions and then discusses methods of data transformations. The chapter also discusses the properties of standard scores and how to use a z score table.

Chapter 6 introduces the process in hypothesis testing. The chapter discusses the differences between one-tailed and two-tailed research hypotheses, errors in hypothesis testing, levels of significance, and confidence interval. The chapter then

CHAPTER 1

Overview of Methodological Terms

LEARNING OBJECTIVES

1. Understand variables and their levels of measurement
2. Understand null and alternative hypotheses
3. Understand reliability and validity of instruments
4. Understand descriptive and inferential statistics
5. Understand types of relationships between variables

INTRODUCTION

Perhaps you already have learned about the research process and research design in other research courses. You may know about identifying and defining a researchable social problem, variables and their levels of measurement, research questions and hypotheses, probability and nonprobability sampling methods, test construction, and data collection methods. However, you probably have not covered in depth how to code data and enter them in a statistical computer program, analyze the data, and interpret and write the results. Data analysis methods, interpretations, and discussion of the results are the next steps in the research process.

This book is all about data analysis methods. It includes a step-by-step discussion of data analysis, starting with preparation of data for entry in a statistical program such as the Statistical Package for the Social Sciences (SPSS) and ending with selection of appropriate statistical techniques to analyze the data and discuss the results. However, because data analysis is a continuation of the research process, basic research methodological terms will be reviewed, especially those that are significant to data analysis, including: variables and constants, levels of measurement, research hypotheses, reliability and validity, descriptive and inferential statistics, and relationships between variables.[1]

---

[1]For more discussion of the research process, research design, and methodological terms, see Fortune & Reid (1999), Rubin & Babbie (2005), and Weinbach & Grinnell (2004).

VARIABLES AND CONSTANTS

Variables

The main reason to conduct any statistical analysis is to examine whether relationships exist among two or more variables under investigation. Variables are anything that can vary among subjects, events, or objects, such as the following:

1. Gender: an individual can be male or female.
2. Race: an individual can be White, African American, Native American, or other.
3. Age: an individual can be 25 years old, 28, 30, 36, and so on.
4. Income: an individual can earn $20,000, $26,500, $37,800, $50,000 a year, and up.
5. Level of Anxiety: an individual can be very anxious, somewhat anxious, somewhat not anxious, or not at all anxious.
6. Life Satisfaction: an individual can be very satisfied with life, somewhat satisfied, somewhat not satisfied, or not at all satisfied.

There are four types of variables: independent, dependent, extraneous, and control.

Independent Variable: It is a variable that researchers can control or manipulate according to the purpose of the study. It is a variable believed to cause an effect. For example, if you believe that a higher level of education leads to more annual income, then education will be the independent variable. If you believe better physical health leads to a lower level of depression, then physical health will be the independent variable.

Dependent Variable: This is a measure of the effect of the independent variable. It is dependent upon and is the outcome of the independent variable. Annual income is the dependent variable in the first example above, and level of depression is the dependent variable in the second example.

Extraneous Variable: This represents an alternative explanation for any relationship observed between the independent and dependent variables. It is a third variable that is not part of the analysis, but is believed to influence the relationship between the independent and dependent variables under study.

Extraneous variables are considered major threats to the internal validity of a research study. While many factors may influence internal validity (the relationship between the independent and dependent variables), researchers have identified seven possible sources of threats. These are: history, maturation, testing, instrumentation, statistical regression, selection, and ambiguity about the direction of causal influence.[2]

---

[2]For more on threats on internal validity see Bloom, Fischer, & Orme (2003) and Rubin & Babbie (2005).

In the above examples, the relationship between education and annual income could also be affected by an individual's gender, and the relationship between physical health and level of depression could be affected by an individual's age. Gender and age could thus be viewed as extraneous variables that may influence the relationship between education and income, or between physical health and levels of depression.

Control Variable: It is a variable that researchers assume has an effect on the dependent variable. In a sense, it is an extraneous variable that researchers can control to determine its effect on the dependent variable. To do so, researchers first treat it as a control variable (also called *covariance*) and then choose the appropriate statistical technique (such as partial correlation or analysis of covariance) to examine the relationship between the independent and dependent variables. In our examples, if researchers collect data on gender and age, they can statistically control for their effect on the dependent variables. Thus, gender will serve as a control variable, or covariance, in the first example, and age will serve as a control variable in the second example.

To control for the effect of gender on the relationship between education and annual income, for example, researchers may also conduct two separate statistical analyses, one for men and another for women. To control for the effect of age on the relationship between physical health and levels of depression, researchers may recode age into young, middle, and old age, then conduct three separate analyses, one for each category.

Constants

Unlike variables, constants are anything that does not vary among the subjects, events, or objects under study. A constant is a characteristic that all participants under investigation have in common. For example, if all people were Christian, then religion would be treated as a constant. But people may belong to many religious groups, such as Christians, Muslims, Jews, Buddhists, and others, so religion is not a constant but a variable. The speed of light, on the other hand, is a constant; it remains steady. In geometry, Π (Greek capital letter pi) is a constant because it is a fixed value: 3.14. To compute the area of a circle, square the radius then multiply by Π: area = $r^2 \times \Pi$. In regression analysis (see chapter 12), the a in the regression equation is a constant.

LEVELS OF MEASUREMENT

Measurement is the assignment of numerical values to the attributes of categorical variables according to a set of rules. For example, a researcher may assign 0 to represent females and 1 to represent males; 1 for White, 2 for African American, 3 for Native American, 4 for Asian, and 5 for Other.

Variables are classified under four levels of measurement: nominal, ordinal, interval, and ratio. Table 1.1 summarizes the levels of measurement and their characteristics.

Table 1.1:   Characteristics of Levels of Measurement

Level of Measurement	Exhaustive/ Mutually Exclusive	Rank Order	Equal Distance	Absolute Zero
Nominal	x			
Ordinal	x	x		
Interval	x	x	x	
Ratio	x	x	x	x

Nominal

Nominal variables are those variables with attributes that are exhaustive and mutually exclusive. To be *exhaustive,* every participant in the study should be classifiable according to one of the variable's attributes. For example, a person can be a Christian, Muslim, Jew, or Other. If Other is not one of the attributes of religion, then you may not represent participants who are Buddhist or those who have no religious affiliation. *Mutually exclusive* means that you must classify every participant in one and only one of the variable's attributes. In other words, an individual cannot select more than one attribute: Here, a person can be male, female, or transgender but not more than one attribute; Christian or Muslim but not both. Thus, nominal variables are those variables whose attributes can be classified in qualitative categories, or discrete groups.

Examples: gender (attributes: male, female); race (attributes: White, African American, Hispanic, Native American, Other); religion (attributes: Christian, Jewish, Muslim, Buddhist, No Preference, Other); hair color (attributes: black, brown, red, other); political party (attributes: Democrat, Republican, Independent, Other); country of birth (attributes: U.S., France, China, Lebanon, Other).

Ordinal

Variables measured on the ordinal level have attributes with the characteristics of nominal variables (mutually exclusive and exhaustive) plus can be *rank-ordered.* Rank-ordered means that one attribute is greater or less than another attribute. However, it is impractical to precisely state how much greater or how much less.

Examples: 5-point Likert scale (attributes: 1 = very dissatisfied, 2 = dissatisfied, 3 = neither satisfied nor dissatisfied, 4 = satisfied, 5 = very satisfied); grading system (attributes: A, B, C, D, F); people in a line (attributes: 1st, 2nd, 3rd, etc.); dress size (attributes: S, M, L, XL, XXL).

Interval

Variables measured on the interval level have attributes with the characteristics of ordinal variables (mutually exclusive, exhaustive, and rank-ordered) plus have an *equal distance.* This indicates that the distance between the first and second attributes is the same as the distance between the second and third, third and fourth, and so on.

Examples: Fahrenheit temperature (attributes: 80°, 70°, 60°, etc.); percentile rank (attributes: 50th, 40th, 30th, 10th, etc.); IQ score (attributes: 110, 100, 90, 80, etc.).

Ratio

Variables measured on the ratio level have attributes with the characteristics of interval variables (mutually exclusive, exhaustive, rank-ordered, and equal distance) plus have an *absolute zero.* In other words, a zero point is possible. For example, if someone has zero income this means he or she has no income, but if someone has zero IQ this does not mean he or she has no intelligence.

Examples: age[3] (attributes: 10, 15, 25, 36, 45 years old, etc.); weight (attributes: 50 pounds, 60, 80, 95, 120, 150, etc.); annual salary (attributes: $20,000, $25,000, $30,000, $45,000, etc.); number of years of education (attributes: 6, 8, 12, 14, 15, 16, 20, etc.).

If feasible, collecting data using interval or ratio levels of measurement is recommended because you can always recode interval or ratio variables into ordinal or nominal variables. However, it is impossible to recode nominal or ordinal variables into interval or ratio variables. That is, it is possible to recode a higher level of measurement to a lower level, but not the opposite.

Example: If you are interested in participants' ages, you may ask them to report their actual age at their last birthday. In this case, age is defined as a ratio level of measurement, which is appropriate for all parametric statistics. You can also recode age into young, middle, or old, which becomes an ordinal level of measurement. Or you could recode it into two groups: Less than 30 years and 30 years or older. In this case, age is treated as a nominal level of measurement.

Why and How to Determine the Level of Measurement of a Variable. Levels of measurement play a fundamental role in choosing the appropriate statistical test. While we have discussed four levels of measurement, interval and ratio levels of measurement are both treated the same way in data analysis. Therefore, we refer to the two levels as interval or higher. As we discuss in chapter 6, one assumption for utilizing any parametric test (such as the Pearson correlation or the independent *t*-test) is that the dependent variable is measured at the interval level or higher. Parametric tests also make assumptions about independent variables. For example, while the Pearson correlation and the dependent *t*-test require that the independent variable be measured at the interval level of measurement or higher, the independent *t*-test and one-way analysis of variance require independent variables to be measured at the nominal level.

---

[3] If age is defined as young, middle, and older, then it will be treated as an ordinal level of measurement.

Determining the level of measurement of a variable is not as straightforward as it may seem. In general, a variable that consists of mutually exclusive and exhaustive categories or discrete groups is measured at the nominal level of measurement. For example: gender (male or female); race (White, African American, Hispanic, Native American, Other); religion (Christianity, Islam, Judaism, Other); sickness (Do you consider yourself sick? Yes or No).

A variable measured by a single item on a 3, 4, 5, or 7-point Likert scale is usually considered an ordinal variable. For example, overall, how satisfied are you with the services you receive? 1 = not at all satisfied, 2 = not satisfied, 3 = satisfied, 4 = very satisfied; Compared to this time last year, how would you rate your health now? 1 = much worse, 2 = worse, 3 = same, 4 = better, 5 = much better; Letter grading system: 1 = A, 2 = B, 3 = C, 4 = D, 5 = F.

A variable measured by a scale (number of items) and a total score is computed to generate a scale score or a variable that requires an exact numeric value, is usually measured at the interval level or higher (ratio). For example, the total scores in the CES-D and Rosenberg Self-Esteem Scale (Appendix A) are considered interval variables. Actual income, actual age, number of years of education, number of children at home, and number of years off welfare are all measured at the interval level or higher.

RESEARCH HYPOTHESES

A hypothesis is an assumption about the relationship among two or more variables under investigation. It provides the general framework for the investigation and describes the problem and the variables. There are two types of hypotheses: null and alternative.

Null Hypothesis (H_0)

A null hypothesis assumes *no significant* relationships among the independent and dependent variables or *no significant* differences among groups (independent variable) with regard to the dependent variable. Researchers usually set out to reject the null hypothesis.

Examples:

H_{01}: There is *no significant* relationship between age of social workers and their level of job satisfaction.

H_{02}: There is *no significant* difference between male and female social workers with regard to their level of burnout.

Alternative Hypothesis (H_a)

The alternative hypothesis assumes *significant* relationships among the independent and dependent variables or *significant* differences among groups (independent variable) with regard to the dependent variable. Researchers usually want to support the alternative hypothesis. It is the complement of the null hypothesis and can be supported *only* by rejecting the null hypothesis.

Examples:

H_{a1}: There is a *significant* relationship between age of social workers and their level of job satisfaction.

H_{a2}: There is a *significant* difference between male and female social workers with regard to their level of burnout.

RELIABILITY AND VALIDITY

Reliability

Reliability is the extent of random variation or random error in the results of the study. It refers to whether a particular measure or test applied repeatedly to the same subjects or objects would yield the same results each time. It does not ensure accuracy. For example, illegal immigrant employees might or might not lie about their immigration status when asked. The question is reliable, but the answer may not be accurate.

The reliability coefficient ranges between 0 and 1. The closer the coefficient is to 1, the more reliable the measure is, with less random errors. How close to 1 must a reliability coefficient be? Some social science researchers use scales with a reliability coefficient of .60. However, a reliability coefficient of .70 is considered more acceptable for a measuring scale.

The three most reported reliability coefficients are the stability coefficient (also known as test-retest reliability), the equivalence coefficient, and internal consistency reliability (also known as coefficient alpha, Cronbach alpha, or simply α). Table 1.2 compares them and describes the source of random error for each type of reliability, data collection methods for evaluating the coefficient, and the statistical techniques used to compute the coefficient.

Validity

Validity refers to whether the observed scores precisely reflect the true scores of the construct or variable under investigation. Does the instrument measure what it intends to measure? For example, a measure of job satisfaction is valid if it accurately measures only job satisfaction and not another construct. In the previous example of the illegal immigrant, the question was reliable, however the true score may not be valid as the response may not be truthful. Thus, an instrument can be reliable, but not necessarily valid.

Validity is improved when researchers control variables that may affect the dependent variable. The most reported types include: face validity, content validity, criterion-related validity, and construct validity.

Face validity refers to whether an instrument appears to measure what it in-

Table 1.2:   Comparison of Reliability Coefficients

Reliability Coefficient	Source of Random Error	Data Collection Methods	Statistical Computation*
Stability Coefficient	Change in subject's score over time	Test, wait, retest (same subjects, same test, two occasions)	Compute Pearson correlation (correlation between scores of time 1 and scores of time 2)
Equivalence Coefficient	Content sampling from test 1 to test 2	Give test 1, give test 2 (same subjects, two tests, one occasion)	Compute Pearson correlation (correlation between scores of test 1 and scores of test 2)
Internal Consistency Coefficient	Content sampling or flawed items	Give one test (same subjects, one occasion)	Divide items into two equal halves. Compute Pearson correlation between the scores of the two halves.

*Statistical computation of reliability is more complicated than it looks in table 1.2. For more on this, see Crocker & Algina (1986).

tends to measure. A life satisfaction scale has face validity if it appears to measure only life satisfaction and not other constructs. The researcher constructing the instrument and experts in the construct are the best judges of face validity.

Content validity refers to whether an instrument measures all possible dimensions of the construct or variable under investigation. A depression scale will measure a person's mood, as well as interest or pleasure in activities, excessive sleep, fatigue, stress, feelings of worthlessness or guilt, ability to concentrate, or suicidal thoughts. It is assessed by professionals and experts in the construct and by a sample from the population being studied.

Criterion-related validity refers to whether an instrument can predict concurrent criterion (concurrent validity) or future criterion (predictive validity). For example, a written driving test that predicts how well a person will drive soon after passing the written test demonstrates concurrent validity; a GRE score that predicts how well a student will do in future graduate studies demonstrates predictive validity. Concurrent validity is assessed by examining the relation between the construct and concurrent criterion. Predictive validity is assessed by examining the relation between the construct and future criterion.

Construct validity refers to whether an instrument has high correlation with existing instruments that measure the same construct (convergent validity) or has low correlation with instruments that measure other constructs (discriminant validity). For example, a new self-esteem scale is said to have convergent validity if it is highly correlated with, for example, the Rosenberg Self-Esteem Scale,[4] a well-

---

[4]Royse (1999).

known standardized scale. The new scale is said to have discriminant validity if it has low correlation with, for example, the Life Satisfaction Index,[5] also a well-known standardized scale. Convergent validity is assessed by examining the relation between the construct measured by the new instrument and the same construct as measured by an existing instrument. Discriminant validity is assessed by examining the relation between one construct and another as measured by a different instrument.

Well-developed instruments should establish at least content validity and construct validity (one does not replace the other), and also have a high reliability coefficient.

DESCRIPTIVE AND INFERENTIAL STATISTICS

Descriptive Statistics

Descriptive statistics describe, characterize, or classify data by summarizing it into understandable terms without losing or distorting information.

Descriptive statistics include: summary tables, graphs (bar graphs, histograms, stem-and-leaf plots, and others), frequencies, percentages, measures of central tendency (mean, median, mode), and measures of variability (range, variance, standard deviation).

Example: Descriptive statistics summarize the number of males and females in a study, the mean (average) age, the most frequent score for a specific variable (mode), and the percentage of Whites and non-Whites in a study.

Inferential Statistics

Inferential statistics consist of parametric statistical techniques such as the Pearson correlation, student's t-tests, or analysis of variance, and nonparametric statistical techniques like Spearman rho, Mann-Whitney U, Wilcoxon signed rank, and Kruskal-Wallis H tests, which are used to make generalizations about population characteristics by studying a sample from a given population. Researchers then make inferences from the statistics of a sample to the parameters of a population.

Statistics describe the characteristics of a sample selected from a population. They are symbolized by Roman letters. *Example:* $\overline{X}$ = mean, S^2 = variance, SD = standard deviation, and r = correlation coefficient.

Parameters describe the characteristics of the population from which a sample is drawn. They are symbolized by Greek letters. *Example:* μ (mu) = mean, σ^2 (sigma squared) = variance, σ (sigma) = standard deviation, and ρ (rho) = correlation coefficient.

---

[5]Wood, Wylie, & Sheafor (1969).

Figure 1.1:   Scatterplot for Burnout and Turnover

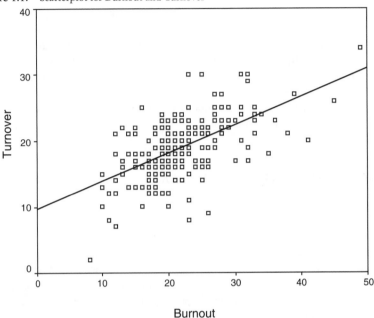

Burnout

Figure 1.1 illustrates the relationship between burnout and turnover. The fit line runs from the lower left side to the upper right side, indicating a positive relationship.

CORRELATION BETWEEN TWO VARIABLES

Statistical analyses examine the relationships or correlations among independent and dependent variables. These relationships can be positive, negative, curvilinear, or no correlation.[6]

Positive (Direct) Correlation

A positive correlation occurs when an increase or decrease in the independent variable leads to an increase or decrease in the dependent variable; in other words, when both variables move in the same direction at the same time. For example, the higher the level of burnout among social workers, the greater the rate of turnover. This demonstrates a significant positive (direct) correlation between burnout and turnover (Figure 1.1).

---

[6]Correlation between two variables does not necessarily indicate that one variable causes the other variable to occur. For conditions of causality, see chapter 7.

Negative (Inverse) Correlation

A negative correlation occurs when an increase in the independent variable leads to a decrease in the dependent variable, or vice versa. In other words, both variables move in the opposite direction at the same time. For example, the higher the level of burnout, the lower the level of job satisfaction. This demonstrates a significant negative (inverse) correlation between burnout and job satisfaction (Figure 1.2).

Curvilinear Correlation

A curvilinear correlation occurs when the relationship between the independent and dependent variables changes at certain levels. In other words, two variables could have a positive correlation at one time, but later become negative. For example, physical ability changes with age (Figure 1.3).

Figure 1.2:   Scatterplot for Job Satisfaction and Burnout

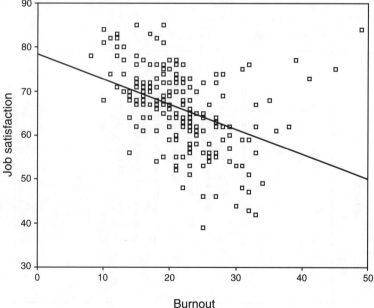

Figure 1.2 illustrates the relationship between burnout and job satisfaction. Unlike Figure 1.1, the fit line in Figure 1.2 runs from the upper left side to the lower right side. This pattern indicates a negative relationship.

Figure 1.3: Scatterplot for Age and Physical Ability

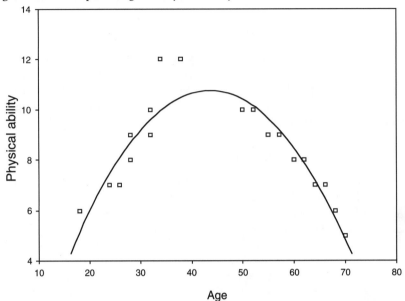

Figure 1.3 shows a curvilinear relation between age and physical ability. From birth until midforties the variables have a positive correlation, then the correlation is negative from mid-forties until death.

Figure 1.4: Scatterplot for Job Satisfaction and Workload

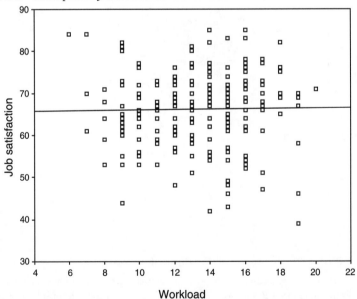

Figure 1.4 illustrates the relationship between job satisfaction and workload. The fit line runs parallel to the x axis, which indicates that no correlation exists between the two variables.

No Correlation

No correlation occurs when a change in the independent variable has no affect on the dependent variable. In other words, the two variables are not correlated.
(Figure 1.4)

SUMMARY

This chapter defined the main research methodological terms used in data analysis.
Data analysis employs a variety of statistical techniques to organize, summarize,
and test hypotheses regarding relationships between dependent and independent
variables at different levels of measurement.

Chapter 1 defined constants and variables, discussed different types of variables, and outlined levels of measurement. Null and alternative hypotheses, reliability and validity of instruments, the use of descriptive and inferential statistics,
and types of relationships between variables were also discussed.

Chapter 2 will introduce SPSS and describe its role in data analysis. You will
learn how to create an instrumentation codebook, start SPSS, and create variable
names, labels, value categories, and SPSS templates, as well as the process of data
cleaning, data recoding, and creating total scores.

PRACTICAL EXERCISE

Review a current empirical-research–based article in a professional social work or
related journal that is of some interest to you and answer the following questions.
Attach the article along with your answers.

1. Summarize the article's main purpose, methods, and major findings.
2. What are the null and alternative hypotheses?
3. What are the independent and dependent variables under study?
4. What are their levels of measurement?
5. Which instrument(s) was/were used to measure the dependent variable(s)?
6. Discuss the reliability and validity of the instrument(s).
7. Discuss the statistical methods (descriptive or inferential) used to analyze
    the data.
8. Discuss the relationships among the dependent and independent variables
    and their directions.
9. Discuss the strengths and limitations of this study.
10. In your judgment, what could be done differently?

Creating SPSS Data Files

LEARNING OBJECTIVES

1. Understand SPSS and syntax files
2. Understand how to create an instrumentation codebook
3. Understand how to start SPSS
4. Understand how to create variable names, labels, and value categories
5. Understand how to create SPSS templates
6. Understand the data cleaning process
7. Understand how to recode and compute total scores for a scale

INTRODUCTION

Statistics has traditionally been a tough subject for social work students. Many experience anxiety about statistics, especially about memorizing mathematical formulas or using a paper and pencil to create graphs, calculate means, or compute complex analyses such as analysis of variance, covariance, regression, or others.

Today, students still need to be able to do simple calculations but most of the data analyses and statistical tests are conducted by computer programs. This means you can focus on understanding the rationale for using a specific statistical test, utilize the computer to run the test, and learn to read and make sense of the results, as well as understand the theoretical application of the test. This technology reduces anxiety over statistics and social workers are more apt to apply it in their practice.

Many programs are available for data analysis. They may be used for small data sets and simple calculations or for more advanced and complex analysis with larger data sets. The most popular computer program used in the social sciences is the Statistical Package for the Social Sciences (SPSS). Other popular software programs include SAS and Excel.[1]

This chapter introduces SPSS for Windows and SPSS syntax file. It discusses how

---

[1]See Gilmore (2004); SAS Publishing (2001); Walkenbach (2003); Carlberg (2004).

to prepare data for entry in SPSS, start the program, and create variable names, labels, value categories, and templates. Chapter 2 also discusses how to enter data in SPSS, check for errors, recode negative scores, and compute total score for a particular scale.

ABOUT THE SPSS PROGRAM

This book utilizes SPSS for Windows Version 12.0 as the main software to organize, describe, and analyze data. While some may use older versions of SPSS, most of the SPSS 12.0 commands discussed here are the same as the commands of SPSS 11.5.[2] All SPSS syntax commands in this book can be used with SPSS Versions 9 through 12.0.

SPSS for Windows was chosen because it is a powerful statistics program that can run most bivariate and multivariate statistics. It is the most widely used statistical program in academic and professional organizations.

Like much Windows software (Microsoft Word, Excel, or PowerPoint, for example), SPSS for Windows has simple toolbar and dialog boxes that enable users to easily do most kinds of statistical analysis.

SPSS Main Toolbar

The SPSS main toolbar (figure 2.1) provides easy access to all buttons and functions available in the SPSS program. Use the mouse to scroll up and down or click on the appropriate button to complete the analysis or employ any other function. The *File* menu allows users to open a new data file or SPSS syntax file, an existing data file or SPSS syntax file, save files, and many other options.

To open a new data file, click on *File,* then on *New,* then on *Data.* A new SPSS *Data Editor* screen will open.

To open an existing SPSS data set, click on *File,* then on *Open,* then on *Data.* A new *Open File* dialog box will open. Choose the directory where the data set is located, click on the file name, then on *Open.* This is the same method used to open a Word or PowerPoint file.

The *Analyze* menu allows users to run frequency tables, compare means, run correlations, regression, reliability, and nonparametric tests, and many other functions.

SPSS Syntax File

Another way to run statistical analysis in SPSS is using the SPSS syntax file.[3] This is the SPSS programming language, a text file composed of statistical commands that instruct the program to run a specific analysis. For example, you may

---

[2]The only differences between SPSS 12.0 and 11.5 or earlier relate to variable names and the chart editor, which are discussed in later chapters.

[3]SPSS syntax file is not available in SPSS Student Version.

Figure 2.1: SPSS Main Toolbar and Dialog Boxes

instruct SPSS to run a frequency table for a specific variable, say gender, simply by typing the command *frequency gender* in the SPSS syntax text file. This instructs SPSS to run a frequency table for the variable gender. You may also instruct SPSS to run a frequency table and measures of central tendency (see chapters 3 and 4) for age by typing this command in the SPSS syntax text file: frequency age /statistics = mean, median, mode, sum. This command (frequency) and subcommand (/Statistics)[4] instruct SPSS to run a frequency table for age and the mean, median, mode, and the sum for age.

Use of SPSS syntax file is most appropriate when the same data are collected frequently from new subjects that require a new analysis. In this case, it is recommended to create and save a syntax file for the original data set and reuse it when new data are added. You may use the same syntax file commands with a different SPSS data set, but change the variable names. For example, you can use the above syntax (frequency age /Statistics = mean, median, mode, sum) to request a frequency table and measures of central tendency for the variable *depression* from another data set. In this case, substitute *age* with *depression.*

A third advantage (not available in the SPSS main toolbar) is that you can save all your functions in a syntax file. This enables you to add, edit, or rerun the analysis. A fourth advantage is that a syntax file created with SPSS Version 10.0, for example, can be used with SPSS Version 12.0, while the SPSS Version 10.0 main toolbar may not be the same as that of Version 12.0. You are able to use all syntax commands discussed in this book with earlier versions of SPSS.

The SPSS main toolbar is the main method to run descriptive and inferential statistics and other analyses. The SPSS syntax commands for each function appear throughout the book, presented in boxes. To use them, we illustrate how to open a new SPSS syntax file, type syntax commands, and run them.

CREATING AN INSTRUMENTATION CODEBOOK

Data are usually collected by preconstructed instruments. Participants in a study are asked either to write their answers for each question (open-ended question) or circle one or more answers that best describe their view (closed-ended question).

---

[4]Each subcommand must start with a slash (/). Each command and subcommand must end with a period (.) and be in a separate line. All commands and subcommands can be lowercase or capitals. Variable names must be spelled exactly as they appear in the SPSS data file.

For example, the Welfare Survey (appendix B) asks participants to complete the month, day, and year for the question *When were you born?*, circle male or female for *What is your gender?*, and circle their race for the question *What is your race?*

For these three questions and those remaining, two things must happen before they can be entered in an SPSS file: Each question must be given a name, and each categorical value (such as male and female) must be given a numerical value. All questions, items, and categories included in any questionnaire is given a code prior to data entry in SPSS.

Most statistical software is the same; that is, the first step in preparing data for entry in SPSS is creating an instrumentation codebook. This codebook consists of letters, numbers, or other characters which are then entered in an SPSS data file. For example, *What is your gender?* may be named gender or sex, while male and female may be coded as 1 for male, and 2 for female. These codes follow guidelines set up by SPSS programmers.

SPSS Guidelines for Variable Names and Labels

1. Each question included in the questionnaire represents a variable that will be entered in SPSS.
2. Each variable should be given a name before it is entered in an SPSS file.
3. In SPSS Version 12.0, variable names must be sixty-four characters or less. However, older SPSS versions require variable names of eight characters or less. (In this book we conform to eight characters to be able to work with earlier versions of SPSS).[5]
4. Each variable must have a different name.
5. Variable names must start with a letter. For example, the name **VAR2** is acceptable, but **2VAR** is not.
6. Variable names cannot include spaces, slashes [forward (/) or backward (\)], or hyphens (-). For example, variable names such as **VAR 2, VAR/2, VAR\2,** or **VAR-2** are not acceptable.
7. Variable names can contain periods (.) and underscores (_). For example, **VAR.2** and **VAR_2** are acceptable.
8. Each name can take a label that is not constrained to these conditions. Usually the labels are the same as the questions. In the SPSS *Data View* screen, only the variable names are visible, yet it is easy to access the variable labels.
9. Variable names in SPSS Version 12.0 or higher can be uppercase letters, lowercase letters, or both. Variable names in older SPSS versions will always appear in lowercase.

---

[5]If you try to open a SPSS file that was created with SPSS Version 12.0 using an older SPSS version, only the first eight characters of the variable name will appear.

Value Categories

In chapter 1 we defined variables as concepts consisting of attributes that differ in quantity or quality among the subjects, events, or objects under study. Attributes identify categorical variables; for example, the attributes for gender are typically male and female and the attributes for race are African American, White, Hispanic, Native American, and Other. When attributes of a variable are expressed in words, they are called value categories.

Because quantitative statistical analysis is based on numbers, all value categories must be converted into numerical values. For example, for a variable with two categories, you may assign 1 for the first category and 2 for the second category (1 = male, 2 = female). Or you may assign 0 for the first category and 1 for the second category (0 = male, 1 = female). Once you assign a value, you must consistently enter the same value category throughout the file.

Recommendations for Value Categories.   If the variable consists of two groups, assign 0 to one group and 1 to the other group. This is especially important in multiple regression analysis (see chapter 12), which requires that categorical variables and dichotomous variables (nominal variables with only two groups) be recoded to dummy variables, such as 0 and 1.

If the variable consists of more than two groups, assign 1 to the first group, 2 to the second group, 3 to the third group, and so on. You may use 0 later on if you want to compare one group versus all the others. In this case, you may recode all other groups to 0 and the other group to 1. For example: Let's say that the variable race was coded as 1 = White, 2 = African American, 3 = Native American, 4 = Asian, and 5 = Other. Now you are interested in comparing Whites versus all other groups. In this case, you may recode 2, 3, 4, and 5 to 0, and keep White as 1. If you were interested in comparing African Americans versus all others, then you may recode 1, 3, 4, and 5 to 0, and 2 (African Americans) to 1.

Identification Numbers

Each questionnaire should be given an ID number. This is especially important in case an error occurs during data entry in SPSS (for example, you accidentally enter 99 instead of 9, or 0 instead of 1). If participants supply Social Security numbers or phone numbers, then these may serve as ID numbers. If no ID numbers were supplied, you may create your own. Say you collected data from 200 subjects, you may assign ID numbers starting from 001 to 200.

You may use ID numbers to go back to the instrument, locate, and correct the errors. For example, in a study that examines depression among 300 elderly people who are 65 years of age or older, you notice that the age of one subject is 45. By finding the ID number for this subject, you can go back to that instrument and check the age, and if the subject is indeed 45, you may decide to delete that entry from the analysis, because the study covers age 65 or older.

PRACTICAL EXAMPLE

The instrument in appendix B is used as an example to create variable names, value categories, labels, and assign missing values. The instrument was sent to 200 former welfare recipients in Prince George's County in Maryland. Of 200, 107 completed and returned the instruments. No Social Security or other identification numbers were collected. The following describes the process for preparing an instrumentation codebook:

For the purpose of data entry, a new variable called **ID** is created for each instrument. This ID number will range from 1 to 107 (total number of completed surveys).

Using SPSS guidelines previously discussed, assign a variable name for each question. It is recommended to designate a name that is easy to remember. Then, assign value categories for categorical variables, such as gender, race, level of education, and so on. Table 2.1 summarizes the variable names and value categories for all items in appendix B.

STARTING THE SPSS PROGRAM

Starting SPSS may differ from one computer to another. It will also depend on the Windows configurations set up by the administrator for computers where SPSS is installed. There are two ways to access SPSS:

1. In Windows, click on *Start,* click on *Program,* click on *SPSS for Windows,* and click on *SPSS 12.0 for Windows* (or follow the same steps if you have an earlier version of SPSS).

2. If there is an SPSS shortcut icon on the desktop, double-click on the icon.

These steps will open a new SPSS spreadsheet called *SPSS Data Editor* (screen 2.1.A). Depending on the computer configuration, a dialog box called *SPSS 12.0 for Windows* will open (screen 2.1.B). If this dialog box opens, click on *Cancel* to close it. (You may check *Don't show this dialog in the future.*) There are two tabs in the lower left corner of the SPSS spreadsheet: *Data View* and *Variable View* (screen 2.1.C). These tabs allow you to switch between the data view screen and variable view screen.

Variable View

Before entering data in the SPSS spreadsheet, first define the variables in the study. Transfer the information created in the instrumentation codebook to the *Variable View* screen (screen 2.2) by clicking on the *Variable View* tab.

Each row in the *Variable View* screen represents a variable; each column represents a variable property, which allows you to define and edit all variables in the study, according to their type (numeric, date, string, and so on), width, decimals,

Table 2.1:   Welfare Survey—Instrumentation Key

Question/Label	Variable Name*	Value Categories, if any
ID number	**ID**	none (ID ranges between 001 to 107)

When were you born?	**DOB**	mm/dd/yy
		    two digits for the month/two digits
		    for the day/and two digits for the year
		    (July 1, 2002 = 07/01/02). You may
		    choose a different format (dd-mm-yyyy),
		    but be consistent.

What is your gender?	**GENDER**	0 = male 1 = female
What is your race?	**RACE**	1 = African American 2 = Asian or Pacific Islander 3 = Hispanic 4 = Native American 5 = White 6 = Mix or Multiracial 7 = Other (please specify): _____

How many years of education do you have?	**EDUCAT**	No value categories are needed for
		    variables measured at the interval or
		    ratio level of measurement.

Do you receive government assistance to help pay for your housing?	**HOUSE**	0 = no 1 = yes
IF yes, What type of housing assistance?	**HOUSE_A** (indicating it depends on the previous item)	1 = Section 8 2 = Public housing 3 = Other (please specify): _____
How would you describe your physical health?	**P_HEALTH** (P for physical)	1 = excellent 2 = very good 3 = good 4 = fair 5 = poor

CES-D Scale:
    (The next 20 items
    represent the CES-D
    scale. In this case we
    will assign CESD1 for
    the first item, CESD2
    for the second item,
    until CESD20)
	CESD1
	CESD2
	....
	....
	....
	....
	CESD20
		0 = rarely or none of the time
		1 = some or a little of the time
		2 = occasionally
		3 = most or all of the time
		
		(These values apply for all 20 items.)

*Bold capital letter words hereafter represent variable names.

Screen 2.1:   SPSS *Data Editor* Main Dialog Box

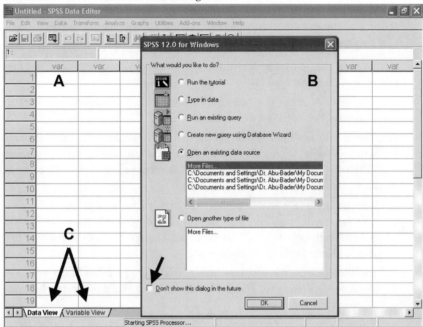

Screen 2.2:   SPSS *Variable View* Dialog Box

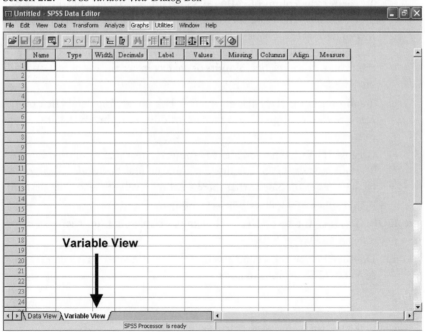

label, value (for categories), missing values, column width, alignment, and level of measurement.

The following describes the steps for creating variable names and their properties for the instrument described in the Practical Example (see table 2.1):

1. **ID:** To enter the first variable name in the codebook, double-click on the first row under *Name* and type ID.[6]

   a. Double-click on the gray box under *Type* (first row). The default *Type* in SPSS is *numeric*. Because ID is a numeric (001 to 107), leave as is and click *OK*.

   b. The default for *Width* is 8. Only the first 8 characters of the variable name will be visible. ID numbers in this case have a maximum of 3 characters (001 to 107). If necessary, change this to more or less than 8. Here, keep all variables at 8 characters.

   c. The default for *Decimals* is 2. Only the first two decimal places of the variable value will be visible. For example, a zero value will appear as .00 and 3.7522 will appear as 3.75. If necessary, change *Decimals* to more or less than 2. Keep *Decimals* at 2 places.

   d. Double-click on the first box under *Label*, to type a label for a variable. Because it is clear what ID stands for, there is no need to create a label for ID; leave this box empty.

   e. There is no need to create *Values* or assign *Missing data* for **ID.** (SPSS treats empty cells as missing.)

   f. To change the column for ID (SPSS default is 8), click on the first box under *Columns* and click the *Up* arrow to increase the width or *Down* arrow to decrease it. *Columns* represents the number of digits or characters that will be visible in the *Data View Screen*, if you change *Columns* to 3, then you will see the first 3 digits or characters for the variable. Leave this box as 8.

   g. To align data for ID, click on the first box under *Align* and click on the *Down* button to align data to the left, middle, or right. By default, all information will be aligned right.

   h. Because ID is used here to identify subjects, treat it as a nominal variable. To replace *Scale* (SPSS default), click on the first box under *Measure* and click on *Nominal*. Notice that there are three levels of measurement: nominal, ordinal, and scale (interval or higher).

2. **DOB:** To enter the second variable name, double-click on the second row under *Name* and type DOB.

   a. Double-click on the second row under *Type*. Because this is a date, change *Numeric* (SPSS default) to *Date*.

---

[6]Remember that bold capital letter words represent variable names.

Screen 2.3:   SPSS *Variable Type* Dialog Box

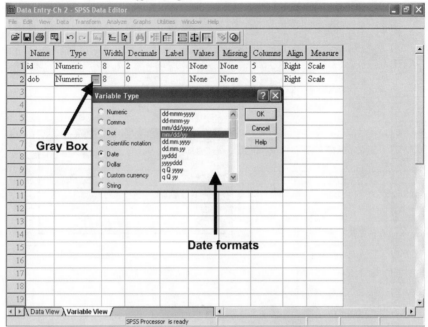

b.   Click on the gray box next to *Numeric*. A new dialog box called *Variable Type* will open (screen 2.3).

c.   Select *Date*. A list of formats will open. Find and click on the one you pre-selected. Click on *mm/dd/yy* and click on *OK* (notice that *Type* for DOB has changed to *Date*).

d.   Leave default for remaining cells as is.

3. **GENDER:** To enter the third variable name, double-click on the third row under *Name* and type GENDER.

a.   Double-click on the third row under *Type*. Because this is a numeric variable (0 = male, 1 = female), leave *Type* as is.

b.   Leave default for *Width* as 8.

c.   Double-click on the third row under *Decimals*. You can type 0, or use the *Up* and *Down* arrows to change the 2 to 0. We will change this to 0 because if we leave it, any value that is 0 will appear as .0 (We may leave it as is . . . this will not affect any of the analyses).

d.   There is no need to create a label for gender.

e.   Because gender is a nominal level of measurement, assign value categories. The values for gender are 0 = male and 1 = female. To assign value

Screen 2.4:   SPSS *Value Labels* Dialog Box

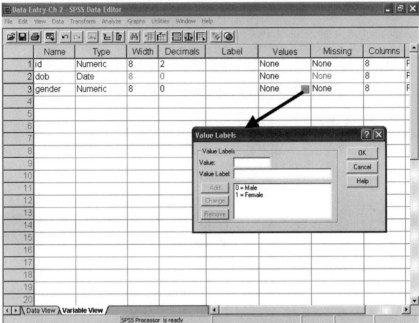

categories, click on the third row under *Values* and click on the gray box next to *None* (SPSS default).

f.   A new dialog box called *Value Labels* will open (screen 2.4).

g.   Type 0 in the *Value* box and type male in the *Value Label* box.

h.   Click on *Add* to confirm the assignment of 0 for male. Click on *Add* each time you add or edit a label.

i.   Type 1 in the *Value* box, type female in the *Value Label* box, and click on *Add* to confirm the assignment of 1 for female.

j.   Click on *OK.*

k.   *Missing:* SPSS for Windows treats empty boxes as missing cases. You do not need to create missing values. However, some researchers may assign values such as 9, 99, 999, or something else, to represent missing data. To assign missing values for **GENDER,** click on the third row under *Missing* and click on the gray box next to *None.* A new dialog box called *Missing Values* will open (screen 2.5).

l.   Check *Discrete missing values.*

m. Type 9, 99, 999, or whatever you choose.

n.   Click on *OK.*

Screen 2.5:   SPSS *Missing Values* Dialog Box

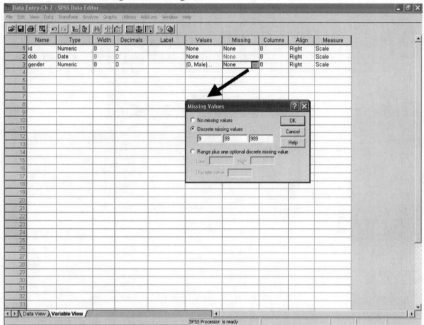

o.   **GENDER** is a nominal variable. Under the *Measure* column, change the level of measurement from *Scale* to *Nominal* (as discussed above).

4. **RACE:** To enter the fourth variable name, double-click on the fourth box under *Name* and type RACE.

  a.   Leave the default for *Type, Width, Decimals,* and *Label* as is.

  b.   Click on the fourth row under *Values* and click on the gray box. A new dialog box called *Value Labels* will open (screen 2.6).

  c.   Type 1 in the *Values* box, type African American in the *Value Label* box, and click on *Add* to confirm the assignment of 1 for African American.

  d.   Repeat step c to assign values to all other races.

  e.   Click on *OK.*

  f.   You may leave *Missing* as is or assign values as discussed above.

  g.   Change *Scale* to *Nominal* under *Measure.*

5. **EDUCAT:** To enter the fifth variable name, double-click on the fifth row under *Name* and type EDUCAT.

  a.   Leave the default for *Type, Width,* and *Decimals* as is.

  b.   Double-click on the fifth row under *Label* and type *Number of years of education.* This will serve as a label for the variable **EDUCAT.**

Screen 2.6:   SPSS *Value Labels* Dialog Box

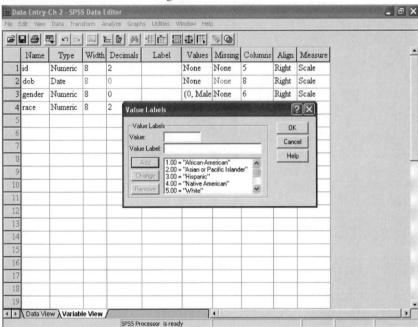

c. Assigning value categories is inappropriate because this is a continuous variable, interval, or higher level of measurement. (Subjects can have any number of years of education.)

d. Because education is measured here at the ratio level (interval or higher), leave *Scale* as is under *Measure*.

6. **HOUSE:** Use the same steps used for **GENDER** to create this variable. It is important to create a label for this variable because there are too many interpretations for HOUSE. For example, you may label it as "Receive government assistance to pay for housing."

7. **HOUSE_A:** Repeat the same steps to create this variable. You may label it as "If yes to **HOUSE,** what type of assistance?"

8. **P_HEALTH:** Repeat the same steps used in **RACE** to create a variable name for **P_HEALTH.** You may need to add a label, such as "How would you describe your physical health?"

9. **CES-D Scale:** For the next 20 items, start by typing CESD1 in the 9th row under *Name* and CESD2 in the 10th box under *Name*. Continue in this manner until you type CESD20 in the 28th row.

10. Double-click in the *Values* box associated with CESD1 (9th row under *Values*) to create value categories for CESD1. Use the same steps used for **GENDER** or **RACE** to create these labels.

Screen 2.7:   SPSS *Variable View* File

	Name	Type	Width	Decimals	Label	Values	Missing	Columns	Align	Measure
1	id	Numeric	8	2		None	None	8	Right	Nominal
2	dob	Date	8	0		None	None	8	Right	Nominal
3	gender	Numeric	8	0		{0, Male}..	9, 99, 999	5	Right	Nominal
4	race	Numeric	8	2		{1.00, African	None	6	Right	Nominal
5	educat	Numeric	8	2	Number of yea	None	None	7	Right	Scale
6	house	Numeric	8	2	Receive govern	{.00, No}...	None	8	Right	Nominal
7	hous_a	Numeric	8	2	If yes to HOUS	{.00, Section	None	8	Right	Nominal
8	p_health	Numeric	8	2	How would you	{1.00, Excellen	None	8	Right	Ordinal
9	cesd1	Numeric	8	2		{.00, Rarely or	None	8	Right	Ordinal
10	cesd2	Numeric	8	2		{.00, Rarely or	None	8	Right	Ordinal
11	cesd3	Numeric	8	2		{.00, Rarely or	None	8	Right	Ordinal
12	cesd4	Numeric	8	2		{.00, Rarely or	None	8	Right	Ordinal
13	cesd5	Numeric	8	2		{.00, Rarely or	None	8	Right	Ordinal
14	cesd6	Numeric	8	2		{.00, Rarely or	None	8	Right	Ordinal
15	cesd7	Numeric	8	2		{.00, Rarely or	None	8	Right	Ordinal
16	cesd8	Numeric	8	2		{.00, Rarely or	None	6	Right	Ordinal
17	cesd9	Numeric	8	2		{.00, Rarely or	None	5	Right	Ordinal
18	cesd10	Numeric	8	2		{.00, Rarely or	None	6	Right	Ordinal
19	cesd11	Numeric	8	2		{.00, Rarely or	None	6	Right	Ordinal
20	cesd12	Numeric	8	2		{.00, Rarely or	None	6	Right	Ordinal
21	cesd13	Numeric	8	2		{.00, Rarely or	None	6	Right	Ordinal
22	cesd14	Numeric	8	2		{.00, Rarely or	None	6	Right	Ordinal
23	cesd15	Numeric	8	2		{.00, Rarely or	None	6	Right	Ordinal
24	cesd16	Numeric	8	2		{.00, Rarely or	None	6	Right	Ordinal

11. After creating values for CESD1, click on the box containing these values (9th box under *Values*).

12. Click on the *right* mouse button and select *Copy*.

13. While holding the *left* mouse button, click on the *Values* box for CESD2 and scroll down until you reach the *Values* box for CESD20. This will highlight all the *Values* boxes for CESD items 2 to 20.

14. Point mouse anywhere in the highlighted area, click on the *right* mouse button, and select *Paste*. This will paste values to all selected items. This function is called *SPSS template*. It simplifies the process for creating value categories, especially when many items have the same one. Items don't have to appear in order. You can copy and paste value categories anywhere in *Variable View*. (Screen 2.7 displays the SPSS *Variable View* File.)

15. Save your work often.

Data View

The next step is to enter all data collected from participants. Click on the *Data View* tab at the lower left corner in the main SPSS screen (screen 2.7). A new spreadsheet with all the variable names, starting with **ID** and ending with

Screen 2.8:   SPSS *Data View* Screen

CESD20 will appear in the top row (screen 2.8).[7] In SPSS *Data View*, each row represents a single case or a single observation and each column represents a variable or an item being measured. To view the label for a specific variable, point mouse on the specific variable name but don't click on it. For example, to view the label for **HOUSE**, point mouse on **HOUSE** and the label will appear (screen 2.8). Double-clicking on the variable will open *Variable View* for this and other variables.

The following describes steps for data entry in SPSS:

1.   Enter the ID number for the first case in the first row under **ID.** Order is not important in data entry. That is, you may first enter case number 15, then number 11, followed by 3, and so on. Let us start with case number 3.

2.   Enter 3 in the first row under **ID.** Once a value is entered in the first row and first column (**ID**), all columns associated with this case fill with dots (.). These dots (SPSS default) represent missing values and will remain missing unless they are replaced with valid data; otherwise, they will be excluded from future analysis.

3.   Click on first row under **DOB.** Type, for example, 02/28/85 in the first box

---

[7]Remember, each column in *Data View* represents a variable and each row represents a case.

Screen 2.9:   SPSS *Data View* File

	id	dob	gender	race	educat	house	hous_a	p_health	cesd1
1	3.00	02/28/78	1	2.00	12.00	.00	1.00	4.00	3.00
2	5.00	03/12/76	0	4.00	10.00	1.00	3.00	1.00	1.00
3	7.00	10/10/83	1	3.00	8.00	.00		2.00	.00
4	11.00	11/12/80	0	1.00	10.00	1.00	1.00	3.00	2.00
5	14.00	07/07/75	2	1.00	7.00	1.00	2.00	3.00	1.00

Data Entry-Ch 2 - SPSS Data Editor

File   Edit   View   Data   Transform   Analyze   Graphs   Utilities   Add-ons   Window   Help

13 : race

Data View / Variable View /

SPSS Processor is ready

under **DOB**. If date does not appear, check that you are using the format you chose for *Date.*

4.   If case number 3 is female, type 1 in the first row under **GENDER**.

5.   Enter remaining data for case number 3.

6.   Save your work after each case.

7.   Enter data for your next subject, say, case number 7.

8.   After finishing this data entry, you may sort cases by ID (or any other format). Click on *Data* on the SPSS main toolbar, scroll down, and click on *Sort Cases.* A new dialog box called *Sort Cases* will open. Click on *ID,* and click on the arrow between the two boxes to move *ID* under *Sort by.*

9.   Click on *OK.* This will sort cases by ID number; case number 3 will be first, followed by case number 5, and so on (screen 2.9).

Data Cleaning

Sometimes, especially if you have a large sample size, you may make errors in data entry. For example, your intention is to click on 0 (male) for GENDER, but you click on 9 because it is nearby on the keyboard. Or you may enter 4 instead of 3 for CESD items. Errors will significantly affect your analysis, so it is necessary to

Screen 2.10:   SPSS *Analyze* Toolbar

clean your data before conducting any descriptive or inferential analyses. The following describes steps for data cleaning:

1. Run frequencies for all variables in the study. Click *Analyze* in the SPSS main toolbar, click *Descriptive Statistics,* then click *Frequencies* (screen 2.10).

2. A new dialog box called *Frequencies* will open (screen 2.11). While holding the *left* mouse button down, click on *ID* in the variables list box, scroll down, and highlight all variables. You may also clean them one by one or every five variables, especially if you have many variables. Click on the arrow button between the two boxes to move variables in the *Variable(s)* box. Make sure the *Display frequency tables* box is checked (SPSS default).

3. Click on *OK.*

SPSS Frequencies Output.   The following is the SPSS output displaying the frequencies for all variables. Because the process for data cleaning is the same, we will only check frequency tables for **ID** (table 2.2), **DOB** (table 2.3), **GENDER** (table 2.4), and **CESD10** (table 2.5).

This study requires a different ID number for each case. Table 2.2 shows that no duplicate ID numbers exist, thus indicating no errors in **ID.**

If partici0pation in the study was limited to welfare recipients 18 years or older, then the latest year of birth should be 1986. Anyone born after 1986 should

Screen 2.11:   SPSS *Frequencies* Dialog Box

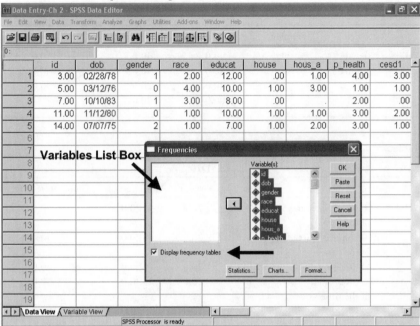

Table 2.2:   Frequency Table for ID

		Frequency	Percent	Valid Percent	Cumulative Percent
			ID		
Valid	3.00	1	20.0	20.0	20.0
	5.00	1	20.0	20.0	40.0
	7.0	1	20.0	20.0	60.0
	11.00	1	20.0	20.0	80.0
	14.00	1	20.0	20.0	100.0
	Total	5	100.0	100.0	

Table 2.3:   Frequency Table for Date of Birth (DOB)

		Frequency	Percent	Valid Percent	Cumulative Percent
			DOB		
Valid	07/07/75	1	20.0	20.0	20.0
	03/12/76	1	20.0	20.0	40.0
	02/28/78	1	20.0	20.0	60.0
	11/12/80	1	20.0	20.0	80.0
	10/10/83	1	20.0	20.0	100.0
	Total	5	100.0	100.0	

Table 2.4:   Frequency Table for Gender

		Frequency	Percent	Valid Percent	Cumulative Percent
			GENDER		
Valid	0 male	2	40.0	40.0	40.0
	1 female	2	40.0	40.0	80.0
	2	1	20.0	20.0	100.0
	Total	5	100.0	100.0	

Table 2.5:   Frequency Table for CESD10

		Frequency	Percent	Valid Percent	Cumulative Percent
			CESD10		
Valid	.00 Rarely or none of the time	1	20.0	20.0	20.0
	1.00 Some or a little of the time	1	20.0	20.0	40.0
	2.00 Occasionally	1	20.0	20.0	60.0
	3.00 Most or all of the time	1	20.0	20.0	80.0
	4.00	1	20.0	20.0	100.0
	Total	5	100.0	100.0	

not be included. Table 2.3 shows that the youngest person in the study was born in 1983 (20 years old), which indicates that **DOB** entries are accurate.

GENDER was coded 0 for male and 1 for female. Any value that is neither 0 nor 1 (unless it is a missing value) is inaccurate and must be corrected.

Table 2.4 shows that two participants were male, two were female, and one was labeled 2. This 2 is an error. To clean the error, follow these steps:

1. Open the SPSS *Data View* file.
2. Click on the variable **GENDER.** This will highlight all data in this category.
3. Click on *Edit* in the SPSS main toolbar.
4. Scroll down and select *Find.* A new dialog box called *Find Data in Variable Gender* will open (screen 2.12).
5. Type 2 in the box labeled *Find what* and click *Find Next.*
6. The number 2 under **GENDER** will appear.
7. Find the case number associated with this 2, in this case, ID number 14.
8. Go back to instrument number 14 and confirm the gender for this participant. Let us say it was female.
9. Return to SPSS *Data View* file and double-click on 2, delete it, and type 1.
10. Save your file. Repeat steps if there are other errors under **GENDER.**

Screen 2.12:   SPSS *Find Data* Main Dialog Box

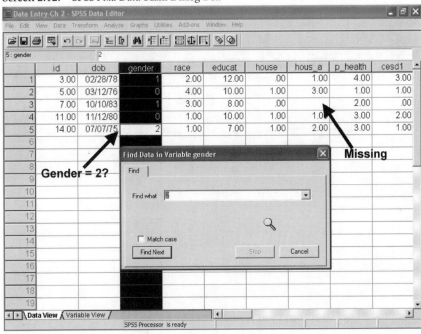

CESD items were coded as 0, 1, 2, or 3. As with **GENDER,** any other value is inaccurate and will need to be corrected.

Table 2.5 presents the frequency for CESD10. It shows one participant with a score of 4. This score is outside the possible range, and represents an error. To clean this error, follow the same steps used to clean **GENDER.**

Finally, because data entry is so time consuming and computer failure is always possible, it is recommended that you save the clean SPSS data file in the hard drive as well as on an external drive or disk.

Recoding Values

A scale is a set of items where some items are positively worded and others are negatively worded. For example, the CES-D scale (appendix B) is used as a screening tool to gauge frequency of depressive symptoms in the preceding week. The scale consists of 20 items measured on a 4-point Likert scale. Of them, items number 4, 8, 12, and 16 (I felt that I was just as good as other people, I felt hopeful about the future, I was happy, and I enjoyed life) are positively worded: Higher scores in these items indicate less depression, while higher scores in the remaining 16 items indicate greater depression. To be sure all items indicate the same direction (that higher scores indicate greater depression), the scores for items 4, 8, 12, and 16 must be reversed before any further statistical analysis. In this case, reverse a score of 3 to 0, 2 to 1, 1 to 2, and 0 to 3. This procedure is referred to in SPSS as *Recode.*

Screen 2.13:   SPSS *Transform* Toolbar

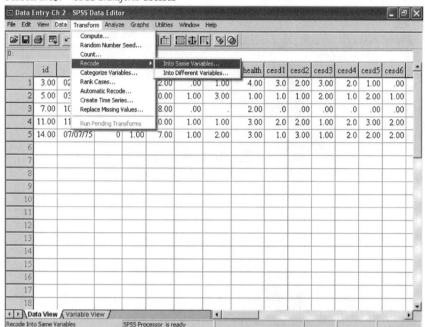

Two methods may be used to run SPSS commands: SPSS main toolbar and SPSS syntax file.

1. To use the SPSS main toolbar to recode values of above items, follow these steps:

    a. Open the SPSS data file with the variable(s) you wish to recode.

    b. Click on *Transform,* scroll down to *Recode,* and click on *Into Same Variables* (screen 2.13).

    c. A new dialog box called *Recode Into Same Variables* will open (screen 2.14.A). From the variables list in the left box, scroll down and click on *CESD4,* then click on the arrow button to move it in the *Numeric Variables* box.

    d. Repeat step c to move *CESD8, CESD12,* and *CESD16.*

    e. Click on *Old and New Values.* A new dialog box called *Recode Into Same Variables: Old and New Values* will open (screen 2.14.B).

    f. Type 3 in the *Value* box under *Old Value.* Type 0 in the *Value* box under *New Value.*

    g. Click on *Add* to confirm this recode. This will transfer the old and new values in the *Old . . . New* box.

    h. Repeat steps e and f to recode 1 to 2, 2 to 1, and 3 to 0.

    i. Click on *Continue,* then click on *OK.*

Screen 2.14:   SPSS *Recode Into Same Variables* Dialog Box

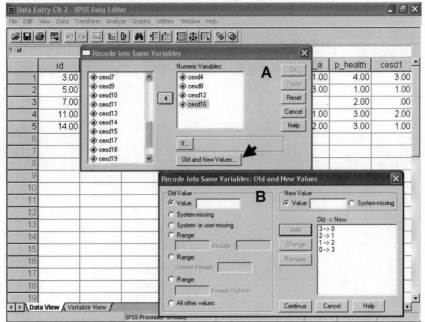

2. To use the SPSS syntax file, follow these steps:

    a. Open the SPSS data file that contains the variable(s) you wish to recode.

    b. Click on *File* in the SPSS main toolbar and click on *New*.

    c. Click on *Syntax* (screen 2.15). A new SPSS syntax file will open.

    d. Type the following SPSS syntax exactly:

        RECODE CESD4 CESD8 CESD12 CESD16 (0 = 3) (1 = 2)
        (2 = 1) (3 = 0). EXECUTE.

    e. Highlight this syntax.

    f. Click on the *right* mouse button and click on *Run Current* (screen 2.16).
        You may also click on the arrow button on the toolbar at the top of the
        screen (also called *Run Current*).

After all recodes are completed, save this file in a new SPSS data file (for example, SPSS Welfare Analysis), which ensures access to the original SPSS raw data
file as well as to the new SPSS data file on which future analysis will be conducted.

Remember: You can use the *Recode* function to combine groups, change categorical values, and other changes. For example, if **RACE** was defined as 1 = White,
2 = African American, 3 = Hispanic, 4 = Native American, you can compare
Whites against all others by creating a new variable using the *Recode* function.
Recode 2, 3, and 4 to 0 (0 = Non-Whites) and keep 1 (Whites) as 1 in a new variable (for example, RACE_REC). The syntax file for this would read as follows:

Screen 2.15:   SPSS Syntax Main Toolbar

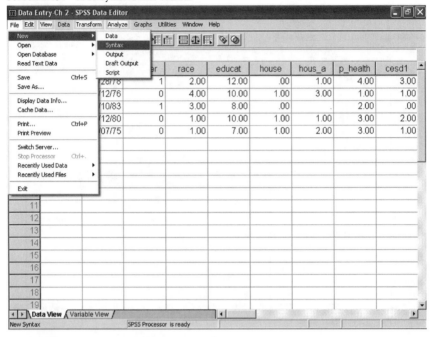

Screen 2.16:   SPSS Syntax Screen

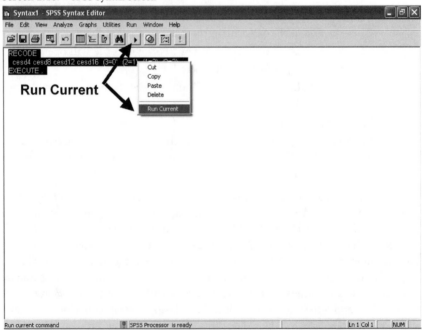

RECODE RACE (1 = 1) (2 = 0) (3 = 0) (4 = 0) INTO RACE_REC.
EXECUTE.

Computing a Total Score for Scale

Many social constructs are measured using a scale, which is a set of items or questions. The scores for these items are generally summed to generate a total score for the specific construct. For example, the potential total score for the CES-D scale ranges from 0 to 60, where higher scores indicate greater levels of depression. A score of 16 is generally used as a cutoff score, indicating high levels of symptoms, or clinical depression. Researchers may collect information on multiple items to measure depression, but they are usually most interested in the total score.

Like most SPSS functions, you can use the SPSS main toolbar or the SPSS syntax file to compute total score. To compute the total score for the CES-D in our example, follow these two methods:

1. To use the SPSS main toolbar, follow these steps:
    a. Open the SPSS data file that contains the scale items you wish to tally to compute a total score.
    b. Click on *Transform.*
    c. Click on *Compute.* A new dialog box called *Compute Variable* will open (screen 2.17).
    d. Type the name of the new variable you want to create in the *Target Variable* box in the upper left corner of the *Compute Variable* dialog box. In this case, name it *CESD.*
    e. Scroll down under *Function* and click on *SUM(numexpr,numexpr, . . .).*
    f. Click on the arrow button next to *Functions* to move this function in the *Numeric Expression* box.
    g. Scroll down under *Type & Label* and highlight CESD1.
    h. Click on the arrow button in the right side of *Type & Label* to move CESD1 to replace the first "?" in the *Numeric Expression* box.
    i. Repeat steps g and h to replace the second "?" with CESD2.
    j. Repeat these steps until you have moved all 20 CESD variables.
    k. Make sure there is a comma (,) between each CESD item (screen 2.18).
    l. Click on *OK.*
2. To use the SPSS syntax file to compute a total score, follow these steps:
    a. Open the SPSS data file that contains the scale items you wish to tally to compute a total score.
    b. Click on *File* in the SPSS main toolbar.
    c. Click on *New* and click on *Syntax* to open a new SPSS syntax file.
    d. Type the following syntax exactly:

Screen 2.17:   SPSS *Compute Variable* Dialog Box

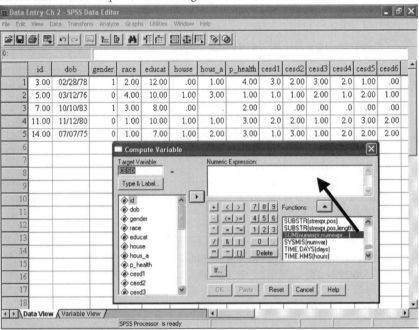

Screen 2.18:   SPSS *Compute Variable* Function

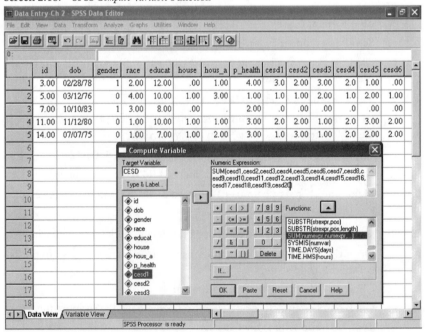

Screen 2.19:   SPSS *Data View* File

COMPUTE CESD = SUM (CESD1, CESD2, CESD3, CESD4,
CESD5, CESD6, CESD7, CESD8, CESD9, CESD10, CESD11,
CESD12, CESD13, CESD14, CESD15, CESD16, CESD17,
CESD18, CESD19, CESD20). EXECUTE.

Note: If all items to be summed are sorted in order in the SPSS *Data View*
screen and no other items are between them, simply type:

COMPUTE CESD = SUM (CESD1 TO CESD20). EXECUTE.

e.   Highlight this syntax.

f.   Click on the *right* mouse button and click on *Run Current.* You may also
     click on the arrow button located in the toolbar at the top of the screen
     (also called *Run Current*).

Both SPSS methods will create and add a new variable called **CESD** to the
SPSS data file. This file will be located in the last column in the *Data View* screen
(screen 2.19).

SUMMARY

This chapter introduced the SPSS program, SPSS main toolbar, and SPSS syntax
file. The chapter discussed the importance of creating an instrumentation code-

book prior to data entry. This codebook defines variable names, types, and labels, and assigns numerical codes for categorical values.

The process of transferring these codes in SPSS files using two SPSS computer screens was described. The *Variable View* screen shows where variables and their categories are defined and edited, and the *Data View* screen is where data are entered.

Finally, the chapter discussed the importance and the practical steps for data cleaning, recoding items, and computing total scores for a scale.

Chapter 3 presents methods for organizing and summarizing data. The chapter will discuss frequency tables and graphs, including the bar graph, histogram, and stem-and-leaf, and how to use SPSS to create frequency tables and graphs.

PRACTICAL EXERCISE

The following data were collected from a random sample of 40 subjects who went off welfare and went to work under new welfare reforms. Participants completed a self-administered survey, which measured the following variables:

1. **D1: AGE.**
2. **D2: GENDER:** M = male, and F = female.
3. **D3: RACE:** AFA = African American, H = Hispanic, W = White.
4. **D4: MARITAL STATUS:** M = married, S/N = single/never married, D = divorced, W = widowed, and S = separated.
5. **D5: HEALTH IN GENERAL:** Since you left welfare and went to work, would you say your health is MB = much better, SB = somewhat better, AS = about the same, SW = somewhat worse, or MW = much worse?

Participants also completed the Rosenberg Self-Esteem Scale (appendix C). This consists of 10 items (E1 to E10). They rated their general feelings about each item on a 4-point Likert scale (SA = strongly agree, A = agree, D = disagree, and SD = strongly disagree). Items number 1, 3, 4, 7, and 10 are positively worded and all others are negatively worded. A total score was computed for each subject, ranging from 10 to 40, with higher scores indicating greater self-esteem.

Directions:

1. Create an instrumentation codebook. Include a name for each variable, label, and value categories.
2. Using the SPSS *Variable View* file, define each variable, its type, and assign values for each category.
3. Using the SPSS *Data View* file, enter data.
4. Clean and save the data.
5. Recode scores for the five positive self-esteem items.
6. Compute total score for self-esteem.
7. Run frequencies for all variables.

D1	D2	D3	D4	D5	E1	E2	E3	E4	E5	E6	E7	E8	E9	E10
24	M	AFA	S/N	SB	A	SA	SA	SA	A	SA	SA	A	SA	SA
24	M	H	M	AS	A	SA	A	A	SA	A	A	D	SA	SA
25	F	AFA	S/N	MB	SA	SA	SA	SA	SA	SA	SD	SD	SA	SA
25	F	H	S/N	SB	D	A	SA	SA	SA	A	SA	D	SA	SA
25	F	AFA	M	AS	SA	SA	SA	SA	SA	SA	SA	SA	SA	SA
26	M	AFA	S/N	AS	SA	SA	SA	SA	SA	D	A	SA	SA	SA
26	M	AFA	D	AS	SA	SA	SA	SA	SA	SA	SA	SA	SA	SA
26	F	W	D	AS	D	A	A	A	A	D	A	D	A	A
26	M	W	S/N	AS	D	SA	A	A	A	A	A	SD	A	A
27	M	H	S/N	AS	D	A	A	SA	A	A	SA	A	SA	SA
28	M	W	M	AS	A	A	SA	SA	A	A	SA	A	A	SA
29	F	AFA	S/N	AS	A	A	SA	D	SA	SA	SA	SA	SA	SA
29	M	AFA	S	AS	A	A	A	A	A	A	A	A	SA	SA
31	M	H	S	SB	A	D	SA	SA	D	D	D	SD	D	D
32	M	AFA	S/N	AS	SA	A	SA	SA	SA	SA	SA	SA	SA	SA
32	M	H	S/N	AS	SA	SA	SA	SA	A	A	SA	D	SA	SA
32	F	W	S/N	AS	A	D	A	A	A	A	A	D	A	D
33	M	H	W	AS	SA	SA	SA	SA	SD	SA	SA	SA	SA	SA
35	M	AFA	S/N	SB	D	SA	SA	SA	A	D	SA	SA	SA	A
35	M	AFA	S/N	MB	A	SA	SA	SA	SA	SA	SA	SA	SA	SA
35	M	W	S	AS	A	D	SA	A	A	SA	A	A	SA	A
36	M	AFA	S/N	SB	A	SA	A	A	D	D	A	A	A	A
36	M	H	W	MB	SA	SA	SA	SA	SA	SA	A	SA	SA	SA
36	F	H	S	SB	SA	SA	SA	SA	SA	SA	SD	SA	SA	SA
36	F	W	S	MB	A	A	SA	SA	A	A	SA	A	A	SA
37	M	AFA	S	SB	A	SA	A	A	A	SA	A	D	SA	A
37	F	W	W	SB	SA	SA	A	A	A	A	A	A	A	SA
38	F	AFA	D	AS	D	D	SA	A	D	D	D	D	D	D
38	M	AFA	S	MB	SA	SA	SA	A	SA	SA	SD	SA	SA	SA
38	F	H	M	MW	SA	SA	D	SD	SA	SA	D	SA	SA	A
39	M	AFA	S/N	AS	A	A	SA	A	A	D	A	D	A	A
40	F	H	S/N	MB	SA	D	SA	SA	SA	D	A	SA	SA	SA
41	M	AFA	D	AS	SA	SA	SA	SA	SA	A	SA	SA	SA	SA
42	M	AFA	M	MB	SA	A	SA	SA	A	A	SA	A	A	SA
42	M	AFA	W	AS	SA	SD	SA	SA	SA	SD	SA	SD	SD	SA
42	F	AFA	D	MB	A	SA	SA	A	SA	SA	A	SA	SA	SA
44	M	AFA	S/N	MB	SA	SA	SA	A	SA	SA	A	A	SA	SA
44	F	AFA	D	SB	A	A	A	A	A	A	A	D	A	A
45	F	W	S	SW	SA	SA	SA	A	SA	A	SA	SA	SA	SA
45	M	H	S/N	SB	A	A	SA	A	A	D	A	D	SA	A

CHAPTER 3

Data Organization and Summary

LEARNING OBJECTIVES

1. Understand a frequency distribution table and its components
2. Understand the different types of graphs and their uses
3. Understand how to create frequency distribution tables and graphs in SPSS

Data Set: *Job Satisfaction* (Appendix A)

INTRODUCTION

The purpose of any research study is to examine the characteristics of a population and how they are related. Researchers select representative samples from the population to which generalizations will be made, then collect data from subjects who agree to participate in surveys or interviews (face-to-face, or by telephone or Internet).

After data are collected (see chapter 2), the particulars are coded, entered into statistical software such as SPSS, and checked for data entry errors. Some items may need to be recoded to ensure that all scale items progress in the same direction. The last step in preparing data for statistical analysis is to compute the total scores for scales and subscales.

Now the process of data analysis and interpretation begins. The first step is to organize and summarize data in a way that is easy to understand and interpret. Two simple ways to accomplish this are frequency distribution tables and graphs.

This chapter discusses frequency distribution tables and their components, then presents three types of graphs. You will also learn how to work with SPSS to create frequency distribution tables and graphs.

FREQUENCY DISTRIBUTION TABLES

A frequency distribution is an arrangement of values (attributes) that shows the number of times (frequency) a given value (score) or group of values occurs. It details how the research sample or population's values are distributed.

For example, a frequency distribution will show the frequency of males and females for **GENDER** (dichotomous variable, nominal level of measurement); frequency of Whites, African Americans, Native Americans, Hispanics, or Others for **RACE** (categorical variable, nominal level of measurement); and the number of participants who are 30, 40, 50, or 60 years old for **AGE** (continuous variable, ratio level of measurement).

There are four components of frequency distributions:

1. *Absolute frequency distribution (f):* This refers to the actual number of times each score or value occurs. It is symbolized by a *lowercase italic f.* The sum (Σ or sigma) of all frequencies will always equal the number of cases in the study ($\Sigma f = N$).

2. *Cumulative frequency distribution (cf):* This refers to the number of cases at and below a given score or value. It is symbolized by lowercase italic *cf.* The cumulative frequency distribution for the maximum score will always equal the total number of cases in the study (N).

3. *Percentage distribution (%):* This refers to the percentage of cases for each score or value. The sum of all percentages will always equal 100%.

4. *Cumulative percentage distribution (c%):* This refers to the percentage of cases at and below a given score or value. The cumulative percentage distribution for the maximum score is always 100%.

How to Create a Frequency Distribution Table. The first step is to arrange the raw data (observed scores) in an array. In this case, scores must be arranged from the lowest value (minimum score) to the highest (maximum score).

Example: The following are final grades (raw data 3.1) for 20 students who took a data analysis course last year:

Raw Data 3.1

| 86 | 80 | 82 | 86 | 88 | 90 | 88 | 90 | 94 | 92 |
| 84 | 88 | 84 | 88 | 86 | 92 | 88 | 96 | 90 | 88 |

To create a frequency distribution table, first arrange scores in an array, by sorting from lowest to highest (array data 3.1).

Array Data 3.1

| 80 | 82 | 84 | 84 | 86 | 86 | 86 | 88 | 88 | 88 |
| 88 | 88 | 88 | 90 | 90 | 90 | 92 | 92 | 94 | 96 |

The next step is to construct a table with five columns, shown in table 3.1.

1. In the first column, under *X,* enter the grades or scores as they appear in the array data starting with the minimum score (80) and ending with the maximum score (96). Enter each score only one time.

Table 3.1:   Frequency Distribution Table

X	f	cf	%	c%
80	1	1	5%	5%
82	1	2	5%	10%
84	2	4	10%	20%
86	3	7	15%	35%
88	6	13	30%	65%
90	3	16	15%	80%
92	2	18	10%	90%
94	1	19	5%	95%
96	1	20	5%	100%
Total (Σ)	20		100%	

X = score; f = frequency; cf = cumulative frequency; $\%$ = percentage; $c\%$ = cumulative percentage

2. In the second column, under f, enter the number of times each score occurs. Remember, the sum of all frequencies (Σf) must equal the total number of students in the study; in this case, 20.

3. In the third column, under cf enter the total number of students at and below each score. For example, the cf for the score 80 is 1 because only one student scored 80 or below. The cf for the score 82 is the number of students who scored 82 plus the number who scored less than 82; that is, $1 + 1 = 2$. The cf for 84 is the number of students who scored 84 plus the number of students who scored less than 84; that is, $2 + 1 + 1 = 4$.

    Remember, the cf for the maximum score (in this case, 96) is equal to the number of subjects in the study (N); in this case, 20. In other words, all students scored 96 or less.

4. In the fourth column, under $\%$, enter the percentage of times that each score occurs. To compute percentage, divide the number of times a score occurs (f) by the total number in the sample (N). In our example, the percentage of students who scored 80 is $1/20 = .05$, or 5%. The percentage who scored 84 is $2/20 = .10$, or 10%, and the percentage who scored 88 is $6/20 = .30$, or 30%.

Formula: $\% = \dfrac{f}{N}$

f = frequency
N = sample size

Example: What percentage of students scored 86 in table 3.1?

Answer: $\% = f/N = 3/20 = 15\%$

5. In the fifth column, under $c\%$, enter the total percentage of students at or be-

low each score. For example, the *c%* for 80 is 5% because only 5% of students scored 80 or below; the *c%* for 82 represents the percentage of students who scored 82 plus the percentage who scored less than 82; 5% + 5% = 10% (You can also compute *c%* by dividing the *cf* for 82 by N; 2/20 = .10, or 10%). The *c%* for 84 is the percentage of students who scored 84 plus the total percentage of students who scored less than 84; that is, 10% + 5% + 5% = 20% (or, divide the *cf* for 84 by N; 4/20 = .20, or 20%).

Remember, the *c%* for 96 (maximum score) is 100%. In other words, 100% of students scored 96 or less. To compute *c%,* divide the cumulative frequency (*cf*) by the total number of cases in the study (N).

$$c\% = \frac{cf}{N}$$

Formula: $c\% = \dfrac{cf}{N}$

cf = cumulative frequency

N = sample size

Example: What is the cumulative percentage for a score 86 in table 3.1 (in other words, what percentage of students scored 86 or less)?

Answer: $c\% = cf/N = 7/20 = 35\%$

How to Create a Frequency Distribution Table in SPSS.   For this purpose, we will use the variables of level of education (**EDUCAT**) and workload (**LOAD**)[1] from the SPSS *Job Satisfaction* data file as a practice exercise. As taught in chapter 2, two methods may be used to run a frequency distribution table: the SPSS main toolbar or an SPSS syntax file.

To create a frequency table in SPSS, follow these steps:

a. Open the SPSS *Job Satisfaction* data file.
b. Click on *Analyze* in the SPSS main toolbar.
c. Click on *Descriptive Statistics* and click on *Frequencies* (screen 3.1). The dialog box *Frequencies* will open (screen 3.2).
d. From the variables list (left box), scroll down and click on **EDUCAT**.
e. Click on the arrow button between the two boxes to move **EDUCAT** in the *Variable(s)* box.
f. Repeat steps d and e to find and move **LOAD** in the *Variable(s)* box.
g. Make sure that the box in the right side of *Display frequency tables* is checked (SPSS default).
h. Click on *OK.*

[1]Bold capital letter words represent variable names as they appear in SPSS data files.

Screen 3.1: SPSS *Analyze* Toolbar

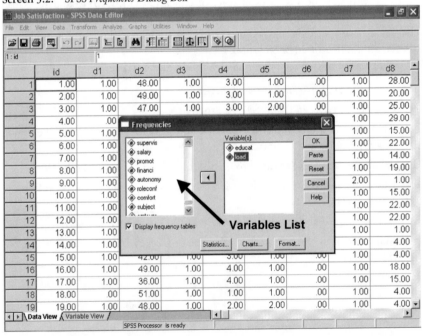

Screen 3.2: SPSS *Frequencies* Dialog Box

SPSS syntax for frequency distribution:

Frequency **EDUCAT LOAD.**

The following tables describe the SPSS output. They include Statistics (table 3.2) and Frequency Tables (table 3.3.A and table 3.3.B). The Statistics table summarizes the number of valid and missing cases for each variable in the analysis; in this example, **EDUCAT** and **LOAD**.

As shown in table 3.2, there are 218 valid cases for each variable and no missing cases. All subjects in the study have valid scores in both variables. If, however, two participants had failed to provide levels of education, then the valid number for **EDUCAT** would be 216 and the missing number would be 2.

The frequency table shows the frequencies, percentages, and cumulative percentages for each score (value) in each variable. There is one frequency table for each variable in the analysis; in this case, one table for **EDUCAT** and one for **LOAD**.

Unlike in table 3.1, SPSS 12.0 (and earlier versions) does not produce the cumulative frequency distribution. Instead, SPSS produces two columns for percentage: *Percent* and *Valid Percent*. *Percent* represents the percentage of times each score (value) occurs assuming there are no missing cases. *Valid Percent* represents the percentage of times each score (value) occurs when taking into account only cases with no missing scores (values). If there are no missing cases, then the *Percent* and *Valid Percent* will be identical. It is recommended to report the *Valid Percent*.

According to table 3.3.A: Frequency Table for Level of Education, 185 participants have undergraduate degrees and 33 participants have graduate degrees. In other words, 84.9% have undergraduate degrees and the remaining 15.1% have graduate degrees. Notice that *Percent* and *Valid Percent* are equal in this case. This is because there are no missing values. Remember that the sum of all frequencies is equal to the total sample size (N = 218), and the total percentage is 100%.

Table 3.3.B: Frequency Table for Workload shows the lowest score for workload is 6 and the maximum score is 20. One subject (.5%) has a score of 6, 18 subjects (8.3%) have a score of 10, and 25 subjects (11.5%) have a score of 16. The *Cumulative Percent* shows that 20.6% of subjects have a score of 10 or less, 51.4% have a score of 13 or less, 94% have a score of 17 or less, and 100% of subjects have a score of 20 or less.

Table 3.2:   Statistics

	EDUCAT (Level of Education)	LOAD
N Valid	218	218
Missing	0	0

Table 3.3.A: Frequency Table for Level of Education

EDUCAT

			Frequency	Percent	Valid Percent	Cumulative Percent
Valid	.00	Undergraduate	185	84.9	84.9	84.9
	1.00	Graduate	33	15.1	15.1	100.0
		Total	218	100.0	100.0	

Table 3.3.B: Frequency Table for Workload

LOAD

		Frequency	Percent	Valid Percent	Cumulative Percent
Valid	6.00	1	.5	.5	.5
	7.00	3	1.4	1.4	1.8
	8.00	7	3.2	3.2	5.0
	9.00	16	7.3	7.3	12.4
	10.00	18	8.3	8.3	20.6
	11.00	15	6.9	6.9	27.5
	12.00	27	12.4	12.4	39.9
	13.00	25	11.5	11.5	51.4
	14.00	26	11.9	11.9	63.3
	15.00	31	14.2	14.2	77.5
	16.00	25	11.5	11.5	89.0
	17.00	11	5.0	5.0	94.0
	18.00	6	2.8	2.8	96.8
	19.00	6	2.8 .	2.8	99.5
	20.00	1	.5	.5	100.0
	Total	218	100.0	100.0	

GRAPHIC PRESENTATIONS OF DATA

Presentation of data in frequency distribution tables is sometimes discouraged if the audience is not familiar with basic statistics and won't understand what these tables represent. In this case, it is more helpful to present the data in a way that will communicate to the average person.

Graphic presentation is another way to organize data. Graphs can help visualize data. Unlike frequency distribution tables, however, graphs do not give detailed information and they can be misleading as different people interpret them based on their own understanding.

There are many types of graphs, but only the four most commonly used styles are introduced in this book. This chapter presents the bar graph, histogram, and stem-and-leaf plot. The box plot chart is introduced in the following chapter.

Bar Graph

A bar graph is used to display the frequency or percentage of cases under value categories; that is, variables that are measured at the nominal level of measurement. These variables have values that represent categories with no intrinsic ranking, such as gender, race, or religious affiliation.

A bar graph can be useful to display the frequency or percentage of cases for variables measured at the ordinal level. These variables have values that represent categories with intrinsic ranking, such as the 5-point Likert scale (1 = strongly disagree, 2 = disagree, 3 = neither agree nor disagree, 4 = agree, 5 = strongly agree).

In a bar graph, the y axis represents the frequency or percentage of cases associated with each category and the x axis represents the value categories. To construct a bar graph, draw the same number of vertical bars as the number of categories associated with the nominal variable: Draw four bars to represent four race categories, and two bars to represent two gender categories. All bars should have equal width, and they should not touch each other, as the categories are mutually exclusive. Figure 3.1 is an example of a bar graph representing three categories:

Figure 3.1:   Bar Graph for Treatment Evaluation

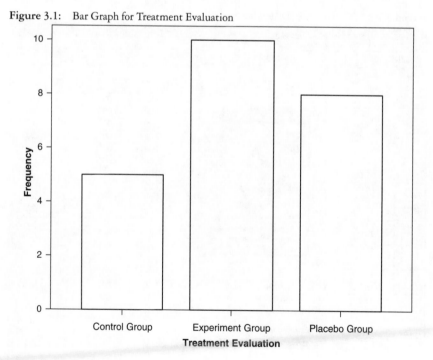

control group, experiment group, and placebo group. The graph shows that there are more subjects in the experiment group (n = 10) than the control group (n = 5) or the placebo group (n = 8). Notice that the three bars are the same width and do not touch each other, indicating that these are three mutually exclusive groups.

How to Create a Bar Graph in SPSS.   To illustrate this, run a bar graph for gender (**D1**) from the *Job Satisfaction* data file. As with frequency distribution tables, there are two ways to generate bar graphs: the SPSS main toolbar and SPSS syntax file.

To create a bar graph in SPSS, follow these steps:

a.   Open the SPSS *Job Satisfaction* data file.

b.   Click on *Graphs* in the SPSS main toolbar.

c.   Scroll down and click on *Bar.* A dialog box called *Bar Charts* will open (screen 3.3).

d.   Click on *Simple* (SPSS default).

e.   Make sure that *Summaries for groups of cases* under *Data in Chart Are* is checked (SPSS default). If not, check it.

f.   Click on *Define.* A new dialog box, *Define Simple Bar: Summaries for Groups of Cases,* will open (screen 3.4.A).

Screen 3.3:   SPSS *Bar Charts* Dialog Box

Screen 3.4:   SPSS *Bar Charts* Dialog Box

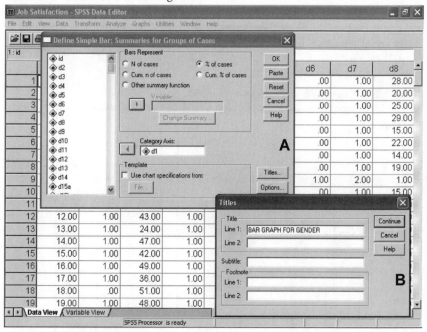

g. Find and highlight **D1** in the variables list and click on the arrow button in the left side of *Category Axis.*

h. Check *N of cases* under *Bars Represent* to request frequencies, *% of cases* to request percentage, or other options.

i. To add a title to the graph, click on *Titles.* A new dialog box called *Titles* will open (screen 3.4.B). Type the title (e.g., Bar Graph for Gender).

j. Click on *Continue,* then *OK.*

```
                    SPSS Syntax for Bar Graph
        (syntax 1 for frequencies; syntax 2 for percentages):

Syntax 1: GRAPH
            /BAR(SIMPLE) = COUNT BY D1
            /MISSING = REPORT
            /TITLE = 'Frequency of Males and Females'.

Syntax 2: GRAPH
            /BAR(SIMPLE) = PCT BY D1
            /MISSING = REPORT
            /TITLE = 'Percentages of Males and Females'.
```

The following outputs show two bar graphs for gender: The first bar graph (figure 3.2.A) presents frequencies for males and females (36 and 182). The second bar graph (figure 3.2.B), which is identical to the first, presents percentages of males versus females (16.5% and 83.5%).

Figure 3.2.A: Bar Graph for Gender—Frequency

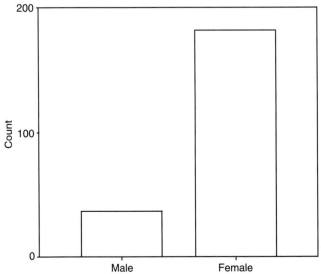

Figure 3.2.B: Bar Graph for Gender—Percentage

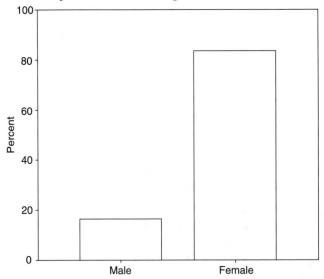

Histogram

A histogram is used to graphically display a distribution of scores or values for continuous data, usually variables measured at the interval level of measurement. These variables have values that represent ordered categories with equal distance between values; for example, IQ scores or Fahrenheit temperature. Histograms can also display ratio variables, which share the above properties, plus meaningful zero; for example, age, years of education, or annual income.

A histogram, like a bar graph, uses the y axis to display frequency of cases for a given score and the x axis to display scores (figure 3.3). Unlike a bar graph, the bars in a histogram touch each other, indicating continuous data.

To construct a histogram, draw a vertical bar for each score or group of scores. All bars should have equal width.

How to Create a Histogram in SPSS.   To illustrate this, run a histogram for workload (**LOAD**) from the SPSS *Job Satisfaction* data file.

To create a histogram in SPSS, follow these steps:

a.   Open the SPSS *Job Satisfaction* data file.

b.   Click on *Graphs* in the SPSS main toolbar.

c.   Click on *Histogram.* A new dialog box called *Histogram* will open (screen 3.5.A).

d.   Find and highlight **LOAD** in the variables list and click on the arrow button in the middle of the dialog box to move **LOAD** in the *Variable* box.

Figure 3.3:   Histogram for Comfort at Work

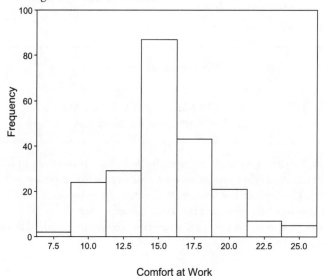

Comfort at Work

Screen 3.5:   SPSS *Histogram* Dialog Box

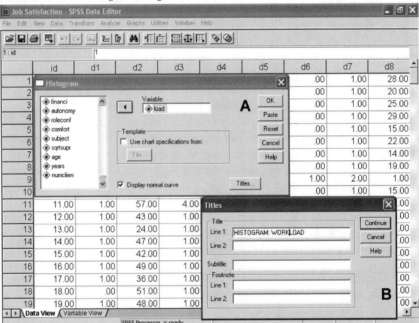

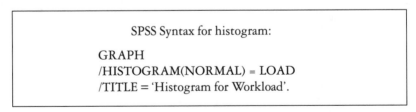

e.   Click on *Titles.* This will open a new dialog box (screen 3.5.B). Type a title and click *Continue* (you need this step only if you wish to add a title to the graph).

f.   You can also check the box next to *Display normal curve,* to examine the shape of the distribution (see chapter 5).

g.   Click on *OK.*

SPSS Syntax for histogram:

GRAPH
/HISTOGRAM(NORMAL) = LOAD
/TITLE = 'Histogram for Workload'.

Figure 3.4 displays the SPSS output for workload. It shows eight bars of equal width representing eight continuous values for workload (minimum = 6 and maximum = 20). The highest bar represents the most frequent score (mode, see chapter 4); the shortest bar represents the least frequent score.

Figure 3.4 also shows overall distribution, the mean, standard deviation, and sample size (see chapter 4).

Figure 3.4:   Histogram for Workload

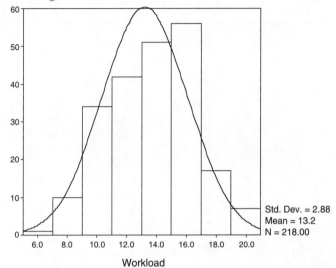

Workload

Std. Dev. = 2.88
Mean = 13.2
N = 218.00

Stem-and-Leaf Plot

Like a histogram, a stem-and-leaf plot displays the distribution of scores or values for a continuous variable. Each observed score or value is subdivided into two components: the leading digits (stem), and the trailing digits (leaf). A stem-and-leaf plot shows each value, a group of values, frequency for each value, frequency for each group of values, and the total sample size. A stem-and-leaf plot is especially useful for comparing two or more groups under one variable (e.g., comparing Whites and Others with regard to their levels of depression). Another advantage of a stem-and-leaf plot is if it is turned counterclockwise it will form a histogram.

How to Create a Stem-and-Leaf Plot.   To illustrate this, use data from table 3.4, depression scores collected from 39 subjects age 65 and older. The minimum score is 2 and maximum score is 47.

To construct a stem-and-leaf plot, first decide on the stem, then on the leaf. In this example, use the "tens" digits for the stems and the "ones" digits for the leaves. For example, the "tens" digit for the score of 2 is 0, and becomes the stem, and the "ones" digit, 2, will serve as the leaf; the "tens" digit for the score of 47 is 4, and becomes the stem, and the "ones" digit, 7, will serve as the leaf; and so on.

The next step is to present the frequency for each group of scores. Figure 3.5 displays a stem-and-leaf plot for these data.

This graph provides the following information:

1.   Minimum score = 2 (stem = 0 and leaf = 2).

2.   Maximum score = 47 (stem = 4 and leaf = 7).

Table 3.4:   Frequency Table for Depression

Score	f	%	c%
2.00	2	5.1	5.1
3.00	1	2.6	7.7
4.00	1	2.6	10.3
5.00	1	2.6	12.8
7.00	2	5.1	17.9
8.00	6	15.4	33.3
9.00	1	2.6	35.9
10.00	1	2.6	38.5
11.00	1	2.6	41.0
12.00	5	12.8	53.8
15.00	3	7.7	61.5
17.00	2	5.1	66.7
18.00	2	5.1	71.8
20.00	2	5.1	76.9
21.00	2	5.1	82.1
22.00	2	5.1	87.2
23.00	1	2.6	89.7
24.00	1	2.6	92.3
30.00	1	2.6	94.9
33.00	1	2.6	97.4
47.00	1	2.6	100.0
Total	39	100.0	

3. Interval frequency: 14 people scored between 2 (stem = 0 and leaf = 2) and 9 (stem = 0 and leaf = 9), 14 between 10 (stem = 1 and leaf = 0), and 18 (stem = 1 and leaf = 8), 8 between 20 and 24, 2 between 30 and 33, and one person scored 47 (stem = 4 and leaf = 7).

4. Individual frequency: the exact frequency for each score. 6 people have a score of 8 (the number 8 appears six times under Leaf with a Stem of 0); 3 people have a score of 15 (the number 5 appears three times under Leaf with a Stem of 1).

5. Sample size: N = 39. This represents the sum of all frequencies.

6. Shape of the distribution: Rotating this graph counterclockwise 90° will produce a histogram displaying the same data.

   How to Create a Stem-and-Leaf Plot in SPSS.   To illustrate this, run a stem-and-leaf for quality of supervision at work (**SUPERVIS**) from the SPSS *Job Satisfaction* data file.

   To create a stem-and-leaf plot in SPSS, follow these steps:

a. Open the SPSS *Job Satisfaction* data file.

b. Select *Analyze*.

Figure 3.5:   Stem-and-Leaf Plot for Depression

Frequency	Stem	Leaf
14	0	2 2 3 4 5 7 7 8 8 8 8 8 8 9
14	1	0 1 2 2 2 2 2 5 5 5 7 7 8 8
8	2	0 0 1 1 2 2 3 4
2	3	0 3
1	4	7
Total 39		

c.   Click on *Descriptive Statistics,* then *Explore.* A new dialog box called *Explore* will open (screen 3.6.A).

d.   Find and highlight **SUPERVIS** in the variables list and click on the top arrow button to move it in the *Dependent List* box.

e.   Check *Plots* under *Display* in the lower left corner.

f.   Click on *Plots* in the lower right corner.

g.   A new dialog box called *Explore: Plots* will open (screen 3.6.B).

Screen 3.6:   SPSS *Explore* Dialog Box

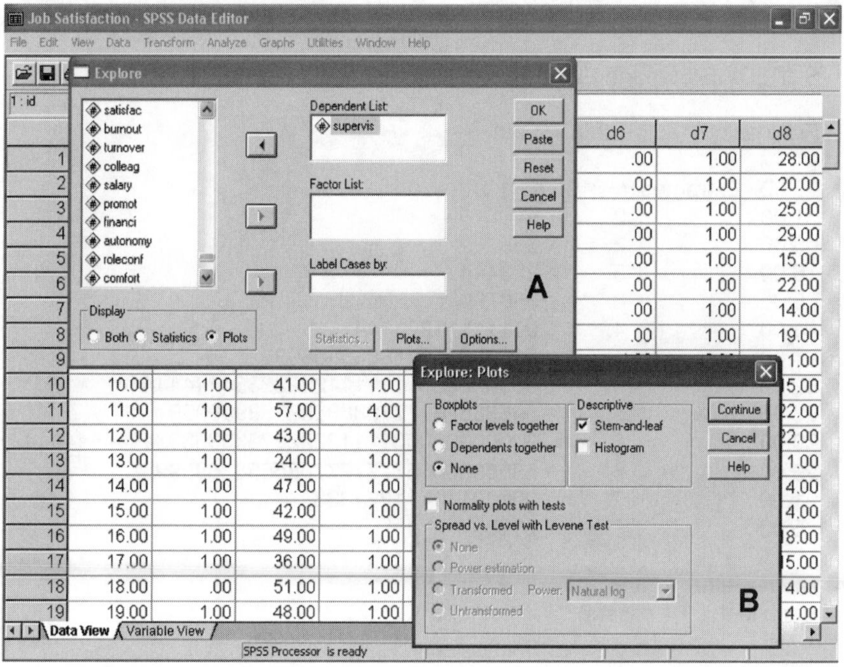

h.   Make sure the *Stem-and-Leaf* box under *Descriptive* is checked (SPSS default).

i.   Choose *None* under *Boxplots* (see chapter 4).

j.   Click *Continue.*

k.   Click *OK.*

SPSS syntax for a stem-and-leaf plot:

EXAMINE SUPERVIS
/PLOT STEMLEAF

Table 3.5:   Explore for Supervision

	Case Processing Summary					
	Cases					
	Valid		Missing		Total	
	N	Percent	N	Percent	N	Percent
SUPERVIS	214	98.2%	4	1.8%	218	100%

Figure 3.6:   Stem-and-Leaf Plot for Supervision

```
SUPERVIS Stem-and-Leaf Plot

Frequency        Stem    Leaf

    9.00   Extremes  (=<19)
    1.00      2.     4
    3.00      2.     789
    6.00      3.     223444
    6.00      3.     556799
   14.00      4.     00111111223344
   21.00      4.     555556677778888888999
   32.00      5.     00000000011111112223333444444444
   28.00      5.     5556666677778888888888999999
   39.00      6.     000000000001111222222333333334444444444
   29.00      6.     55556666667777777888888889999
   21.00      7.     000001111112223333444
    5.00      7.     56889

Stem width:   10.00
Each leaf:    1 case(s)
```

The above two items describe the SPSS output. The first part is a case processing summary (table 3.5) showing the valid number of cases, missing cases, and the total sample size. The second part of the output is a stem-and-leaf plot (figure 3.6). Unlike constructing a stem-and-leaf by hand, SPSS quickly determines upper and lower extreme scores. All cases with lower extreme scores are grouped together at the top of the plot, and upper extreme scores are grouped and shown at the end of the plot. Here, 9 cases have lower extreme scores of 19 or less. There are no cases with upper extreme scores.

In this example, each interval of scores (0–9, 10–19, 20–29, etc.) is divided into two halves: 0–4 and 5–9. The score of 20–24 falls under the first grouping for the 2 stem, while 25–29 falls under the second grouping for the 2 stem.

This stem-and-leaf plot shows that 1 person scored 24 (frequency = 1, stem = 2, and leaf = 4), 3 people scored between 27 and 29 (frequency = 3, stem = 2, and leaf = 7, 8, 9), 14 people scored between 40 and 44, 39 people scored between 60 and 64, and so on.

SUMMARY

This chapter discussed two methods for summarizing and presenting data: frequency distribution tables and graphs. A frequency distribution table summarizes the frequency for each score, cumulative frequency, percentage, and cumulative percentage. Graphs are used to visually display the distribution of scores. Three types were discussed: bar graphs, histograms, and stem-and-leaf plots. A bar graph is used to illustrate the distribution of categorical data. The histogram illustrates a distribution for continuous data. A stem-and-leaf plot illustrates both the frequency and the shape of a distribution for continuous data. SPSS methods of computing and creating frequency tables and graphs were discussed throughout.

Chapter 4 presents the next step in data organization and summary: measures of central tendency, variability, and percentiles; as well as the boxplot chart and its use in data description. The chapter will outline the steps involved in computing these measures and creating boxplot charts in SPSS.

PRACTICAL EXERCISES

I.   The following are the final scores of 40 students who took Basic Research Methods courses in the past two years.

68	65	75	73	80
68	65	76	82	80
86	66	88	75	81
70	67	79	75	74
72	68	100	82	82
72	76	91	96	84
84	89	94	100	88
86	90	96	80	82

The instructor used the following grading system to determine final grades:

A = 90 or higher   B = 80 to 89

C = 70 to 79   F = 69 or less

Directions:

1. Create a frequency distribution table to summarize the raw scores.
2. What percentage of students failed the course (F)?
3. What percentage of students received a grade of A or B?
4. How many students scored A? B? C? F?
5. Use your answer for question 4 to construct a bar graph.
6. Construct a stem-and-leaf plot for the raw scores. Explain the process in creating a stem-and-leaf plot.

II. Access the SPSS *Depression-Elderly* data file (see appendix A for variables list) and answer the following questions:

1. Run frequency distributions for all variables.
2. Describe participants in terms of their gender, race, education, marital status, level of education, and whether they consider themselves sick.
3. What percentage of subjects are considered clinically depressed (a score of 16 or above on the **CES-D**)?
4. How many were older than 75 years old?
5. Create a new column and compute the cumulative frequency for negative recent life events (**NRLEV**).
6. What percentage had between 4 and 7 negative recent life events?
7. From the variables list, choose one categorical variable and one continuous variable. For each variable, create a graph. What information does each graph provide?

CHAPTER 4

Descriptive Statistics: Measures of Central Tendency, Variability, and Percentiles

LEARNING OBJECTIVES

1. Understand measures of central tendency
2. Understand measures of variability
3. Understand percentiles
4. Understand boxplot charts
5. Understand how to compute these measures and create a boxplot in SPSS

Data Set: *Job Satisfaction* (Appendix A)

INTRODUCTION

Chapter 3 discussed two methods for organizing and summarizing research data: frequency distribution tables and graphs. These are two useful methods that visually show how values are distributed, but they do not describe where the values or scores of variables are centered. For example, a social work researcher who examines levels of anxiety among sexually abused young females might like to know which level of anxiety score appears the most, falls at the middle, or is average.

This chapter presents three measures of central tendency that provide information about the point around which a distribution's values are clustered: the mode, median, and mean. Three other measures of variability describe the dispersion of each value or score from the mean: range, variance, and standard deviation. Percentiles and boxplot charts are also discussed.

Consider the raw data from table 3.1 (see chapter 3). The data show student test scores, as follows (raw data 4.1):

Raw Data 4.1

86	80	82	86	88	90	88	90	94	92
84	88	84	88	86	92	88	96	90	88

MEASURES OF CENTRAL TENDENCY

Mode

The mode is the simplest measure of central tendency. It is the most frequently occurring score in a distribution.

To determine the mode in the example (raw data 4.1), count the number of times (frequency) each value occurs. It is easier if we arrange the data in an array (array data 4.1):

Array Data 4.1

80	82	84	84	86	86	86	88	88	88
88	88	88	90	90	90	92	92	94	96

Evaluating this data, the value 88 occurs six times, followed by 86 which occurs three times. Therefore, in the above example, 88 is the mode. Also, find the mode by looking at the absolute frequency (f) column in table 3.1 (chapter 3). The most frequent score is 88; it occurred six times, the highest frequency.

The following dataset (raw data 4.2) represents burnout among 19 social workers employed at a child protective services agency in Virginia. The scores range between 31 and 60, with a score of 45 and above indicating greater levels of burnout. What is (are) the mode(s) of these data?

Raw Data 4.2

60	55	38	39	42	58	42	43	47	54
45	31	43	42	48	31	54	56	43	

To determine the mode(s), arrange data in an array, from the lowest to the highest score, as follows:

Array Data 4.2

31	31	38	39	42	42	42	43	43	43
45	47	48	54	54	55	56	58	60	

The score 42 occurs three times, as does 43. This distribution has two modes: 42 and 43.

The mode is simple to figure out; it is the most occurring score. It is easy to compute and not affected by outlier scores, the extremes at either end of the distribution, which may demand special consideration.

Unlike other measures of central tendency (mean and median), one disadvantage of the mode is that a given distribution may include more than one mode. A distribution with one mode, which is desired, is called *unimodal.* A distribution with two modes is called *bimodal,* and a distribution with three or more modes is called *multimodal.* Another disadvantage of the mode is that it does not provide information about the variation of scores.

Median

The median is a value in a distribution below and above where half of the values fall. The median divides an array of values into two equal groups. Like the mode, median is not affected by outlier scores.

To determine the median, first arrange raw data in an array.

If the distribution has an odd number of cases, the median will be the middle value.

If the distribution has an even number of cases, the median will be the sum of the two middle scores divided by two.

Since there are 20 cases in raw data 4.1, the median will be the sum of the two middle scores divided by 2. Looking at array data 4.1, we found that the two middle scores are 88 and 88. Thus, the median is 88 + 88/2 = 88.

Example: What is the median in raw data 4.2?

Answer: Because there are 19 cases in this distribution, the value associated with the middle case is the median; that is, the value associated with the 10th case (9 cases below and 9 cases above). The score for the 10th case is 43, the median. In other words, 50% of social workers in this example have a score of 43 or below and 50% have a score of 43 or above.

Mean

The mean is the most reported measure of central tendency. It is the arithmetic average of the scores in a distribution: the sum of all values (ΣX) divided by

$$\text{Formula: } \overline{X} = \frac{\Sigma f X}{N}$$

$\overline{X}$ = mean

Σ (sigma) = sum

f = frequency

X = score

N = number of cases

Table 4.1:   Frequency Scores Table

X	f	fX
80	1	80
82	1	82
84	2	168
86	3	258
88	6	528
90	3	270
92	2	184
94	1	94
96	1	96
Σ	20	1760

X = score, f = frequency

the number of cases (N). The main disadvantage of the mean, unlike the mode or median, is that it is very sensitive to outlying scores. Data should be carefully evaluated for outlying scores before a decision is made to report the mean. In such cases, the mean may not be appropriate to report. The symbol for the population mean is μ (mu) and the sample mean is $\overline{X}$ (X bar).

Example: Compute the mean score for raw data 4.1.

Answer: First, arrange data in a frequency table, presenting the scores and their absolute frequencies (table 4.1). Second, add a column to present the outcomes of multiplying each score (X) by its frequency (f). Third, add the values in the fX column (that is, ΣfX). Finally, divide this value by the number of cases in the study (N).

$$\overline{X} = \frac{\Sigma fX}{N} = \frac{1760}{20} = 88$$

If you do not wish to create a frequency table, you can compute the mean as follows:

$$\overline{X} = \frac{\begin{array}{c}(80 \times 1) + (82 \times 1) + (84 \times 2) + (86 \times 3) \\ + (88 \times 6) + (90 \times 3) + (92 \times 2) + (94 \times 1) + (96 \times 1)\end{array}}{20}$$

$$\overline{X} = \frac{1760}{20} = 88$$

Example: What is the mean for Raw Data 4.2?

$$\begin{aligned}\text{\textit{Answer:} } \overline{X} = &(31 \times 2) + (38 \times 1) + (39 \times 1) + (42 \times 3) + (45 \times 1) \\ &+ (47 \times 1) + (48 \times 1) + (54 \times 2) + (55 \times 1) \\ &\frac{+ (56 \times 1) + (58 \times 1) + (60 \times 1)}{19}\end{aligned}$$

$$\overline{X} = \frac{871}{19} = 45.84$$

Thus, the mean is 45.84, which falls slightly above the cutoff score of 45. This indicates that social workers in this child protective services agency tend to experience great levels of burnout.

Measure(s) of Central Tendency to Report

The three measures of central tendency each provide different information about the distribution. However, the type of data, their levels of measurement, and their distribution will determine what is most appropriate to report.

With nominal variables, the mode is the only measure of central tendency to report.

Example: If the variable **RACE** is classified as 1 = White, 2 = African American, 3 = Hispanic, 4 = Native American, 5 = Other, it is meaningless to report the median or the mean. However, if we found that the majority of participants in a study are African American, then we can safely report that the mode is African American, or 3, the value label associated with it.

With ordinal data, both the mode and the median could be reported.

Example: We asked 50 subjects to rate their physical health on a 5-point Likert scale (1 = poor, 2 = fair, 3 = good, 4 = very good, 5 = excellent). Seven subjects rated their physical health as 1, 8 as 2, 10 as 3, 15 as 4, and 10 as 5. Here, the mode is 4 because 4 is the most frequent score (15 subjects chose 4); the median is 3.5, the middle score in an even number of cases (25 subjects, or 50%, chose 3 or less; 25 subjects, or 50%, chose 4 or above).

With interval or ratio data, the mean could be reported along with the mode and median. However, the mean is very sensitive to outlying cases. For example, if we asked 10 undergraduate students their ages and found that 9 of them were between 18 and 24 and the 10th student was 36, this increases the mean from where it should be to a higher score. If this student was 14, then the mean would be lower than it should be. In either case, the mean is not a good representation of the data. The researcher may want to treat this case as missing and report the mean for the 9 students within a normal range.

MEASURES OF VARIABILITY

Range

The range is the simplest measure of variability. It is the number of units on a distribution of scores that include the maximum and minimum scores. For example, the number of units on a scale of 1 to 10 is 10 (1, 2, 3, 4, 5, 6, 7, 8, 9, and 10; there are 10 values). The number of units on a scale of 25 to 33 is 9 (25, 26, 27, 28, 29, 30, 31, 32, and 33; there are 9 values). A range is defined mathematically as:

Formula: Range = (Maximum Score − Minimum Score) + 1

Example: Compute the range for raw data 4.1 and raw data 4.2.

Answer: To find the range for each data set, first find the minimum and maximum scores, then apply them in the range formula as follows:

Raw Data 4.1:   Range = (96 − 80) + 1 = 17
Raw Data 4.2:   Range = (60 − 31) + 1 = 30

Variance

The second measure of variability is variance. It is a statistic that measures how spread out a distribution of scores is from the mean. The more spread out a distribution is, the greater the deviation is from the mean.

Mathematically, the variance is defined as the average (mean) of the sum of squared deviations around the mean. The symbol for the variance in a population is σ^2 (sigma squared) and in a sample it is S^2.

Formula: $S^2 = \dfrac{\Sigma f(X - \overline{X})^2}{N - 1}$

S^2 = variance
Σ = sum
f = frequency
X = score
$\overline{X}$ = mean
N = sample size

To obtain the variance, first compute the mean ($\overline{X}$) for the data. Second, compute the mean deviation for each case by subtracting the mean from each raw score $(X - \overline{X})$. Third, square each mean deviation $(X - \overline{X})^2$. Fourth, sum all squared deviations $[\Sigma f(X - \overline{X})^2]$. Finally, divide this sum by $(N - 1)$.

Remember: The sum of all mean deviations is always zero: $\Sigma f(X - \overline{X}) = 0$.

Example: What is the variance of student test scores presented in table 3.1 (see chapter 3)?

Answer: To compute the variance, first add two columns to the table: the mean deviation $(X - \overline{X})$ and the squared mean deviation $(X - \overline{X})^2$ (as shown in table 4.2).

$$\overline{X} = \frac{\Sigma fX}{N} = \frac{1760}{20} = 88$$
$$\Sigma f(X - \overline{X})^2 = 64 + 36 + 32 + 12 + 0 + 12 + 32 + 36 + 64 = 288$$

Table 4.2:   Frequency Distribution Table

X	f	fX	$f(X - \overline{X})$	$f(X - \overline{X})^2$
80	1	80	$1(80 - 88) = -8$	$1(80 - 88)^2 = 1 \times (-8)^2 = 64$
82	1	82	$1(82 - 88) = -6$	$1(82 - 88)^2 = 1 \times (-6)^2 = 36$
84	2	168	$2(84 - 88) = -8$	$2(84 - 88)^2 = 2 \times (-4)^2 = 32$
86	3	258	$3(86 - 88) = -6$	$3(86 - 88)^2 = 3 \times (-2)^2 = 12$
88	6	528	$6(88 - 88) = 0$	$6(88 - 88)^2 = 6 \times (0)^2 = 0$
90	3	270	$3(90 - 88) = 6$	$3(90 - 88)^2 = 3 \times (2)^2 = 12$
92	2	184	$2(92 - 88) = 8$	$2(92 - 88)^2 = 2 \times (4)^2 = 32$
94	1	94	$1(94 - 88) = 6$	$1(94 - 88)^2 = 1 \times (6)^2 = 36$
96	1	96	$1(96 - 88) = 8$	$1(96 - 88)^2 = 1 \times (8)^2 = 64$
Σ	20	1760	zero	288

$$\text{Variance} = S^2 = \frac{\Sigma f(X - \overline{X})^2}{N - 1} = \frac{288}{19} = 15.16$$

Standard Deviation

Standard deviation is the most-used measure of variability. Reported along with the mean, it indicates how closely scores in a distribution cluster around the mean. The larger the standard deviation, the larger the variability around the mean. It is measured in the same units as the mean. For example, if the mean age is 25, a standard deviation could be ±5 years.

The standard deviation is most appropriate when data approach a normal distribution (see chapter 5). In this case, 68.26% of subjects will fall within ±1 standard deviation of the mean, 95.44% of subjects fall within ±2 standard deviations of the mean, and 99.74 percent of subjects will fall within ±3 standard deviations of the mean. We return to this in the next chapter when we discuss normal distribution and z scores.

Mathematically, standard deviation is the square root of the variance ($\sqrt{S^2}$). The symbol for the standard deviation for a population is σ and for a sample is SD.

As with any value produced by the square root, standard deviation is always reported with + and − signs, which indicate that a given score in a distribution can be above or below the mean.

Example: Compute the standard deviation for the data in table 4.2.

Answer: Because the variance for these data is 15.16, the standard deviation will be as follows:

$$SD = \sqrt{S^2} = \sqrt{15.16} = \pm 3.89$$

Percentile

A percentile is a point or score in a distribution, at or below which a given percentage of scores is found. It is symbolized by the capital letter P with a subscript number indicating the percentile desired. For example, P_{35} indicates the 35th percentile; 35% of cases fall at or below the given score. The 50th percentile (P_{50}) is the score that 50% of cases fall at or below. This is also called the median (median = 50th percentile).

Example: John's score on a statistics test was at the 75th percentile; 75% of all students who took the test scored at or below his score, and 25% scored higher than John. This does not mean that John passed or failed the test.

To find the percentile for a specific score in a distribution, locate the cumulative percentage ($c\%$) in a frequency distribution table (see chapter 3). The cumulative percentage for a given score represents the percentile for this score.

For example, using raw data 3.1 (chapter 3), a student who scored 88 in the data analysis course falls at the 65th percentile (p_{65}): 65% of students scored at or below 88. A student who scored 84 falls at the 20th percentile: 20% scored at or below 84; 65% and 20% are the cumulative percentages for 88 and 84 (see table 3.1).

Quartiles.   The quartiles are the 25th, 50th (median), and 75th percentiles, symbolized by Q1, Q2, and Q3. Quartiles divide a distribution of scores into four equal parts.

To find a quartile, first find the median, or 50th percentile, which divides a distribution into equal groups. Treat each half as a separate distribution. For all scores below the median, find the middle point. This will be the 25th percentile. Now locate the middle point for all scores above the median. This is the 75th percentile.

Interquartiles Range.   The distance between the 75th percentile (Q3) and the 25th percentile (Q1), symbolized by IQR, is computed by subtracting the 25th percentile from the 75th percentile.

Formula: IQR = Q3 − Q1

IQR = interquartiles range
Q3 = 75th percentile
Q1 = 25th percentile

Figure 4.1:   Boxplot for Job Satisfaction by Gender

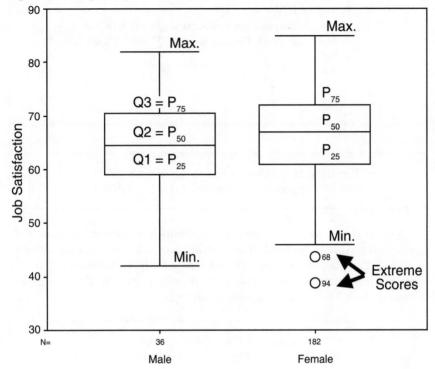

Boxplot

A boxplot is a graphical presentation that illustrates the median (P_{50}), the range (minimum and maximum), and quartiles (Q1 and Q3). It is also used to identify unusual or outlying scores in a distribution. A boxplot does not provide as much information as a histogram or stem-and-leaf plot.

Figure 4.1 displays two boxplots comparing male and female social workers with regard to job satisfaction. The median of job satisfaction for females (67) was slightly higher than that of males (65.5). The 75th and 25th percentiles for females were both slightly higher than those for males. These numbers indicate that female social workers are more satisfied with their jobs than male social workers.

The figure also shows two minor outlier cases associated with the female's boxplot. These are case #68 and case #94 in the *Job Satisfaction* data file.

How to Construct a Boxplot.   First, identify minor or extreme outlying cases on the distribution. A score is considered an extreme outlier if it is more or less than three times the interquartiles (IQR). A score is considered a minor outlier if it is more or less than 1.5 times the IQR.

Formulas: IQR = Q3 – Q1
Extreme Outlier Score > Q3 + 3 × (IQR)
Extreme Outlier Score < Q1 – 3 × (IQR)

IQR = interquartile range
$Q3 = P_{75}$
$Q1 = P_{25}$

Formulas: Minor Outlier Score > Q3 + 1.5 × (IQR)
Minor Outlier Score < Q1 – 1.5 × (IQR)

Outlier scores fall at either end of a distribution (minimum and maximum scores), and need to be adjusted. If no outlying cases exist, no adjustment should be made. This adjustment is referred to as Reasonable Upper Boundary (RUB), the adjusted maximum score, and Reasonable Lower Boundary (RLB), the adjusted minimum score. They are computed as follows:

Formulas: RUB = Q3 + 1.5 (IQR)
RLB = Q1 – 1.5 (IQR)

Example: Construct a boxplot for Array Data 4.1.
Answer:

1. Compute the P_{50} (median).

    $$P_{50} = \frac{(88 + 88)}{2} = 88$$

2. Find P_{25}.
    Treat the first 50% of cases as a new distribution, as follows:

    80   82   84   84   86   86   86   88   88   88

    The two middle scores are 86 and 86. The middle point is (86 + 86)/2 = 86.

3. Find P_{75}.
    Treat the second 50% of cases as a second distribution.

    88   88   88   90   90   90   92   92   94   96

    The two middle scores are 90 and 90. The middle point is (90 + 90)/2 = 90.

4. Compute the Reasonable Upper and Lower Boundaries (RUP and RLB).

$$IQR = Q3 - Q1 = P_{75} - P_{25} = 90 - 86 = 4$$
$$RUB = Q3 + 1.5(IQR)$$
$$90 + 1.5 \times 4 = 90 + 6 = 96$$
$$RLB = Q1 + 1.5(IQR)$$
$$86 - 1.5 \times 4 = 86 - 6 = 80$$

Any score above 96 or below 80 is considered an outlier score, and will be represented on the boxplot by (E) for extreme outliers and (M) for minor outliers. In the example, no scores fall below 80 or above 96, the values for RUB and RLB. This indicates no outlier cases in this distribution.

The values needed to construct a boxplot are as follows:

1. Adjusted minimum score (RLB) = 80

2. $Q1 = P_{25} = 86$

3. $Q2 = P_{50} = $ median $= 88$

4. $Q3 = P_{75} = 90$

5. Adjusted maximum score (RUB) = 96

To construct a boxplot, first draw a line parallel to the x axis to convey the minimum score (RLB = 80). Second, draw a line of the same length to convey the maximum score (RUB = 96). Third, draw three lines parallel to the x axis but slightly longer than the previous two lines to convey Q1, Q2, and Q3. Fourth, connect the ends of these three lines to form a rectangle. Fifth, connect the midpoint of the minimum with Q1 and another line to connect the midpoint of the maximum with Q3. Figure 4.2 illustrates this boxplot.

Figure 4.2:   Boxplot for Raw Data 4.1

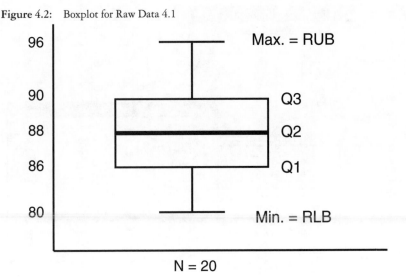

How to Run Measures of Central Tendency and Variability in SPSS.   To illustrate this, we will use the variable job satisfaction (**SATISFAC**) from the SPSS *Job Satisfaction* data file as a practice exercise.

To run measures of central tendency and variability in SPSS, follow these steps:

a.   Open the SPSS *Job Satisfaction* data file.

b.   Click on *Analyze* in the SPSS main toolbar.

c.   Click on *Descriptive Statistics.*

d.   Click on *Frequencies.* A new dialog box called *Frequencies* will open (screen 4.1.A).

e.   Scroll down in the variables list and click on **SATISFAC.**

f.   Click on the arrow button between the two boxes to move the **SATISFAC** in the *Variable(s)* box.

g.   Click on *Statistics* in the bottom of the *Frequencies* dialog box (screen 4.1.A). A new dialog box called *Frequencies: Statistics* will open (screen 4.1.B).

h.   Check the *Mean, Median,* and *Mode* under *Central Tendency.*

i.   Check *Quartiles* under *Percentile Values* to get the 25th, 50th, and 75th percentiles. You may also check *Percentile(s)* to request a specific percentile. Let us request the 10th, 20th, and 60th percentiles. After you check the *Percentile(s),* type 10 in the *Percentile(s)* box and click on *Add,* type 20 and click on *Add,* type 60 and click on *Add.*

Screen 4.1:   SPSS *Frequencies: Statistics* Dialog Box

Screen 4.2:   SPSS *Frequencies: Charts* Dialog Box

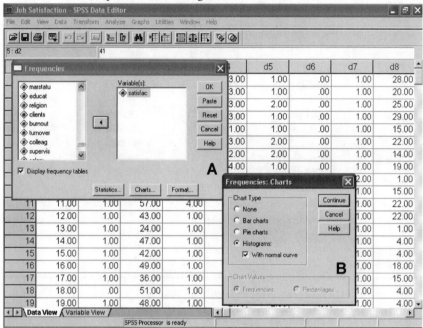

j.   Check *Std. Deviation, Variance, Range, Minimum,* and *Maximum* under *Dispersion.*

k.   Click on *Continue* to return to *Frequencies* dialog box.

l.   You can also click on *Charts* to request a chart. A new dialog box called *Frequencies: Charts* will open (screen 4.2.B).

m.   If you have a categorical variable, you may check *Bar Charts* or *Pie Charts.* For continuous variables like **SATISFAC,** you may request a histogram. Check *Histograms* and check *With normal curve.*

n.   Click on *Continue* and click on *OK.*

SPSS syntax for central tendency and variability:

FREQUENCIES SATISFAC
/NTILES = 4
/PERCENTILES = 10 20 60
/STATISTICS = STDDEV VARIANCE RANGE MINIMUM
MAXIMUM
MEAN MEDIAN MODE
/HISTOGRAM NORMAL.

Table 4.3:   Statistics Table for Job Satisfaction

SATISFAC		
N	Valid	218
	Missing	0
Mean		66.1606
Median		67.0000
Mode		64.00
Std. Deviation		8.82534
Variance		77.88655
Range		46.00
Minimum		39.00
Maximum		85.00
Percentiles	10	54.0000
	20	59.0000
	25	61.0000
	50	67.0000
	60	69.0000
	75	72.0000

To analyze more than one variable, type the variable name(s) after **SATIS-FAC,** with a space between variable names.

Tables 4.3 and 4.4 and figure 4.3 display the SPSS output.

The statistics table (table 4.3) reports the number of valid and missing cases, measures of central tendency (mean, median, mode), measures of variability (standard deviation, variance, range,[1] minimum, and maximum), and percentiles.

Table 4.4 displays the frequency, percent, valid percent, and cumulative percent for each score in job satisfaction (see chapter 3).

The last part of the output displays a histogram with a normal curve (see chapter 5) for job satisfaction. Figure 4.3 also reports the standard deviation, mean, and number of cases (N).

How to Create a Boxplot in SPSS.   Create a boxplot for overall workload (**LOAD**) and workload by level of education (**EDUCAT—BSW vs. MSW**). Both variables are from the SPSS *Job Satisfaction* file.

To create a boxplot in SPSS, follow these steps:

a.   Open the SPSS *Job Satisfaction* data file.

b.   Click on *Graphs* in the SPSS main toolbar.

c.   Click on *Boxplot*. A dialogue box called *Boxplot* will open (screen 4.3).

---

[1]SPSS computes range by subtracting the minimum score from the maximum score (it does not add 1 to the formula). In this case, it is recommended to report the minimum and maximum scores.

Table 4.4:   Frequency Table for Job Satisfaction

		SATISFAC		
		Frequency	Percent	Valid Percent	Cumulative Percent
Valid	39.00	1	.5	.5	.5
	42.00	1	.5	.5	.9
	43.00	1	.5	.5	1.4
	44.00	1	.5	.5	1.8
	46.00	2	.9	.9	2.8
	47.00	1	.5	.5	3.2
	48.00	2	.9	.9	4.1
	49.00	1	.5	.5	4.6
	51.00	2	.9	.9	5.5
	52.00	1	.5	.5	6.0
	53.00	6	2.8	2.8	8.7
	54.00	3	1.4	1.4	10.1
	56.00	6	2.8	2.8	15.6
	57.00	2	.9	.9	16.5
	58.00	3	1.4	1.4	17.9
	59.00	7	3.2	3.2	21.1
	60.00	3	1.4	1.4	22.5
	61.00	9	4.1	4.1	26.6
	62.00	12	5.5	5.5	32.1
	63.00	3	1.4	1.4	33.5
	64.00	17	7.8	7.8	41.3
	65.00	5	2.3	2.3	43.6
	66.00	6	2.8	2.8	46.3
	67.00	16	7.3	7.3	53.7
	68.00	11	5.0	5.0	58.7
	69.00	8	3.7	3.7	62.4
	70.00	12	5.5	5.5	67.9
	71.00	8	3.7	3.7	71.6
	72.00	12	5.5	5.5	77.1
	73.00	7	3.2	3.2	80.3
	74.00	8	3.7	3.7	83.9
	75.00	4	1.8	1.8	85.8
	76.00	9	4.1	4.1	89.9
	77.00	6	2.8	2.8	92.7
	78.00	3	1.4	1.4	94.0
	80.00	2	.9	.9	95.0
	81.00	2	.9	.9	95.9
	82.00	3	1.4	1.4	97.2
	83.00	2	.9	.9	98.2
	84.00	2	.9	.9	99.1
	85.00	2	.9	.9	100.0
	Total	218	100.0	100.0	

Figure 4.3:   Histogram for Job Satisfaction

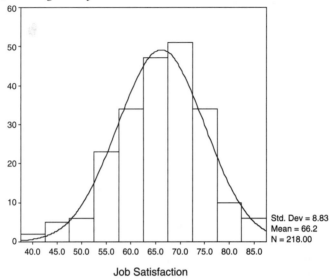

Job Satisfaction

Screen 4.3:   SPSS *Boxplot* Dialog Box

Screen 4.4:   SPSS *Define Simple Boxplot* Dialog Box

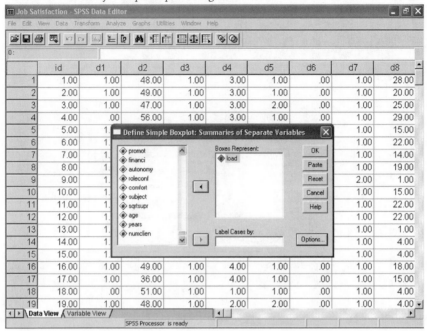

d. Click on *Simple* (SPSS default).

   i. To create a boxplot for one continuous variable (**LOAD**):

   a. Check *Summaries of separate variables.*

   b. Click on *Define.* A new dialog box called *Define Simple Boxplot: Summaries of Separate Variables* will open (screen 4.4).

   c. Scroll down in the variables list and click on **LOAD,** click on the arrow button between the two boxes to move **LOAD** in the *Boxes Represent* box.

   d. Click on *OK.*

   ii. To compare two or more groups with regard to a continuous variable (**LOAD** by **EDUCAT**—undergraduate vs. graduate workload), follow steps *ia* to *ic* above and then:

   a. Click on *Define* (make sure that *Summaries for groups of Cases* under *Data in Chart Are* is checked (SPSS default). A new dialog box called *Define Simple Boxplot: Summaries for Groups of Cases* will open (screen 4.5).

   b. Scroll down in the variables list, click on **LOAD** (dependent variable), and click on the upper arrow button to move **LOAD** in the *Variable* box.

   c. Scroll down in the variables list, click on **EDUCAT** (independent variable), and click on the middle arrow button to move **EDUCAT** in the *Category Axis* box.

Screen 4.5:   SPSS *Define Simple Boxplot for Groups* Dialog Box

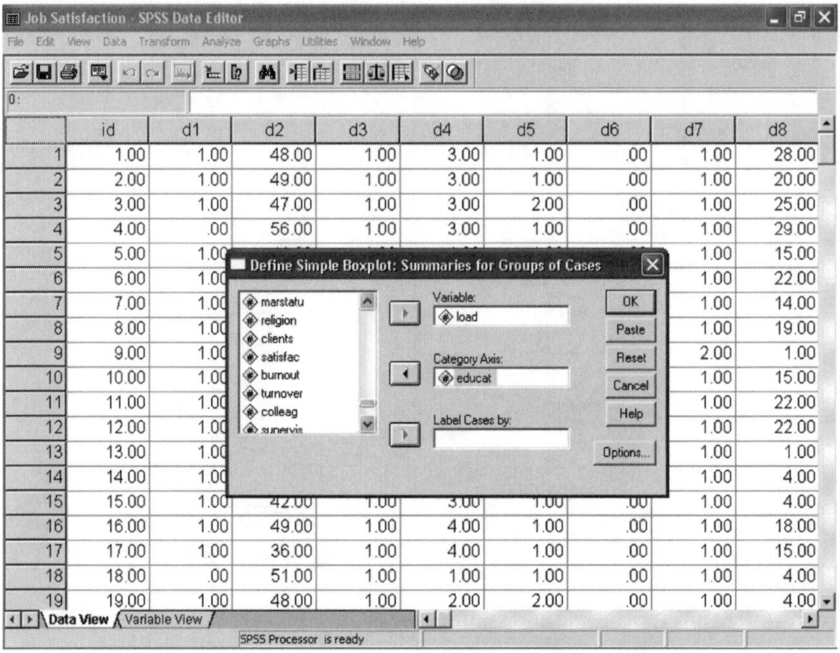

d. Click on *OK*.

SPSS syntax for Boxplot (one continuous variable):

EXAMINE LOAD
/PLOT=BOXPLOT.

SPSS syntax for Boxplot (one continuous variable
by one categorical variable):

EXAMINE LOAD BY EDUCAT
/PLOT=BOXPLOT.

The following SPSS output displays the results of the boxplot commands:

The explore table (table 4.5) reports the number and percentage of valid, missing, and total cases for workload; 218 social workers completed the workload scale. No missing cases were reported.

Figure 4.4. displays a boxplot for workload. The y axis displays the scores for workload. The figure shows that the minimum score was 6 and maximum score was 20; the 25th, 50th, and 75th percentiles are 11, 13, and 15; there were no outlier cases.

Table 4.6 reports the number and percentage of valid, missing, and total cases

Table 4.5:   Explore Table for Workload

	Cases					
	Valid		Missing		Total	
	N	Percent	N	Percent	N	Percent
LOAD	218	100.0%	0	.0%	218	100.0%

Figure 4.4:   Boxplot for Workload

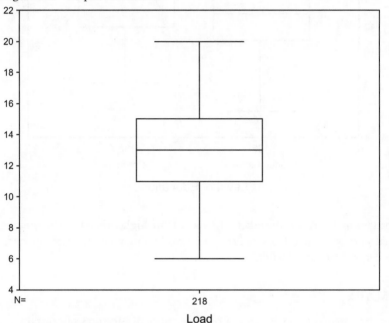

Table 4.6:   Explore Table for Workload by Education

| | EDUCAT | Cases | | | | | |
	(Level of Education)	Valid		Missing		Total	
		N	Percent	N	Percent	N	Percent
LOAD	.00 Undergraduate	185	100.0%	0	.0%	185	100.0%
	1.00 Graduate	33	100.0%	0	.0%	33	100.0%

for workload by levels of education; 185 undergraduate and 33 graduate social
workers completed the workload scale. No missing cases were reported.

Figure 4.5 displays two boxplots for workload: one for undergraduate and another for graduate social workers. Undergraduate workload ranges between 6 and
20; graduate workload ranges between 8 and 18; the 25th and 50th percentiles of

Figure 4.5:   Boxplot for Workload by Education

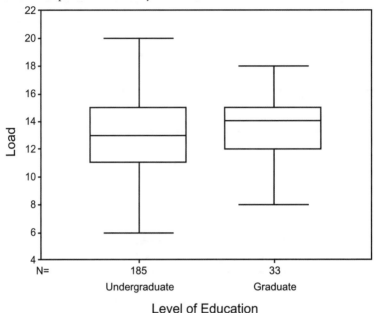

workload for graduate social workers (12 and 14) are higher than for undergraduate social workers (11 and 13). Graduate social workers may have higher workloads than undergraduate social workers.

SUMMARY

Chapter 4 presented two measures of data description. Measures of central tendency are mode, median, and mean. The mode is the most frequent score in a distribution; the median is the score in a distribution that 50% of scores fall at or below; the mean is the average score. Measures of variability consist of the range, variance, and standard deviation. The range is the number of units in a distribution; variance is the sum of the squared deviations around the mean; standard deviation is the square root of the variance.

The chapter also presented the percentile, a point in a distribution at or below which a percentage of cases fall. The boxplot graph visually displays measures of central tendency and variability. How to utilize SPSS to compute measures of central tendency, variability, and percentile, and boxplot construction were also presented.

Chapter 5 discusses the properties of normal and skewed distributions, methods of data transformation into normal distributions, and the properties of standard scores (z scores).

PRACTICAL EXERCISES

I. Use the data from Question 1 in chapter 3 and answer the following questions:

1. Compute the mean, median, and mode.

2. Compute the range, variance, and standard deviation.

3. What are the 25th, 50th, and 75th percentiles?

4. Construct a boxplot for these scores. Explain the process for constructing a boxplot.

II. Access the SPSS *Depression-Welfare* data file (Appendix A) and answer the following questions:

1. Run measures of central tendency and variability for all variables.

2. Report the appropriate measures of central tendency and variability for age (**AGE**), marital status (**MSTATUS**), physical health (**PH**) and levels of depression (**CES_D**).

3. What are the 25th, 40th, 50th, and 80th percentiles for self-esteem (**S_ESTEEM**)?

4. What is the interquartile (**IQR**) for self-esteem?

5. Run a boxplot graph for self-esteem based on race (**RACE_REC**). What group (African Americans or Others) appears to have higher self-esteem? Explain.

6. Run a boxplot for levels of depression (**CES_D**). Explain what this graph tells you.

CHAPTER 5

Normality of Distributions, Data Transformations, and Standard Scores

LEARNING OBJECTIVES

1. Understand normal distributions and their properties
2. Understand skewed distributions
3. Understand data transformations process
4. Understand standard scores (z scores) and their properties

Data Set: *Depression-Elderly* (appendix A)

INTRODUCTION

The previous chapter raised the issue of outlier cases that could severely increase or decrease the mean score as well as the standard deviation. Outlier cases can also significantly affect the shape of the distribution of scores.

The importance of a normal distribution is based on two assumptions: First, many social science constructs, such as life satisfaction, self-esteem, or anxiety approach a normal distribution. Statisticians refer to this as the central limit theorem, which indicates the following:

> As the sample size (N) increases, the sampling distribution of the mean for simple random samples of N cases, taken from a population with a mean equal to μ and a finite variance equal to σ^2, approximates a normal distribution.[1]

According to the central limit theorem, if many samples are drawn from a population, their mean scores tend to approach the true mean of the population;

---

[1]Hinkle, Wiersma, & Jurs (1994), 150.

that is, the distribution of mean scores approaches a normal curve. The more samples are studied, the closer the mean score will be to the true population mean.

Second, as will be seen in the following chapters, parametric statistical techniques like the Pearson product-moment correlation coefficients, student's *t*-tests, analysis of variances, and multiple regression analysis are best utilized when the distribution of the dependent variable (measured at the interval level of measurement or higher) approaches a normal curve. These statistics use the mean score to compute the correlation coefficients. As mentioned in chapter 4, the mean best represents a population if a distribution has no outlier cases and it approaches a normal curve.

This chapter examines the normal distribution and its properties, positively and negatively skewed distributions, and statistical methods to evaluate whether a distribution is considered normal or skewed, as well as methods of data transformation. The chapter ends with a discussion of standard scores (*z* scores) and their uses.

NORMALITY OF DISTRIBUTIONS

Standard Normal Distribution

A standard normal distribution has the following characteristics:

1. It is unimodal. That is, it has only one mode. (Recall from chapter 3 that a distribution may have one, two, or multiple modes.)
2. It is symmetrical; the left and right halves are mirror images.
3. It is bell-shaped, with its maximum height at the mean of the scores.
4. All measures of central tendency (mean, median, and mode) are equal.
5. It is continuous. In other words, there is a value of y (the height) for every value of x, where x is assumed to be a continuous variable (e.g., weight and height).
6. It is asymptotic to the x axis. The farther away from the mean, the closer it gets to the x axis; yet it never touches the x axis. Figure 5.1 displays a standard normal distribution.

In reality, although many constructs approach a normal shape, they may never have a perfect standard, normal shape. The question is then when is a distribution considered normal? A distribution may be considered normal if it is not severely skewed, that is, asymmetrical. An asymmetrical distribution has a mean that is not in the center of the distribution. There are two types of skewed distributions: positively and negatively skewed.

Positively Skewed Distribution

This distribution is skewed to the right; the right tail is longer than the left. The mean of a positively skewed distribution is greater than the median and the

Figure 5.1:   Standard Normal Distribution

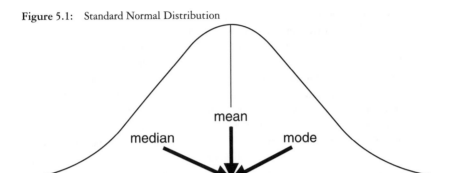

Figure 5.2:   Positively Skewed Distribution

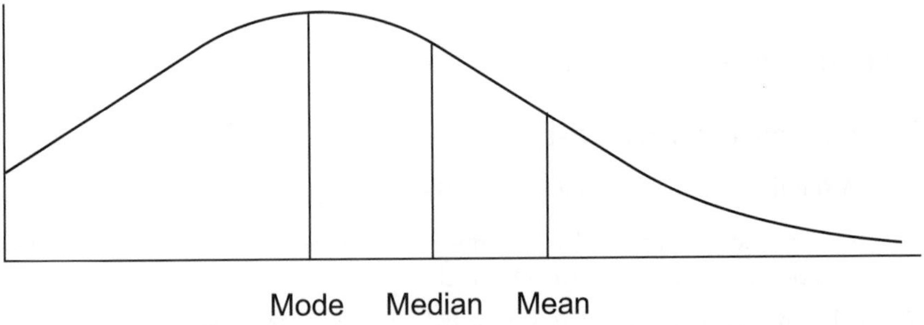

median is greater than the mode (mode < median < mean). In this distribution, most cases fall to the left (see figure 5.2).

To determine if a distribution is positively skewed, subtract the median from the mean. If the result is a positive value, then the distribution is positively skewed.

Mean – Median = Positive Value

Negatively Skewed Distribution

This distribution is skewed to the left; the left tail is longer than the right. The mean is smaller than the median, which is smaller than the mode (mean < median < mode). Most cases fall to the right of the distribution (see figure 5.3).

To determine if a distribution is negatively skewed, subtract the median from the mean. A negative value indicates that the distribution is negatively skewed.

Mean – Median = Negative Value

Figure 5.3:   Negatively Skewed Distribution

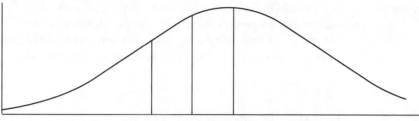

Mean Median Mode

Fisher's Skewness Coefficient

Skewness is a measure of the asymmetry of a distribution. A standard normal distribution is symmetric and has a skewness value of 0. As a rough guide, a skewness value that is more than twice its standard error indicates a significant departure from symmetry and is severely skewed. A distribution may approach a normal curve if it satisfies this formula.[2]

$$\text{Formula: } -1.96 < \frac{\text{Skewness}}{\text{SES}} < 1.96$$
$$\text{SES} = \text{standard error of skewness}$$

Fisher's measure of skewness is sensitive to outlier scores, so should be interpreted with caution. Thus, it is also recommended to eyeball the distribution to evaluate whether it is severely skewed.

Fisher's Kurtosis Coefficient[3]

This is a measure of the extent to which observations cluster around a central point. Kurtosis measures whether the shape of a distribution is too flat or too peaked. For a standard normal distribution, the value of the kurtosis statistic is 0. A positive kurtosis indicates that the observations cluster more and have longer tails than those in the normal distribution. A negative kurtosis indicates that the observations cluster less and have shorter tails.

---

[2]Due to the complexity of their computations, skewness and standard error of skewness (SES) are usually computed by statistical software like SPSS.

[3]Because kurtosis is less commonly used in social sciences than skewness, we define it but won't use it in this book to evaluate normality of a distribution.

Example: Table 5.1 and figures 5.4 and 5.5 display SPSS output that illustrates the use of a skewness coefficient to evaluate the shape of a distribution.

Use skewness to evaluate whether these distributions are significantly skewed. As it appears in table 5.1, the first distribution has a skewness coefficient of .268 and a standard error of skewness of .243. Apply these numbers in the formula.

$$Skewness: -1.96 < \frac{skewness}{SES} < 1.96$$
$$skewness = .268; SES = .243$$
$$\frac{skewness}{SES} = \frac{.268}{.243} = 1.10$$
$$-1.96 < 1.10 < 1.96$$

Conclusion: The distribution of physical health is not severely skewed; that is, it approaches the shape of a normal curve.

Use the same formula to evaluate the shape of the distribution of depression. Table 5.1 shows that the distribution has a skewness coefficient of 1.10 and the standard error of skewness of .243.

$$Skewness: \frac{1.10}{.243} = 4.53$$
$$1.96 < 4.53$$

Conclusion: The distribution of depression is severely skewed.

Data Transformation

If the distribution of levels of depression is severely skewed, parametric statistics may not be appropriate to use with the raw scores of depression. In such cases, consider data transformation: Convert the raw scores of a variable that is significantly skewed into another type of score. This produces a distribution that approaches the shape of a normal curve, without affecting the original meaning of the data.

A number of transformation methods are available in SPSS and other statistical software. To transform raw data into another form, two issues must be addressed: (1) the direction of skewness: Is the distribution positively or negatively skewed? and (2) severity of skewness. How severe is the skewness?

If the distribution is negatively skewed, first reverse the raw scores so the distribution becomes positively skewed. Reversing raw scores also reverses the interpretation. If higher scores indicate greater values in the original data, then higher scores will indicate lower values in reversed data (e.g., if higher scores in the original data indicate greater depression, higher scores in reversed data will indicate

Table 5.1:   Statistics Table for Physical Health and Depression

		ph (physical health)	ces_d (depression)
N	Valid	99	99
	Missing	0	0
Mean		15.4040	13.9899
Median		14.0000	12.0000
Mode		14.00	8.00
Std. Deviation		4.66406	9.10987
Skewness		.268	1.100
Std. Error of Skewness		.243	.243

Table 5.1 displays the number of valid and missing cases, measures of central tendency (mean, median, mode), standard deviations, skewness and standard error of skewness, for physical health (**PH**) and depression (**CES_D**).

Figure 5.4:   Histogram for Physical Health

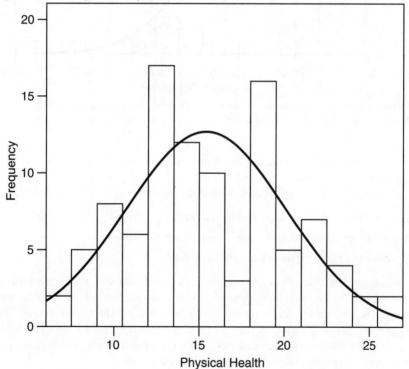

Figure 5.4 shows a histogram with a normal curve for physical health. Its shape appears to approach the shape of a normal curve, yet it is not a <u>standard</u> normal curve.

Figure 5.5:   Histogram for Depression

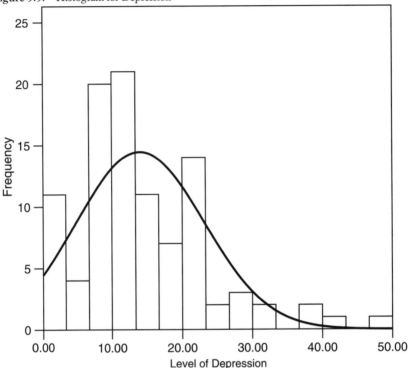

Figure 5.5 shows a histogram with a normal curve for levels of depression (**CES-D**). It is skewed to the right, a positively skewed distribution.

lower depression). If the original distribution is positively skewed, there is no need to reverse the raw data.

To reverse raw scores, follow these three steps:

1.   Find the maximum score for the raw data.

2.   Add 1 to the maximum score. This will serve as a constant.

3.   Subtract each raw score from the constant.

Once a distribution is reversed to be positively skewed, the next step is to transform it to one that may produce a distribution that approaches a normal curve. The most common methods of transformation are the square root and the logarithm. Transformation by the square root is generally conducted with distributions that have moderate skewness, while transformation by the logarithm is employed for distributions that are severely skewed.

Try both methods to see which one produces a distribution closer to the normal curve. Create a histogram with a normal curve then run measures of central tendency, variability, skewness, and kurtosis after each transformation is com-

Table 5.2:   Statistics for Depression and Square Root of Depression

		CES-D (depression)	SQRTCESD (square root CESD)
N	Valid	99	99
	Missing	0	0
Mean		13.9899	3.5172
Median		12.0000	3.4641
Mode		8.00	2.83
Std. Deviation		9.10987	1.27906
Skewness		1.00	−.156
Std. Error of Skewness		.243	.243

pleted to evaluate the shape of the transformed distribution and whether another transformation is needed. The following example compares raw scores for depression and transformed scores for depression.

Example: Depression (CES-D) in the previous example, has a positive skewness. Thus, there is no need to reverse the raw scores. First, transform depression to a square root. Call the transformed variable **SQRTCESD**. Table 5.2 displays statistics for depression and the transformed variable. Figure 5.6 displays the transformed distribution of depression.

Now evaluate whether this distribution is significantly skewed by computing the Fisher's skewness coefficient. Table 5.2 shows that the distribution of the transformed data has a skewness coefficient of −.156 and a standard error of skewness of .243. To evaluate skewness, apply these values in the formula.

$$Skewness: -1.96 < \frac{skewness}{SES} < 1.96$$
$$\frac{-.156}{.243} = -.642$$
$$-1.96 < -.642 < 1.96$$

Conclusion: The results of applying the formula together with eyeballing the distribution of transformed depression scores indicate that it is not severely skewed and approaches the shape of a normal curve. Thus, it is recommended that the square root be used in any future analysis to represent levels of depression.

How to Run Measures of Skewness and Transformation in SPSS. Use the variable social support (SS) from the SPSS *Depression-Elderly* data file. First, run measures of skewness and a histogram with a normal curve to evaluate whether a transformation is needed.

To run measures of skewness in SPSS, follow these steps:

a.   Open the SPSS *Depression-Elderly* data file.

b.   Repeat the steps discussed in chapter 4 to run measures of central tendency

Figure 5.6:   Histogram for Depression—Transformed Scores

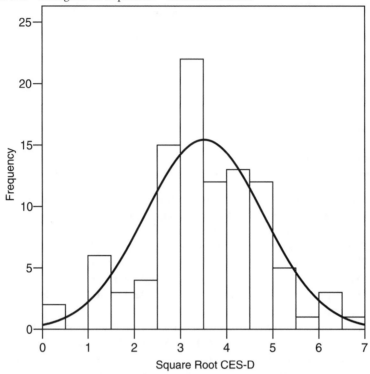

Recall that figure 5.5 shows the distribution of depression as severely skewed. Figure 5.6 displays the distribution of the transformed data, which approaches the shape of a normal curve.

and variability (screen 5.1). In the *Frequencies: Statistics* box (screen 5.1.B), check *Mean, Median,* and *Mode* under *Central Tendency.*

c.   Check *Std. Deviation* under *Dispersion.*

d.   Check *Skewness* under *Distribution.*

e.   Click on *Continue* and click on *Charts.*

f.   Check *Histograms* and check *With normal curve.*

g.   Click on *Continue* and click on *OK.*

SPSS syntax for Measures of Skewness:

FREQUENCY SS
/STATISTICS = STD MEAN
MED MOD SKEW SES
/HISTOGRAM NORMAL.

Screen 5.1:   SPSS *Frequencies: Statistics* Dialog Box

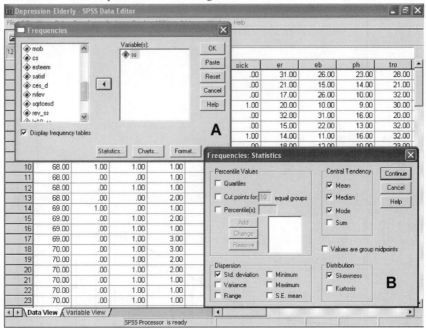

Table 5.3:   Statistics for Social Support

		(SS) Social Support
N	Valid	99
	Missing	0
Mean		27.3333
Median		29.0000
Mode		32.00
Std. Deviation		5.39841
Skewness		−1.475
Std. Error of Skewness		.243

Number of valid and missing cases, measures of central tendency (mean, median, mode), measures of variability (standard deviation), skewness, and standard error of skewness for social support.

You can run analyses on more than one variable at once. To do so, simply type each variable name after SS.

Table 5.3 and figure 5.7 display measures of central tendency, measures of variability, and skewness, coefficient produced by SPSS and a histogram with a normal curve for social support. The distribution of social support is skewed to the left (negatively skewed). A negatively skewed distribution includes a mode greater

Figure 5.7:   Histogram for Social Support

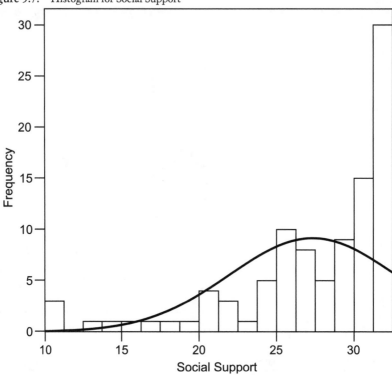

Figure 5.7 shows a histogram with a normal curve for social support.

than the median and a median greater than the mean (mean < median < mode). The statistics table (table 5.3) confirms this: The mode (32) is greater than the median (29); the median is greater than the mean (27.33). Subtract the median (29) from the mean (27.33) and the result is a negative value (–1.67). Is this a severely skewed distribution?

To answer this question, evaluate the skewness of the distribution. Table 5.3 shows a skewness of –1.475 and a standard error of .481. Apply these values in the formula to produce the following results:

$$Skewness: -1.96 < \frac{skewness}{SES} < 1.96$$
$$\frac{-1.475}{.243} = -6.07$$
$$-6.07 < -1.96$$

Conclusion: Eyeballing the chart and considering the results of the skewness indicate that the distribution is significantly skewed. A transformation is thus needed to change the shape of the distribution to approach the shape of a normal curve.

Screen 5.2:   SPSS: *Compute Variable* Dialog Box

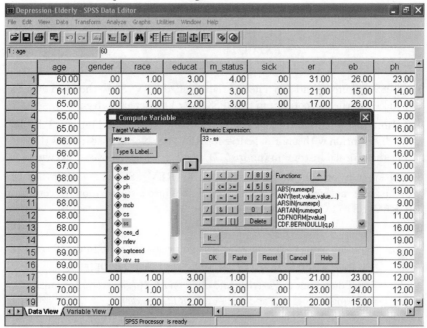

Transformation of Social Support Statistics.   The social support distribution shows a significant negative skewness, so two transformations are necessary.

1. Reverse the raw scores:[4] Add 1 to the maximum score in social support. This will serve as a constant. The maximum score is 32; thus, the constant is $32 + 1 = 33$.

2. Subtract each raw score from the constant (33). This transforms the distribution from severe negative skewness to severe positive skewness. To do this in SPSS, follow these steps:

    a. Open the SPSS *Depression-Elderly* Data file.

    b. Click on *Transform* in the SPSS main toolbar.

    c. Click on *Compute.* A new dialog box called *Compute Variable* will open (screen 5.2).

    d. Type the name of the new variable in the *Target Variable* box. In this case, type **REV_SS** (reversed social support).

    e. Type the formula you want to use under *Numeric Expression.* In this case type 33-SS.

    f. Click on *OK.*

---

[4]Remember that higher scores in the reversed variable will indicate lower social support and lower scores will indicate greater social support.

> SPSS syntax for computing a new variable:
>
> COMPUTE REV_SS = 33-SS.
> EXECUTE.

3.   SPSS will create and add a new variable called **REV_SS** to the SPSS data file, placed in the last column in the SPSS *Data View* screen (screen 5.3).

4.   Run a histogram for the new reversed variable (**REV_SS**). Figure 5.8 displays a distribution with a normal curve for **REV_SS**. Notice that it looks the same as the original histogram (figure 5.7); however, it has a positive skewness.

5.   Next, transform the new reversed variable (**REV_SS**) to a logarithm 10. Use the same methods to transform the variable into a square root. To transform **REV_SS** to **LG10**, follow these steps:

   a.   Repeat steps 2a to 2c above.

   b.   Type the name of the new variable you want to create in the *Target Variable* box (screen 5.4): LG10_SS (logarithm of social support).

   c.   Scroll down under *Functions* and click on *LG10(numexpr)*. To transform it in a square root, find and click on *SQRT(numexpr)*.

Screen 5.3:   SPSS *Depression-Elderly* Data File

	ss	esteem	satisf	ces_d	nrlev	sqrtcesd	rev_ss	var	var
1	29.00	18.00	11.00	17.00	2.00	4.12	4.00		
2	25.00	26.00	4.00	20.00	5.00	4.47	8.00		
3	26.00	34.00	7.00	11.00	11.00	3.32	7.00		
4	29.00	26.00	12.00	8.00	2.00	2.83	4.00		
5	13.00	32.00	10.00	12.00	3.00	3.46	20.00		
6	32.00	35.00	13.00	21.00	4.00	4.58	1.00	**Reversed**	
7	29.00	23.00	13.00	30.00	4.00	5.48	4.00	**Social**	
8	30.00	23.00	10.00	38.00	6.00	6.16	3.00	**Support**	
9	28.00	26.00	11.00	22.00	4.00	4.69	5.00		
10	24.00	27.00	9.00	7.00	4.00	2.65	9.00		
11	14.00	28.00	8.00	10.00	3.00	3.16	19.00		
12	30.00	28.00	10.00	15.00	6.00	3.87	3.00		
13	32.00	30.00	11.00	12.00	4.00	3.46	1.00		
14	26.00	30.00	8.00	7.00	4.00	2.65	7.00		
15	32.00	32.00	10.00	15.00	6.00	3.87	1.00		
16	29.00	30.00	12.00	22.00	6.00	4.69	4.00		
17	22.00	29.00	3.00	23.00	7.00	4.80	11.00		
18	27.00	34.00	8.00	8.00	1.00	2.83	6.00		
19	25.00	27.00	4.00	26.00	5.00	5.10	8.00		

Figure 5.8:   Histogram for Social Support (Reversed Scores)

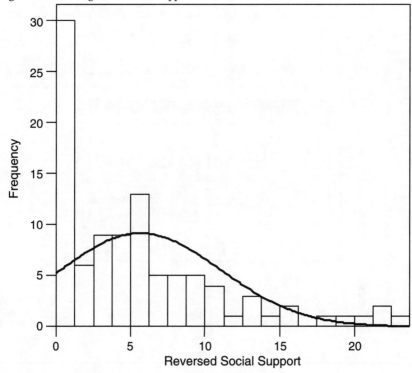

d. Click on the arrow button in the right side of *Functions* to move *LG10 (numexpr)* in the *Numeric Expression* box.

e. Scroll down in the variable list, click on **REV_SS**, and click on the arrow button in the upper middle dialog box to move it in the parentheses after *LG10* and replace the question mark, or simply type variable name inside parentheses, like this: LG10(REV_SS).

f. Click on *OK.*

SPSS syntax for transformation into *log:*

COMPUTE LG_SS = LG10(REV_SS).
EXECUTE.

SPSS syntax for transformation into *square root:*

COMPUTE SQUIRT_SS = SQRT(REV_SS).
EXECUTE.

Screen 5.4:   SPSS *Compute Variable* Dialog Box

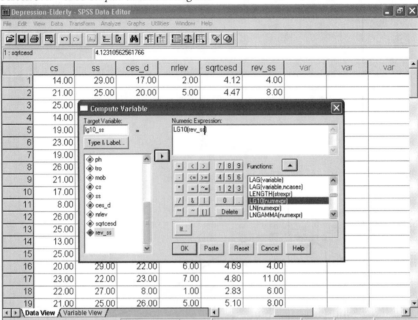

Table 5.4:   Statistics for Logarithm of Social Support

	LG_SS	
N	Valid	99
	Missing	0
Mean		.5526
Median		.6021
Mode		.00
Std. Deviation		.43759
Skewness		.015
Std. Error of Skewness		.243
Kurtosis		−1.268
Std. Error of Kurtosis		.481

These SPSS functions will create and add a new variable called **LG10_SS** in the SPSS *Depression-Elderly* data file. This variable will appear in the last column in the SPSS *Data View* screen.

Next, compute skewness and create a histogram with a normal curve for the transformed variable. Table 5.4 displays the statistics and figure 5.9 displays the distribution for transformed social support (**LG_SS**).

Figure 5.9:   Histogram for Logarithm of Social Support

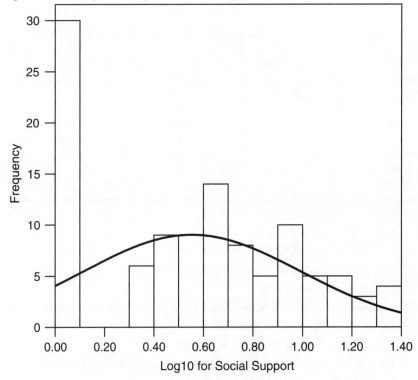

In figure 5.9, the shape of the distribution of the transformed variable approaches the shape of a normal curve, yet it appears too flat.

Evaluation of the skewness coefficient supports this conclusion. The distribution has a skewness coefficient of .061 (.015/.243 = .061), which falls between ± 1.96. This indicates that the distribution is not significantly skewed.

STANDARD SCORES (Z SCORES)

Standard scores, also called z scores, are raw scores converted into standard deviation units. They indicate how many standard deviation units a corresponding raw score, or observation, falls above or below the mean. A raw score greater than the mean will always have a positive z score. A raw score smaller than the mean will always have a negative z score. A raw score exactly on the mean will always have a z score of zero.

Table 5.5:   Frequencies: Statistics Table for Economic Resources (Raw and z Scores)

		ER (Economic Resources)	zer Zscore: (Economic Resources)
N	Valid	99	99
	Missing	0	0
Mean		22.5354	.0000000
Median		22.0000	−.0894716
Mode		21.00	−.25660
Std. Deviation		5.98350	1.00000000
Skewness		−.399	−.399
Std. Error of Skewness		.243	.243
Minimum		5.00	−2.93062
Maximum		32.00	1.58179

Properties of Standard Scores

1. The shape of the distribution of standard scores is identical to that of the distribution of the raw scores.

2. The mean of the standard scores is equal to 0, regardless of the mean of the raw scores.

3. The variance of the standard scores is equal to 1.

4. Because the standard deviation is the square root of the variance, the standard deviation of the standard scores is equal to 1.

5. The sum of all z scores is equal to 0.

By transforming raw scores to standard scores, we transform the original distribution of raw scores to a distribution with an identical shape but with a mean of 0 and a standard deviation of 1.

To illustrate this, we will use SPSS to compare two distributions; the first shows raw data of economic resources (**ER**) and the second shows z scores of the raw data. The following SPSS output contains three parts: Frequencies: Statistics Table (table 5.5); a histogram for economic resources (figure 5.10.A); and a histogram for z scores for economic resources (figure 5.10.B).

Table 5.5 shows measures of central tendency, variability, and skewness for the raw scores and z scores of economic resources. The mean score for the z scores is 0 with a variance of 1 (standard deviation = 1). The table also shows that the skewness, standard error of skewness, for both economic resources and its z scores are identical, therefore the shapes of both distributions are identical.

Figure 5.10.A: Histogram for Economic Resources (Raw Scores)

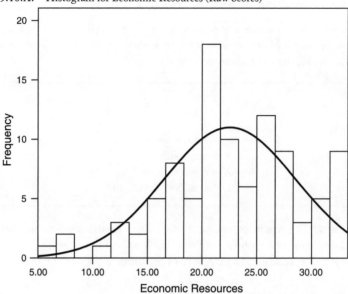

Figure 5.10.A displays the distribution of economic resources. It is negatively skewed, but not severely skewed, as demonstrated by the measures of skewness.

Figure 5.10.B: Histogram for Economic Resources (z Scores)

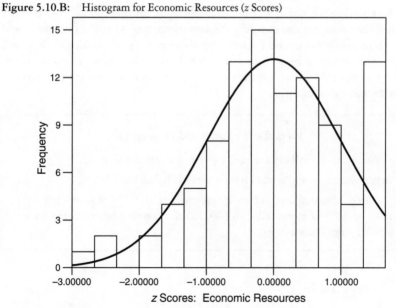

Figure 5.10.B displays the distribution of the z scores for economic resources. It is identical to the distribution of economic resources (negatively skewed, but not severely).

Transformation of Raw Scores to z Scores

Transformation of raw scores to z scores is simple. All you need to know is the mean and the standard deviation for the raw scores (see chapter 4). To convert a raw score to a z score, use the following formula.

Formula: $z_X = \dfrac{X - \overline{X}}{SD}$

z_X = z score for X
X = raw score
$\overline{X}$ = mean
SD = standard deviation

Example: The mean score for last year's Data Analysis course was 86 with a standard deviation of 3. John's score was 92. What is John's z score?

Answer: John's score was greater than the mean, a positive z score.

John's z score: $z_{X=92} = \dfrac{92 - 86}{3} = \dfrac{6}{3} = 2$

Why Standard Scores

By knowing the number of standard deviation units each raw score is above or below the mean, we can compute the area (percentage) between the mean and each z score, area between two z scores, area above each z score, and area below each z score. The area at or below which a z score falls is also known as the *percentile*. Thus, by computing a z score for each raw score, we can determine the percentile for each subject in a study.

Facts about z Scores and Percentiles

A positive z score will always have a percentile greater than 50.

A negative z score will always have a percentile less than 50.

A z score of zero will always have a percentile of 50 (50% of scores fall below and 50% of scores fall above it). In other words, the percentile for the mean score is always 50.

z Scores Table

The z Scores Table (appendix D) presents the area between a z score and the mean, and the area beyond a z score.

Things to Remember

% beyond a positive z score = % beyond a negative z score

% below a positive z score = 50% + % between the mean and the z score

% below a negative z score = 50% − % between the mean and the z score

The z Scores Table shows the following information (figure 5.11):

1. 50% of area is above the mean and 50% is below the mean (a normal distribution is symmetrical; the left and right halves are mirror images).

2. 34.13% is between the mean and 1 standard deviation above the mean; 34.13% is between the mean and 1 standard deviation below the mean (68.26% is between ±1 standard deviation).

3. 47.72% is between the mean and 2 standard deviations above the mean;

Figure 5.11:   Normal Distribution for Percentiles

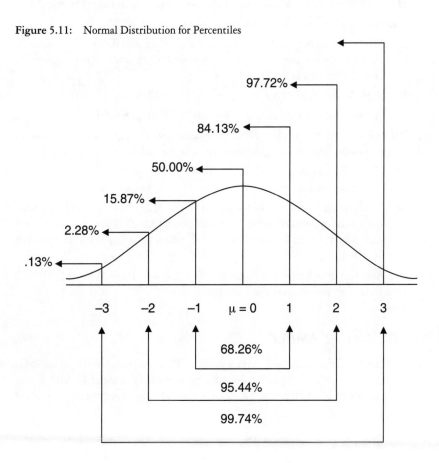

47.72% is between the mean and 2 standard deviations below the mean (95.44% is between ±2 standard deviations).

4. 49.87% is between the mean and 3 standard deviations above the mean; 49.87% is between the mean and 3 standard deviations below the mean (99.74% is between ±3 standard deviations).

The z Scores Table (appendix D) contains three columns: z, Area between $\overline{X}$ and z, and Area beyond z:

1. To find the area (percentage) between a specific z and the mean, first locate the z score in the z column, then find the corresponding area in the Area between $\overline{X}$ and z column.

   Example: To find the area between the mean and a z score of .45, scroll down to .45 in the z column, then move right to the second column, Area between $\overline{X}$ and z. This area is .1736, or 17.36%.

2. To find the area below a positive z (the percentile for +z), locate the z score in the z column, find the area between the z score and the mean, then add .50.

   Example: Find the area below (percentile of) a z score of .85.

   a. Find the area between the mean and z of .85. Scroll down to .85 in the z column, then move right to the second column under Area between $\overline{X}$ and z. This area is .3023.

   b. Add .50 to .3023. That is, .50 + .3023 = .8023.

   c. A z score of .85 falls at approximately the 80th percentile.

3. To find the area below a negative z (the percentile of –z), locate the z score in the z column, find the area between the z score and the mean, then subtract this area from .50.

   Example: Find the area below (percentile of) a z score of –1.25.

   a. Find the area between the mean and a z of –1.25 (identical to the area between the mean and z of 1.25). Scroll down to 1.25 in the z column, then move right to the second column under Area between $\overline{X}$ and z. This area is .3944.

   b. Subtract .3944 from .50. That is, .50 – .3944 = .1056. A z score of –1.25 falls at approximately the 11th percentile.

PRACTICAL EXAMPLE

On the **CES-D** (depression scale) with a mean of 15 and a standard deviation (**SD**) of 2, at approximately what percentile will a person with a score of 18 fall? A person with a score of 13? What percentage of subjects fall between these two scores?

1. To solve for a score of 18:

   a. Compute the z score for 18.

$$z_{X=18} = \frac{X - \overline{X}}{SD} = \frac{18 - 15}{2} = 1.5$$

b. Use the z Scores Table to find the area between the mean and a z of 1.50. The z Score Table shows that the area between the mean and a z of 1.50 is .4332.

c. Because this is a positive z, add .50 to this area.

d. Total area below z of $1.50 = .50 + .4332 = .9332$.

e. A score of 18 falls at approximately the 93rd percentile. This means that about 93% of subjects have scores at or below 18 and about 7% have scores above 18.

2. To solve for a score of 13:

a. Compute the z score for 13.

$$z_{X=13} = \frac{X - \overline{X}}{SD} = \frac{13 - 15}{2} = -1$$

b. Use the z Scores Table to find the area between the mean and a z of -1.0. This is the same as the area between the mean and a z of 1. The z Scores Table shows that this area is .3413.

c. Because this is a negative z score, subtract this area from .50.

d. Total area below a z score of $-1.0 = .50 - .3413 = .1587$, or 15.87%. (see figure 5.11.)

e. Someone with a score of 13 on the **CES-D** scale will fall at approximately the 16th percentile: Almost 16% of subjects will have scores at or below 13 and about 84% will have scores above 13.

3. To solve for percentages of subjects between 13 and 18:

This includes the area between the mean and a z score of 1.50 (the z score for 18) and the area between the mean and a z score of -1.0 (the z score for 13).

a. Area between the mean and $1.50 = .4332$, or 43.32%.

b. Area between the mean and $-1.0 = .3413$, or 34.13%.

c. Area between 1.50 and $-1.0 = 43.32\% + 34.13\% = 77.45\%$. That is, 77.45% of participants have scores between 13 and 18 on the **CES-D** scale.

How to Create z Scores in SPSS.   To illustrate this, compute the z scores for Economic Resources (**ER**) in the SPSS *Depression-Elderly* data file.

To create z scores in SPSS, follow these steps:

a. Open the SPSS *Depression-Elderly* data file.

b. Click on *Analyze* in the SPSS main toolbar.

c. Click on *Descriptive Statistics.*

Screen 5.5:   SPSS *Descriptives* Main Dialog Box

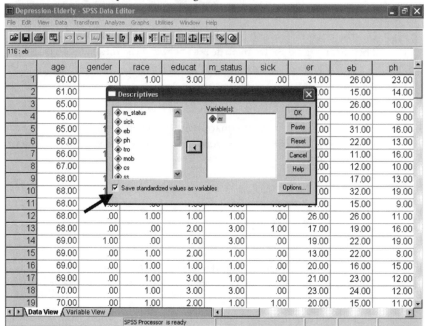

d.   Click on *Descriptives*. A new dialog box called *Descriptives* will open (screen 5.5).

e.   Scroll down in the variables list and move **ER** to the *Variable(s)* box.

f.   Check the box of *Save standardized values as variables*.

g.   Click on *OK*.

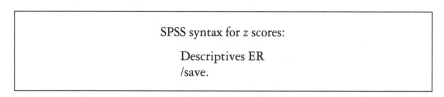

SPSS syntax for z scores:

Descriptives ER
/save.

A new variable called **ZER** will be added to the SPSS *Depression-Elderly* data set. By default, SPSS assigns a name to the new variable. It is the same name as the original variable, now starting with the letter z, indicating z scores.

Now run measures of central tendency, variability, skewness, and create histograms for both economic resources and z scores of economic resources (see SPSS output under *Properties of Standard Scores* above).

SUMMARY

This chapter discussed normality of distributions and their importance for data analysis. Normal distributions are symmetrical and bell-shaped with their mean in the center. Positively skewed distributions have long tails on the right and most cases fall on the left; their mean is greater than the median, and the median is greater than the mode. Negatively skewed distributions have long tails on the left and most cases fall on the right; their mean is smaller than the median, and the median is smaller than the mode.

Two methods to evaluate the severity of skewness are Fisher's skewness and kurtosis coefficients. These coefficients determine whether a transformation of raw scores is needed. Two transformation methods were presented: square root and logarithm. The chapter also discussed standard scores, their importance, and their use in computing the percentile for each raw score, as well as how to utilize the SPSS toolbar and syntax files to compute measures of central tendency, variability, skewness, kurtosis, data transformation, and how to create z scores.

Chapter 6 introduces the next level of data analysis, inferential statistics. It presents one-tailed and two-tailed research hypotheses, errors in hypothesis testing, levels of significance, and levels of confidence interval. Differences between parametric and nonparametric tests and factors to consider in selecting the appropriate statistical test are covered, along with steps in hypothesis testing.

PRACTICAL EXERCISES

I.   Use the data from Question 1 in chapter 3 and answer the following questions:

    1. Convert scores to z scores.

    2. Create two frequency tables. The first summarizes the raw data and the second summarizes the z scores. Are there differences between the two tables? If so, what?

    3. Compute the mean, median, and mode for the z scores.

    4. Compute the range, variance, and standard deviation for the z scores.

II. Access the SPSS *Job Satisfaction* data file (appendix A) and answer the following questions:

    1. Run histograms with normal curve for age (**D2**) and working with colleagues (**COLLEAG**).

    2. What type of distributions are they? Explain.

    3. Are any of these distributions significantly skewed? Justify your answer.

    4. If either one is significantly skewed, what method of transformation would you use to fix their skewness? Use SPSS syntax to run the transformations.

    5. Compare the two distributions. How do the transformed distributions differ from the original distributions?

6. Run measures of central tendency and variability for working with colleagues (**COLLEAG**), satisfaction with supervision (**SUPERVIS**), and satisfaction with promotion (**PROMOT**). Use these measures to answer questions 7 to 11.

7. At approximately what percentile will a person with a score of 44 on the **COLLEAG** scale fall?

8. At approximately what percentile will a person with a score of 54 on the **COLLEAG** scale fall?

9. What percentage of subjects will fall between these two scores (44 and 54)?

10. Adam participated in the *Job Satisfaction* survey. He scored 50 on satisfaction with colleagues; 69 on satisfaction with supervision, and 22 on satisfaction with promotions. What area does Adam appear to be most satisfied with?

11. Given that 218 social workers completed the survey, how many social workers had higher satisfaction than Adam with their promotions?

CHAPTER 6

Hypotheses Testing
and Selecting a Statistical Test

LEARNING OBJECTIVES

1. Understand one-tailed and two-tailed research hypotheses
2. Understand errors in hypothesis testing
3. Understand levels of significance
4. Understand confidence interval
5. Understand parametric and nonparametric tests
6. Understand the process for selecting a statistical test
7. Understand the steps in hypothesis testing

Data Set: *Depression-Welfare* (appendix A)

INTRODUCTION

Chapters 3, 4, and 5 introduced methods of descriptive statistics. Chapter 3 discussed two methods of data organization and summary: frequency tables and graphs. Chapter 4 outlined measures of central tendency and variability. Chapter 5 taught how to evaluate the shape of a distribution and understand standard scores and their importance.

Now we turn to the study of inferential statistics. As described in chapter 1, the goal of quantitative research is to describe the distribution of the sample characteristics (statistics) then make a generalization, or inference, from them to the characteristics of the population (parameters) from which the sample is drawn.

For instance, social work researchers want to know if their treatment or intervention has been effective with clients, and whether it can be replicated to be successful with other clients in similar settings. This can be determined through inferential parametric and nonparametric statistical techniques, such as the Pearson product moment correlation coefficient, student *t*-tests, analysis of variances, chi-square, and other tests.

This chapter reviews research hypotheses and specifically discusses one-tailed and two-tailed versions. Levels of significance, p value, type I and type II errors, and levels of confidence interval are presented, along with parametric and nonparametric tests, selecting a statistical test, and steps in hypothesis testing.

RESEARCH HYPOTHESES

Chapter 1 introduced the null hypothesis and research hypothesis (also known as the alternative hypothesis). The *null hypothesis (H_0)* will have *no significant* relationships between independent and dependent variables, while the *alternative hypothesis (H_a)* shows *significant* relationships between independent and dependent variables.

Why two hypotheses? The main goal of any research study is to find statistical support for the research (alternative) hypothesis, which cannot be supported unless the null hypothesis is statistically rejected. However, that alone will not always provide support for the alternative hypothesis. This will depend on whether the research hypothesis is one-tailed or two-tailed. If one-tailed, two conditions must be met to claim statistical support for the research hypothesis: (1) Significant results must be found; that is, enough statistical evidence to reject the null hypotheses, and (2) The direction of the results is the same as the direction postulated by the alternative hypothesis.

Example: In the welfare-to-work depression study, the researcher hypothesized that former welfare recipients who participated in job training would have significantly lower levels of depression than those who did not. The study found significant differences between the two groups; however, the level of depression for subjects who participated in training were significantly higher than those who did not. The researcher rejected the null hypothesis based on the statistical results, but these results did not support the alternative hypothesis.

One-Tailed Research Hypothesis

A one-tailed research hypothesis, also known as a *directional* hypothesis, clearly predicts the direction of the relationship between independent and dependent variables. Social science researchers may predict *positive* relationships (or *direct*) or *negative* (or *inverse*) relationships.

Figure 6.1 compares positive and negative relationships. *Positive relationships* (see chapter 1) occur when scores in the independent and dependent variables move in the same direction; that is, if the independent variable increases, the dependent variable increases as well (figure 6.1.A), and vice versa (figure 6.1.B). *Negative relationships* occur when scores in the independent and dependent variables go in the opposite directions; if the independent variable increases, the dependent variable decreases (figure 6.1.C), and if the independent variable decreases, the dependent variable increases (figure 6.1.D).

Figure 6.1: Directions of Relationships between Variables

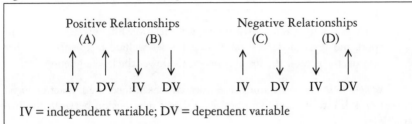

IV = independent variable; DV = dependent variable

Table 6.1: Experimental Pretest-Posttest Group Design

Group	Pretest	Therapy	Posttest
Experimental Group	X_1	Yes	X_2
Control Group	X_3	No	X_4

Example 1: A social work practitioner who conducts group therapy for battered women wishes to help them increase their self-esteem. To test the effectiveness of the therapy, the practitioner conducts an experimental pretest-posttest control group design. Table 6.1 illustrates this experimental design.

Prior to starting group therapy, the practitioner may hypothesize two one-tailed research hypotheses (H_a):

H_{0_1}: There is *no significant* difference between women's level of self-esteem before and after the therapy: $X_1 = X_2$; therapy is ineffective.

H_{a_1}: Women's level of self-esteem at the posttest will be *significantly higher* than their level of self-esteem at the pretest: $X_2 > X_1$; group therapy is effective.

H_{0_2}: There is *no significant* difference between the experimental group and the control group with regard to posttest level of self-esteem: $X_2 = X_4$.

H_{a_2}: Posttest level of self-esteem of the experimental group will be *significantly higher* than the control group: $X_2 > X_4$.

To support the first research hypothesis, the practitioner must show that there is a significant relationship between pretest and posttest scores of self-esteem, and that the posttest scores (X_2) are greater than the pretest scores (X_1).

To support the second research hypothesis, again the practitioner must show a significant difference between the experimental and control groups $(X_2 \neq X_4)$, and that the posttest scores of the experimental group are greater than those of the control group $(X_2 > X_4)$.

Example 2: In the *Depression-Welfare* survey, the researcher examined the impact of social support on clients' levels of depression (**CES-D**). The researcher projected an inverse relationship between the two variables.

H_0: There is *no significant* relationship between social support and levels of depression among former welfare recipients.

H_a: There is a *significant inverse* (or *negative*) relationship between social support and level of depression among former welfare recipients. In other words, the greater the social support, the lower the level of depression.

Example 3: In the same study, the researcher examined the impact of social support on self-esteem, and hypothesized a direct relationship between the two variables.

H_0: There is *no significant* relationship between social support and level of self-esteem among former welfare recipients.

H_a: There is a *significant direct* (or *positive*) relationship: the greater the social support, the higher the level of self-esteem among former welfare recipients.

With one-tailed research hypotheses, researchers use words such as positive, direct, negative, inverse, increase, decrease, higher than, lower than, greater than, or less than to predict the relationships between independent and dependent variables.

Two-Tailed Research Hypothesis

A two-tailed (or *nondirectional*) research hypothesis does not predict the direction of the relationship between independent and dependent variables. In this case, researchers project a significant relationship between the two variables, but stop short of predicting direction. Therefore, researchers need only to reject the null hypothesis to claim statistical support for the alternative hypothesis.

The following illustrates two-tailed hypotheses for the previous three examples:

Example 1:

H_{0_1}: There is *no significant* difference between women's self-esteem at the pretest and posttest: $X_1 = X_2$; therapy is ineffective.

H_{a_1}: Levels of self-esteem at the posttest will be *significantly different* than levels of self-esteem at the pretest: $X_1 \neq X_2$; therapy is not necessarily effective.

Here, the practitioner does not predict whether therapy will be effective, which may affect the decision of subjects to participate in the therapy.

H_{0_2}: There is *no significant* difference between the experimental group and the control group with regard to posttest levels of self-esteem: $X_2 = X_4$.

H_{a_2}: There is a *significant* difference between the experimental group and the control group with regard to posttest levels of self-esteem: $X_2 \neq X_4$.

Again, the practitioner does not predict which group will benefit from the therapy.

Example 2:

H_0: There is *no significant* relationship between social support and level of depression among former welfare recipients.

H_a: There is a *significant* relationship between social support and level of depression among former welfare recipients.

Example 3:

H_0: There is *no significant* relationship between social support and level of self-esteem among former welfare recipients.

H_a: There is a *significant* relationship between social support and level of self-esteem among former welfare recipients.

With two-tailed research hypotheses, researchers use words such as significant relationship, correlation, or association between independent and dependent variables, or significant differences between groups with regard to dependent variables.

ERRORS IN HYPOTHESIS TESTING

Researchers use inferential statistics like the Pearson correlation, *t*-test, chi-square, and others to estimate a population's parameters by studying the statistics of a sample presumed to represent that population. Inferential statistics will also be used to generalize findings from a sample to the population from which it was selected.

We rely on statistics to demonstrate the accuracy of conclusions about relationships between independent and dependent variables in the population. A main concern is to avoid making wrong conclusions, or errors. Two possible errors are the type I and the type II. Table 6.2 describes them.

Type I Error

Type I errors are also known as α (Greek lowercase alpha).[1] These occur when researchers, based on results of the statistical test, decide to reject the null hypothesis (that no relationship exists between the variables) when in fact the null hypothesis is true.

Type II Error

Type II errors are known as β (Greek lowercase beta). These occur when researchers decide not to reject the null hypothesis when in fact it is false.

---

[1] Not to be confused with the Cronbach alpha reliability coefficient.

Table 6.2:   Errors in Hypothesis Testing

Decision	H_0 Is True	H_0 Is False
Reject H_0	Type I error (α)	Correct decision
Do not reject H_0	Correct decision	Type II error (β)

H_0 = Null hypothesis

Correct Decision

Correct decisions occur when researchers decide to reject false null hypotheses or not to reject true hypotheses. Researchers are rarely absolutely confident, so during the research design process, they will set levels of significance to guide them.

Levels of Significance (α)

Levels of significance help determine how close researchers are to making a correct decision, by rejecting a false hypothesis or not rejecting a true hypothesis. Levels of significance are also symbolized by the Greek lowercase α (alpha), which refers to the probability of making a type I error. It is the probability that the observed relationships between variables are due to a chance or sampling error.

Researchers must choose a level of significance prior to collecting and analyzing data. At what level of probability can they claim significant results? Depending on the purpose of the study, they will usually set alpha at .10, .05, .01, or .001.

Traditionally, social science researchers set alpha at .05; that is, the probability of making a type I error is 5 in 100. Medical researchers, for example, whose studies may physically or emotionally risk patients, set alpha lower, usually at .01 (1 in 100) or .001 (1 in 1000), to reduce errors and avoid harming subjects.

Statistical Significance (p value)

All parametric and nonparametric inferential statistical tests produce a p value. As with alpha, a p value indicates how close researchers are to a correct decision. It refers to the probability that relationships between independent and dependent variables could occur by a chance or sampling error.

Mathematically, a p value ranges between 0.00 (the relationship between variables would never occur by chance) and 1.00 (the relationship between variables definitely occurs by chance). The smaller the p value, the less probability that the relationship between variables occurs by a chance or sampling error.

Researchers will compare the computed probability level (p value) with the preset level of significance (alpha). If the p value is *at or below alpha, reject the null hypothesis.* By doing so, statistical support for the alternative hypothesis may be claimed. If the *p* value is *greater than alpha, don't reject the null hypothesis,* or claim statistical support for the alternative hypothesis.

> Reject H_0 only if $p \leq \alpha$.

To reject null hypotheses for the three earlier examples, researchers must show the *p* value for each one is at or below .05 (assuming that alpha was set at .05).

One-Tailed and Two-Tailed Rejection Area

The decision whether to state a one-tailed or two-tailed research hypothesis is made prior to data analysis, because this will determine whether a one-tailed or two-tailed statistical test is required.

The word *tail* refers to the ends of a normal curve, where extreme values are usually found. This may indicate significant relationships between the variables under study. Thus, by stating a one-tailed or two-tailed research hypothesis, researchers are predicting that relationships between variables will fall at the right tail or the left (for a one-tailed hypothesis), or at both tails (for the two-tailed hypothesis).

When a two-tailed hypothesis is examined, the rejection area is divided equally between the two ends, the right and left tails (figure 6.2.A). This is the level of significance, or alpha (α). If alpha was set at .05, then the total rejection area is 5%, which will be divided to two halves of 2.5%. If alpha was set at .01, then the total area is 1%, and the two halves each equal .5%.

As you may recall from chapter 5, standard (*z*) scores indicate how far each raw score is above or below the mean, or indicate the area above or below a given *z*

Figure 6.2.A: Rejection Area for Two-Tailed Hypothesis

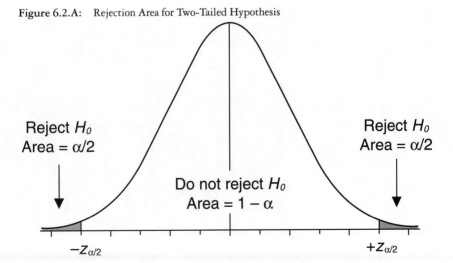

Reject H_0
Area = $\alpha/2$

Do not reject H_0
Area = $1 - \alpha$

Reject H_0
Area = $\alpha/2$

$-Z_{\alpha/2}$ $+Z_{\alpha/2}$

score. Alpha, in this case, represents the area of extreme scores. These areas correspond with a z score, which serves as a cutoff. With a two-tailed hypothesis, researchers reject the null hypothesis if the computed statistic falls beyond the $\pm z$ score; with one-tailed hypotheses, researchers reject the null hypothesis if the computed statistic falls beyond the z score.

To find the z score, use the z Scores Table (appendix D) as discussed in chapter 5.

1.   Determine the area, or percentage, under each tail. For a one-tailed hypothesis, the area is alpha; for a two-tailed hypothesis, divide alpha by 2.

2.   Find this area in the *Area Beyond z* column in the z Scores Table.

3.   Find the z score corresponding with this area in the z column.

Example: If alpha in figure 6.2.A was set at .05, then the area in each tail is .05/2, which is .025. Find this area under the *Area Beyond z* in the z Scores Table. The z score associated with .0250 is ± 1.96. In other words, 95% of cases will fall between -1.96 and $+1.96$, and 5% of cases will fall beyond these z scores.

Assuming $\alpha = .05$, a significant result occurs only if the computed statistic falls at or above $+1.96$ or at or below -1.96. In this case, researchers will reject the null hypothesis. Results will not be significant if the computed statistic falls between -1.96 and $+1.96$. Researchers in this case fail to find statistical support for the two-tailed research hypothesis.

When a one-tailed hypothesis is examined, the rejection area falls at one end, at the right or left tail. Figure 6.2.B presents the rejection area for a one-tailed hypothesis, predicting a positive (direct) relationship between two variables. Figure 6.2.C presents the rejection area for a one-tailed hypothesis, predicting a negative (inverse) relationship between variables.

Figure 6.2.B: Rejection Area for One-Tailed Hypothesis—Positive Relationship

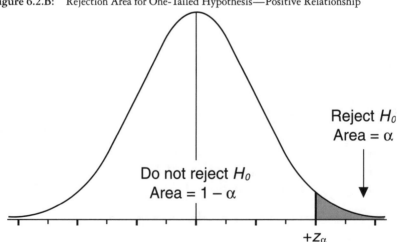

Figure 6.2.C: Rejection Area for One-Tailed Hypothesis—Negative Relationship

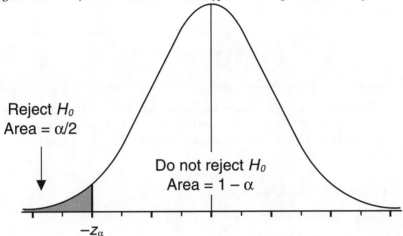

To find the z score associated with the area at either the right or left tail (figure 6.2.B and 6.2.C), use the same methods as used to find z for the area of .025. The area under the right or left tail is .05. Locate this area under the *Area Beyond z* column in the z Scores Table. This area is associated with a z of 1.65.

Assuming α = .05, a significant positive relationship is found only if the computed statistic falls at or above +1.65. A significant negative relationship is found if the computed statistic falls at or below −1.65.

CONFIDENCE INTERVAL

Researchers study a statistic from a sample to estimate parameters of a population, but the sample is only an approximation for the population and so is the statistic. For example, if in the welfare-to-work study (N = 107), the mean (statistics) score of depression among former welfare recipients was 15.56 (SD = 10.14) on a scale of 0 to 60, can the researcher be confident that this score accurately reflects the true mean (parameter) score of the population from which the sample was selected?

The only way to be absolutely confident is to study every person in the population who was on welfare, which is not possible. However, you can use the sample data and the level of significance to estimate a range of values that may contain the true depression score for the population, the true population parameter. This range of scores is referred to as the *confidence interval.*

Confidence interval is a range of upper and lower values, also known as *confidence limits,* that researchers are confident contain the true population parameter.

The level of confidence is the degree of confidence that the confidence interval contains the parameter being estimated. Levels of confidence are usually the complement to the levels of significance (alpha). For example, if alpha is set at .05, then the level of confidence will be .95, or 95%; if alpha is set at .01, then the level of confidence will be .99, or 99%.

> Level of Confidence = 1 − α
> α = alpha

While researchers may compute any level of confidence interval, the most reported ones are at 95% and 99%. They are symbolized by CI_{xx}, where xx represents level of confidence: CI_{95} = 95% confidence interval; CI_{99} = 99% confidence interval.

Computing Confidence Interval

1. Choose the level of confidence: CI_{95} or CI_{99}.
2. Compute the standard error.

> Standard Error: $SE = \dfrac{SD}{\sqrt{N}}$
>
> SD = Standard Deviation

3. Use the following formulas to compute the 90%, 95%, or 99% confidence interval:

> 90% confidence interval: $CI_{90} = \overline{X} \pm 1.65 \times (SE)$
> 95% confidence interval: $CI_{95} = \overline{X} \pm 1.96 \times (SE)$
> 99% confidence interval: $CI_{99} = \overline{X} \pm 2.58 \times (SE)$
> $\overline{X}$ = mean
> SE = standard error

Remember: The sample statistic (mean) must always fall within the confidence interval.

Example: What are the 99%, 95%, and 90% confidence intervals for levels of depression among former welfare recipients?

Answer: The mean score for depression was 15.56 with a standard deviation of 10.14. The sample size (N) was 107.

1. Compute the standard error:

$$SE = \frac{SD}{\sqrt{N}} = \frac{10.14}{\sqrt{107}} = \frac{10.14}{10.34} = .98$$

2. Compute the 99% confidence interval:

$$CI_{99} = \overline{X} \pm 2.58 \times (SE) = 15.56 \pm 2.58 \times (.98)$$
$$CI_{99} = 15.56 \pm 2.53$$
upper limit = 15.56 + 2.53 = 18.09
lower limit = 15.56 – 2.53 = 13.03

Conclusion: We are 99% confident that the interval 13.03 to 18.09 contains the true depression score (parameter) for the population of former welfare recipients.

3. Compute the 95% confidence interval:

$$CI_{95} = \overline{X} \pm 1.96 \,(SE) = 15.56 \pm 1.96 \times (.98)$$
$$CI_{95} = 15.56 \pm 1.92$$
upper limit = 15.56 + 1.92 = 17.48
lower limit = 15.56 – 1.92 = 13.64

Conclusion: We are 95% confident that the interval 13.64 to 17.48 contains the true depression score (parameter) for the population of former welfare recipients.

4. Compute the 90% confidence interval:

$$CI_{90} = \overline{X} \pm 1.65 \,(SE) = 15.56 \pm 1.65 \times (.98)$$
$$CI_{90} = 15.56 \pm 1.62$$
upper limit = 15.56 + 1.62 = 17.18
lower limit = 15.56 – 1.62 = 13.94

Conclusion: We are 90% confident that the interval 13.94 to 17.18 contains the true depression score (parameter) for the population of former welfare recipients from which the sample was selected.

Notice that the 99% confidence interval (13.03 to 18.09) is wider than the 95% confidence interval (13.64 to 17.48), and that the 95% confidence interval is wider than the 90% confidence interval (13.94 to 17.18). Figure 6.3 compares levels of confidence interval and their corresponding intervals.

How to Compute Confidence Interval in SPSS.   Compute the 99% confidence interval for depression (**CES_D**) in the SPSS *Depression-Welfare* file.

To compute confidence interval in SPSS, use the following steps:

a. Open the SPSS *Depression-Welfare* data file.

b. Click on *Analyze,* click on *Descriptive Statistics,* and click on *Explore.* A new dialog box called *Explore* will open (screen 6.1.A).

c. Scroll down on the variables list in the left box, click on **CES_D,** and click on the top arrow button to move **CES_D** in the *Dependent List* box.

d. Check *Statistics* under *Display* to request only statistics.

e. Click on *Statistics* in the right side bottom of the box. A new dialog box called

Figure 6.3: Comparison of Levels of Confidence Intervals

CI_{00} 15.56

CI_{xx} ——

CI_{90} 13.94 ——————— 17.18

CI_{95} 13.64 ————————————— 17.48

CI_{99} 13.03 ————————————————————— 18.09

The higher the level of confidence, the wider the confidence interval.

Screen 6.1: SPSS *Explore* Dialog Box

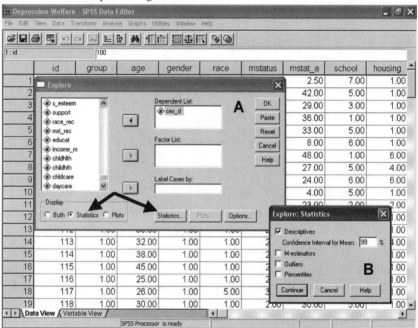

Explore: Statistics will open (screen 6.1.B). Make sure that *Descriptives* is checked and the *Confidence Interval for Mean* is set at 95% (SPSS default).

f.   To compute 99%, simply change 95% to 99%. You can request any level of confidence.

g.   Click on *Continue.*

h.   Click on *OK.*

Tables 6.3.A and 6.3.B display the output produced by SPSS.

Table 6.3.A summarizes the number and percentage of valid, missing, and total cases for depression, and table 6.3.B summarizes the descriptive statistics for

---

SPSS syntax for confidence interval:

EXAMINE CES_D
/PLOT NONE
/CINTERVAL 99.

Table 6.3.A: Explore Table for Depression

Case Processing Summary

	Cases					
	Valid		Missing		Total	
	N	Percent	N	Percent	N	Percent
CES_D (Depression)	107	100	0	0	107	100

Table 6.3.B: Descriptive Statistics for Depression

Descriptives

			Statistic	Std. Error
CES_D Depression	Mean		15.5607	.98007
	99% Confidence	Lower bound	12.9900	
	Interval for mean	Upper bound	18.1315	
	5% Trimmed mean		14.8982	
	Median		14.0000	
	Variance		107.777	
	Std. deviation		10.13790	
	Minimum		.00	
	Maximum		47.00	
	Range		47.00	
	Interquartile range		13.0000	
	Skewness		.985	.234
	Kurtosis		.668	.463

depression, all of which we discussed except the 5% Trimmed Mean. *Trimmed mean* represents the mean score for the middle 90% of cases; that is, scores for the top 5% and lower 5% of cases are eliminated from the analysis. This is especially appropriate when the distribution is severely skewed.

Table 6.3.B shows that the 99% confidence interval is between 12.99 and 18.13. In other words, we are 99% confident that the interval 12.99 to 18.13 contains the true depression score for former welfare recipients from which the sample was selected.

SELECTING A STATISTICAL TEST

This section presents and compares a number of statistical techniques for comput-ing a *statistic* and a p value to examine the null hypothesis. All statistical techniques test whether there is statistical support for the null hypothesis. In other words, by computing the p value, researchers decide to reject or not reject the null hypothesis.

Parametric and Nonparametric Tests

When data collection is complete and ready to be analyzed, researchers de-cide which statistical test is most appropriate. The decision is a critical one because choosing an inappropriate statistical test may lead to inaccurate decision, inter-pretation, and conclusions. Researchers must carefully examine their data to en-sure certain conditions are met, such as normality of distributions.

The many statistical tests to choose from are grouped into two sets: *parametric* and *nonparametric* tests. While each statistical test has its own assumptions and re-quirements, parametric and nonparametric tests assume that the sample from which data are collected represents the population for which generalizations will be made.

A representative sample is essential to estimate the population's parameters. If a nonrepresentative sample is used, generalization of the results to the popula-tion will be questionable. This occurs when the characteristics of the sample (such as gender, race, age, education, income) significantly differ from the characteristics of the population for which generalizations will be made.

Generally, a sample is presumed to be representative of the population if it is drawn through probability sampling methods, such as simple random sampling, systematic random sampling, stratified random sampling, or cluster random sam-pling methods. When a sample is selected through nonprobability sampling methods, such as purposive or convenience sampling, researchers should compare the characteristics of the sample with those of the population to examine whether they are similar.[2]

In addition to the above assumptions, parametric tests assume the following:

1. The dependent variable is continuous data, measured at the interval or ratio levels of measurement.

2. The shape of the distribution of the dependent variable should approach the shape of a normal curve. The distribution should not be severely skewed.

3. The sample size should be large enough. This is important because the larger the sample size, the smaller the standard error of the mean. With a large sample size, the central limit theorem (discussed in chapter 5) ensures that the distribution of the means approximates a normal distribution. "How large is large" will vary from one test to another.

---

[2]For more on sampling methods, see Rubin & Babbie (2005).

at .05 ($\alpha = .05$). Reject the null hypothesis if the p value is equal to or less than alpha.

3. Choose the appropriate statistical test to examine the null hypothesis. First, select the most appropriate parametric and nonparametric tests as outlined in table 6.4. Second, review the parametric assumptions (e.g., distribution, level of measurement, homogeneity of variance, sample size) to determine whether they are met. Third, if necessary, transform the data to the square root, logarithm, or other methods (as discussed in chapter 5). Based on these evaluations and transformations, choose the appropriate test.

    Recommendation: If you choose a nonparametric test, run the corresponding parametric test. If both tests produce the same results, report the results of the parametric test and indicate that the results of the nonparametric test are consistent with the results of the parametric test.

4. Compute the test statistic. This is discussed in detail in the following chapters.

5. Decide whether to reject the null hypothesis (H_0) or not. If the computed p value is equal or less than *alpha,* then reject the null hypothesis. If the computed p value is greater than *alpha,* do not reject the null hypothesis.

6. Summarize your findings and present them in a readable table.

SUMMARY

Chapter 6 discussed the foundation for inferential statistics, essential for all statistical techniques discussed in remaining chapters. We reviewed null and research hypotheses, the difference between one-tailed and two-tailed research hypotheses, errors in hypothesis testing (type I and type II errors), levels of significance (p value), one-tailed and two-tailed rejection areas, and confidence intervals.

The chapter also demonstrated differences between parametric and nonparametric tests and which factors to consider in selecting appropriate statistical tests. Steps in hypothesis testing were outlined.

The next chapter introduces a bivariate statistical test, the Pearson product moment correlation coefficient. Chapter 6 will discuss its purpose, assumptions, coefficient of determination, and the scatterplot. The alternative nonparametric test Spearman rho correlation is presented, along with two practical examples and how to compute statistics, read the output, and summarize and present results of correlation tests.

PRACTICAL EXERCISES

I. Use data from Question 1 in chapter 3 and answer the following questions:

    1. Compute the 95% and 99% confidence interval.

    2. Explain what these intervals tell you.

II. Use the self-esteem data you entered in SPSS in chapter 2 and do the following:

1. State a one-tailed research hypothesis predicting the relationship between age and self-esteem.

2. What are the independent and dependent variables in question 1? What are their levels of measurement?

3. Run a histogram for the dependent variable in question 1. What statistical test appears to be most appropriate to examine the hypothesis you stated in question 1? What is the alternative test?

4. State a one-tailed research hypothesis that predicts the relationship between gender and health in general.

5. What are the independent and dependent variables in question 4? What are their levels of measurement?

6. Run the histogram for the dependent variable in question 4. What statistical test appears to be most appropriate to examine the hypothesis in question 4? What is the alternative test?

7. Use SPSS to compute the 99% confidence interval for self-esteem. What does this interval tell you?

CHAPTER 7

Bivariate Correlation: Pearson Product-Moment Correlation Coefficient

LEARNING OBJECTIVES

1. Understand the purpose of Pearson correlation
2. Understand the coefficient of determination
3. Understand the assumptions underlying the Pearson correlation
4. Understand the scatterplot
5. Understand the alternative nonparametric Spearman rho
6. Understand how to use SPSS to compute statistics
7. Understand how to interpret and present results of the tests

Data Set: *Job Satisfaction* (appendix A)

INTRODUCTION

Up to this point we have reviewed methodological terms and discussed various methods of descriptive statistics, including data organization and presentation, measures of central tendency and variability, and normal and skewed distributions. In chapter 6 we introduced hypothesis testing, selecting an appropriate statistical test, and steps in hypothesis testing.

This and remaining chapters build on chapter 6. Recall that the purpose of any research study is not only to describe characteristics of a sample, but also to examine if these characteristics can be generalized to the population from which the sample is selected. Can relationships between variables observed in the sample be generalized to the population? For example, a social work practitioner who works with welfare recipients may notice that those who have less social contacts are more depressed than recipients who have more contacts. Does this pattern apply to the general population of welfare recipients? Is there a significant inverse relationship between number of social contacts and level of depression among welfare recipients? If this hypothesis proves accurate, it can help the practitioner to develop a treatment approach that will help welfare recipients reduce depression.

The social work practitioner cannot rely on descriptive statistics alone. Further statistical analysis, inferential statistics, must be conducted.

What type of inferential statistics? Table 6.4 in chapter 6 grouped statistical tests in pairs (one parametric and one nonparametric). The first group included Pearson r and Spearman rho.

This chapter presents the Pearson product-moment correlation coefficient and its alternative, Spearman rho coefficient. It discusses the purpose of these tests, defines the coefficient of determination, discusses assumptions underlying the tests, and presents the scatterplot. Two practical examples are presented illustrating how to utilize SPSS to compute correlation coefficients, interpret the output, and write and present the results.

PEARSON CORRELATION COEFFICIENT

Purpose

The Pearson product-moment correlation coefficient (or simply Pearson correlation coefficient or simple correlation) is a bivariate parametric test.[1] It examines the strength and direction of a linear relationship between one continuous dependent variable and one continuous independent variable. The Pearson correlation coefficient is symbolized by a lowercase italic r.

The purpose of Pearson correlation is to examine whether an increase in the independent variable leads to an increase or decrease in the dependent variable. For example, does an increase in the quality of supervision at work lead to a decrease in burnout among social workers? In this question, quality of supervision is the independent variable and burnout is the dependent variable.

Correlation Coefficient

The Pearson correlation coefficient, r, ranges between -1.00 and $+1.00$ ($-1 \leq r \leq 1$). A correlation coefficient of -1.00 indicates a perfect negative correlation; a correlation coefficient of $+1.00$ indicates a perfect positive correlation. A correlation coefficient of 0 indicates that the two variables are not at all correlated.

The sign (+ or −) of the coefficient indicates only the direction of the relationship. That is, a correlation coefficient between 0 and 1 indicates a positive, di-

---

[1]Bivariate statistics examine the relationship between two variables. They do not indicate whether the independent variable causes the dependent variable to occur.

rect, relationship and a correlation coefficient between 0 and −1 indicates a nega-tive, inverse, relationship.

The absolute value of the coefficient $|r|$ indicates the strength of the rela-tionship between the two variables. For example, a correlation coefficient of −.65 is stronger than a correlation coefficient of .60 because the absolute value of −.65 is greater than the absolute value of .60 ($|-.65| = .65 > |.60| = .60$).

Coefficient of Determination

The coefficient of determination measures the strength of the relationship be-tween the two variables. It measures the proportion of variance in the dependent variable, as explained by the independent variable (e.g., burnout as explained by quality of supervision). It is computed by squaring the Pearson correlation coeffi-cient r.

$$\text{Coefficient of determination} = r^2$$

Figure 7.1 contains four Venn diagrams demonstrating different degrees of correlation between two variables. Venn diagram A shows that the two variables are not at all correlated ($r = 0$): The variance in the dependent variable that is ex-plained by the independent variable is zero. Venn diagram B shows a positive cor-relation between the two variables ($0 < r < 1$). Venn diagram C shows a negative correlation between the two variables ($-1 < r < 0$). In both cases, the independent variable explains some of the variance in the dependent variable (r^2). Venn diagram D shows a perfect correlation between the two variables: The independent variable explains 100% of the variance in the dependent variable.

Example: If the correlation between physical health (independent variable) and levels of depression of frail elderly (dependent variable) is −.40 ($r = -.40$), then 16% of the variance in depression is due to physical health [$r^2 = (-.40)^2 = .16$, or 16%]. How strong is this correlation?

The correlation between two variables may be considered *strong, moderate,* or *weak.* To determine the strength of the correlation, first compute the coefficient of determination (r^2). If r^2 is greater than or equal to .64 ($r \geq .80$), then the correla-tion is considered strong. If it is greater than .25 and less than .64 ($.50 < r < .80$), the correlation is considered moderate, and if it is less than or equal to .25 ($r \leq .50$), the correlation is considered weak.

Strong correlation: $\quad r^2 \geq .64$
Moderate correlation: $.25 < r^2 < .64$
Weak correlation: $\quad r^2 \leq .25$

Figure 7.1:   Correlation Between Two Variables

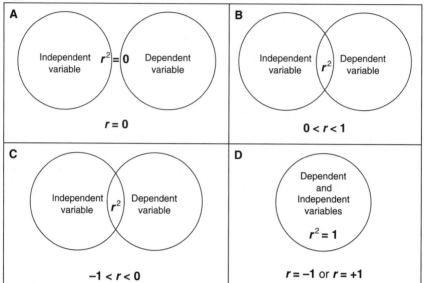

Correlation and Causality

In order to conclude that variable A causes variable B to occur, three require-ments must be demonstrated: (1) the cause, variable A, must precede the effect, variable B, in time; (2) the two variables, A and B, must have empirical correlation; and (3) the correlation cannot be influenced by a third variable. Thus, just because two variables have a high correlation coefficient does not mean that one variable causes the other to occur. For example, the fact that there is a high correlation be-tween job satisfaction and burnout does not mean that higher job satisfaction leads to lower burnout. It could be that lower burnout leads to higher job satisfaction.

Assumptions

As discussed in chapter 6, all parametric tests make assumptions about the population from which the sample is selected.

1. The dependent variable must be measured at the interval level of measure-ment or higher.

2. The shape of the distribution of the dependent variable must approximate the shape of a normal curve.

3. The sample size should be large enough to conduct simple correlation. A sample size of 30 subjects or more is usually suitable to conduct bivariate parametric statistics.

In addition to these general parametric assumptions, Pearson correlation requires the following assumptions:

4. The dependent and independent variables must be paired observations. Data for both variables should be collected from the same subjects at the same time. For example, to examine the relationship between physical health and level of depression of frail elderly, data on both variables must be collected from each subject at the same time.

5. The independent variable must be continuous data (interval or higher).

6. The shape of the distribution of the independent variable must approximate the shape of a normal curve.

To evaluate the assumption of normality, create histograms with normal curves and run measures of central tendency and measures of skewness for both the independent and dependent variables. If the histograms and measures of skewness show severe departure from normality, consider transforming the data to the square root, logarithm, or other transformation methods.

SPEARMAN RHO COEFFICIENT

The Spearman rank correlation coefficient, also called the Spearman rho, is the nonparametric version of the Pearson correlation coefficient. While Pearson correlation compares actual scores (raw scores) of independent and dependent variables, Spearman rho ranks these scores and then examines whether there is a relationship between the two ranks.

Because Spearman rho does not make assumptions about the population from which the sample is selected, it is appropriate to use when either or both the independent and dependent variables are measured at the ordinal level of measurement, or at interval levels that do not meet the assumption of normality. Spearman rho still requires the sample to be representative of the population and the independent and dependent variables to be paired observations.

Like the Pearson r coefficient, the Spearman rho coefficient ranges between −1 and +1, where the sign indicates the direction of the relationship and the absolute value indicates the strength of the relationship. This correlation coefficient is symbolized by r_s.

Scatterplot

A scatterplot (also called scattergram) visualizes whether a linear relationship exists between two continuous variables (interval or ratio). The y axis represents the scores of the dependent variable; the x axis represents the scores of the independent variable. Each point in a scatterplot represents two scores, one for the dependent variable (y) and another for the independent variable (x). There should be one point on the scatterplot for each subject in a study. Figure 7.2 illustrates a

Figure 7.2:   Scatterplot for Burnout and Quality of Supervision

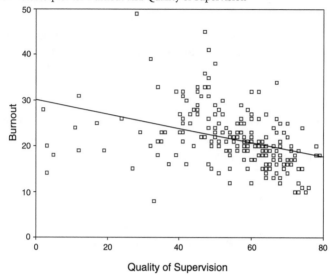

scatterplot for burnout (dependent variable *y*) and quality of supervision (in-dependent variable *x*).

The line in figure 7.2 is called the *fit line*. It indicates that there is a linear neg-ative relationship between quality of supervision and burnout: The greater the quality of supervision, the lower the burnout. A fit line that runs from the upper left side to the lower right side (as in figure 7.2) represents a negative correlation. A fit line that runs from the lower left side to the upper right side represents a posi-tive correlation.

PRACTICAL EXAMPLES

This book is not about statistical formulas (discussed in other statistics books). Here, we present and discuss how to utilize SPSS to run both Pearson correlation and Spearman rho correlation coefficients.

Follow the steps in hypothesis testing discussed in chapter 6. The two ex-amples here illustrate a positive and a negative relationship.

Example 1—Positive Correlation

Use the SPSS *Job Satisfaction* data file (Appendix A) to examine the following research question:

> Is there a significant relationship between opportunities for promotion (**PROMOT**) and job satisfaction (**SATISFAC**) among social workers?

Screen 7.1: SPSS *Bivariate Correlations* Menu

a. Open the SPSS *Job Satisfaction* data file.

b. Click on *Analyze* in the SPSS main toolbar.

c. Click on *Correlate* (screen 7.1).

d. Click on *Bivariate.* A new dialog box called *Bivariate Correlations* will open (screen 7.2).

e. Scroll down in the variable list, click on **SATISFAC,** and click on the arrow button between the two boxes to move **SATISFAC** in the *Variables* box.

f. Repeat step e to move **PROMOT** in the *Variables* box. You can add more than two variables to examine their correlations.

g. Make sure that *Pearson* is checked under *Correlation Coefficients* (SPSS default). If not, check it. Also check *Spearman.*

h. For a two-tailed research hypothesis, make sure that *Two-tailed* is checked under *Test of Significance* (SPSS default). For a one-tailed research hypothesis, check *One-tailed.* In this example, check *One-tailed.*

i. Notice that the box next to *Flag significant correlations* is checked. This means that a correlation that is significant at alpha of .05 will be flagged with a single asterisk and a correlation significant at alpha of 0.01 is flagged with two asterisks. You may uncheck this box to remove any asterisk.

j. Click on *OK.*

Screen 7.2:   SPSS *Bivariate Correlations* Dialog Box

SPSS syntax for Pearson (syntax 1) and Spearman (syntax 2):

syntax 1: CORRELATION SATISFAC PROMOT
/PRINT=ONETAIL NOSIG.

syntax 2: NONPAR CORR SATISFAC PROMOT
/PRINT=ONETAIL NOSIG.

To request a two-tailed *p* value, change ONETAIL to TWOTAIL.

Interpreting the Output.   Tables 7.1.A and 7.1.B display the output of SPSS. The first table displays the results of the Pearson correlation and the second displays the results of Spearman rho.

Table 7.1.A displays three measures: Pearson correlation, Sig. (1-tailed), and N. The Pearson correlation conveys the correlation coefficient *r*. "Sig." conveys the level of significance (*p* value) and "1-tailed" conveys that this is a one-tailed hypothesis. "N" conveys the number of subjects in the study.

The table shows that the correlation coefficient between job satisfaction (**SATISFAC**) and itself is 1 and the correlation coefficient between opportunities for promotion (**PROMOT**) and itself is 1. This is always the case, that the correla-

Table 7.1.A: Results of Pearson Correlation

		SATISFAC	PROMOT
SATISFAC	Pearson correlation	1	.213**
	Sig. (1-tailed)	.	.001
	N	218	218
PROMOT	Pearson correlation	.213**	1
	Sig. (1-tailed)	.001	.
	N	218	218

**Correlation is significant at the 0.01 level.

Table 7.1.B: Results of Spearman rho

			SATISFACT	PROMOT
Spearman rho	**SATISFAC**	Correlation coefficient	1.000	.211**
		Sig. (1-tailed)	.	.001
		N	218	218
	PROMOT	Correlation coefficient	.211**	1.000
		Sig. (1-tailed)	.001	.
		N	218	218

**Correlation is significant at the 0.01 level.

tion between a variable and itself is 1, which is useless information. A correlation should always be between two or more variables (e.g., promotion and satisfaction).

The correlation between job satisfaction (**SATISFAC**) and opportunities for promotion (**PROMOT**) is .213 (round to the nearest decimal, $r = .21$), the p value is .001 (Sig. = .001), and the sample size, N, is 218 subjects. A p that is equal to or less than .05 indicates a significant result. In other words, the correlation between job satisfaction and opportunities for promotion is significant ($p = .001$).

Table 7.1.B displays the results of Spearman rho. Like table 7.1.A, it has three measures: the Spearman rho correlation coefficient, Sig. (1-tailed), and N. The Spearman rho correlation coefficient conveys the rho coefficient. "Sig." conveys the level of significance (p value), and "1-tailed" conveys that this is a one-tailed hypothesis. "N" conveys the number of subjects in the study.

Table 7.1.B shows that the correlation between **SATISFAC** and **PROMOT** is .211 (rho = .211), the p value is .001 (Sig. = .001), and the sample size is 218 subjects. Because the p value is less than .05, the correlation coefficient between job satisfaction and opportunities is significant.

Step 5: Decide whether to reject the null hypothesis.

The results of the Pearson correlation coefficient presented in table 7.1.A show a significant relationship between job satisfaction and opportunities for promotion ($p < .05$). Therefore, reject the null hypothesis.

Writing the Results

When writing the results of the Pearson correlation or Spearman rho, report the correlation coefficient and the p value, as well as the direction and strength of the relationship. You may present results in a Venn diagram or a scatterplot to visually show the relationship between variables. In our example, the results may be summarized as follows:

To examine the relationship between job satisfaction and opportunities for promotion, the Pearson product-moment correlation coefficient was utilized. The results show a significant positive relationship ($r = .21$, $p < .05$), indicating that social workers who have greater opportunities for promotion tend to experience higher levels of job satisfaction than those who have fewer opportunities.

The independent variable (opportunities for promotion) explains less than 5% ($r^2 = .21^2 = 4.4\%$) of the variance in job satisfaction. More than 95% of the variance in job satisfaction is unaccounted for and could be related to extraneous variables. Thus, although the two variables have a significant relationship, this relationship is considered weak. Figure 7.4 is a Venn diagram illustrating the relationship between job satisfaction and opportunities for promotion.

How to Create a Scatterplot in SPSS.   The correlation between job satisfaction and opportunities for promotion can also be shown visually in a scatterplot.

To create a scatterplot in SPSS, follow these steps:

a.   Open the SPSS *Job Satisfaction* data file.

b.   Click on *Graphs* in the SPSS main toolbar.

c.   Scroll down and click on *Scatter.* A new dialog box called *Scatterplot* will open (screen 7.3).

d.   Select *Simple* (SPSS default) and click on *Define.*

e.   A new dialog box called *Simple Scatterplot* will open (screen 7.4.A).

Figure 7.4:   Relationship between Job Satisfaction and Promotion

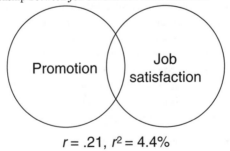

$$r = .21,\ r^2 = 4.4\%$$

This Venn diagram shows the relationship between job satisfaction and opportunities for promotion. The r conveys the Pearson correlation coefficient and the overlap area conveys the variance in job satisfaction that is explained by opportunities for promotion ($r^2 = 4.4\%$).

Screen 7.3: SPSS *Scatterplot* Dialog Box

Screen 7.4: SPSS Simple Scatterplot Dialog Box

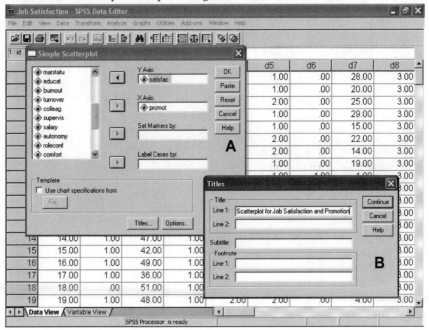

f.   Scroll down in the variable list, click on **SATISFAC** (dependent variable), and click on the top arrow button to move **SATISFAC** in the y *axis* box.

g.   Scroll down in the variable list, click on **PROMOT** (independent variable), and click on the second arrow button to move **PROMOT** in the x *axis* box.

h.   Click on *Titles* and type a title for the scatterplot (screen 7.4.B).

i.   Click on *Continue* and click on *OK.*

SPSS syntax for Scatterplot:

GRAPH
/SCATTER PROMOT WITH SATISFAC
/TITLE= 'Scatterplot for Job Satisfaction and Promotion'.

Figure 7.5 displays the scatterplot for job satisfaction and opportunities for promotion.

Add a fit line to the scatterplot by using the SPSS Chart Editor (only in SPSS Version 12.0).

1.   Point the mouse anywhere in the scatterplot and double-click. A new SPSS window called *SPSS Chart Editor* will open (screen 7.5.B).

Figure 7.5:   Scatterplot for Job Satisfaction and Promotion

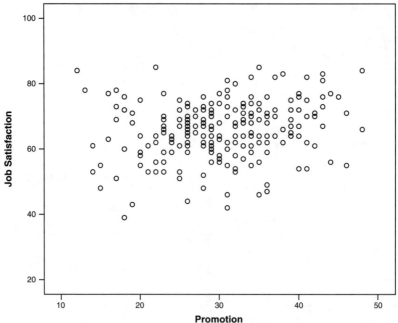

Screen 7.5:   SPSS *Chart Editor* Screen

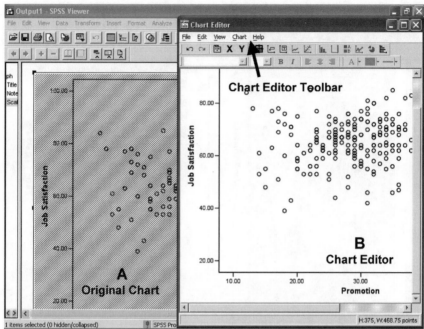

2. Point the mouse and single-click in the scatterplot on *Chart Editor* (screen 7.5.B). This highlights all points in the scatterplot.

3. Click on *Chart* in the *Chart Editor* toolbar. Scroll down and click on *Add Chart Element,* then click *Add Fit Line at Total* (screen 7.6).

4. A fit line will be added to the chart. A new dialog box called *Properties* will open (screen 7.7.A).

5. The *Properties* dialog box allows you to change the size of the chart, weight, color, and type of the fit line.

6. To end, click on *Close,* click on *File* and *Close* in the *Chart Editor* toolbar. This will return you to *Output.*

    To add a fit line in SPSS Version 11.5, follow these steps:

1. Point the mouse anywhere in the plot and double-click. A new SPSS screen called *Chart1—SPSS Chart Editor* will open (screen 7.8.A).

2. Click on *Chart* and *Options* in the SPSS *Chart Editor* toolbar.

3. A new dialog box called *Scatterplot Options* will open (screen 7.8.B).

4. Click on *Total* under *Fit Line.*

5. Click on *Fit Options* to request the coefficient of determination (*r* squared). A new dialog box called *Scatterplot Options: Fit Line* will open (screen 7.8.C).

Screen 7.6: SPSS *Add Fit Line* Toolbar (Version 12.0)

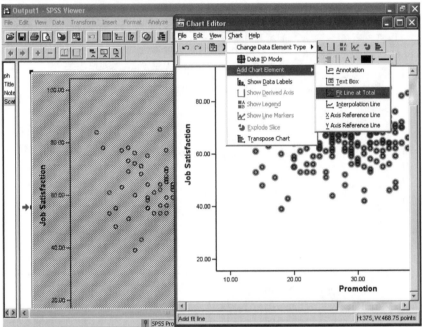

Screen 7.7: SPSS *Fit Line Properties* Dialog Box

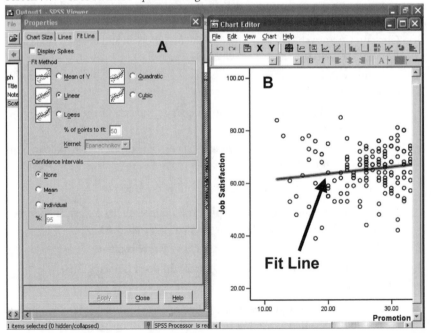

Screen 7.8:   SPSS 11.5 *Chart Editor* Dialog Box

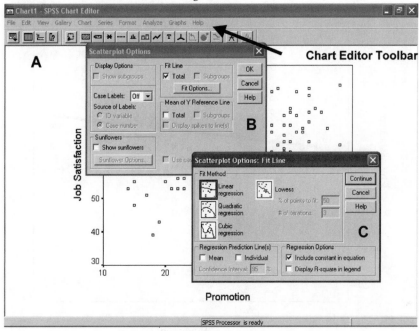

6. Check *Display R-squared in legend.*

7. Click on *Continue* to close *Scatterplot Options: Fit Line* dialog box (screen 7.8.C).

8. Click on *OK.*

9. Click *File* and click *Close* in the *SPSS Editor* toolbar. This will return you to the *Output—SPSS viewer* screen.

Figure 7.6 displays the edited scatterplot for job satisfaction and opportunities for promotion. The figure shows that the two variables have a positive relationship because the fit line runs from the lower left side to the upper right side. The two variables, however, have a weak ($r^2 = .046$) relationship.

Example 2—Negative Correlation

Use the *Job Satisfaction* data file to answer the following research question.

Is there a significant relationship between age (**D2**) and levels of turnover (**TURNOVER**) among social workers?

Step 1: State the null and alternative hypotheses.

H_0: There is no significant relationship between age and level of turnover among social workers.

$r = 0$

Figure 7.6:   Scatterplot for Job Satisfaction and Promotion

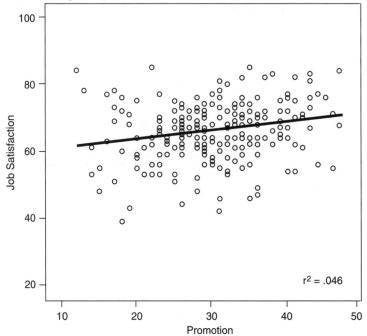

H_a: There is a significant negative (inverse) relationship between age and level of turnover among social workers. In other words, the older the social worker, the lower the level of turnover.

$r < 0$

In this one-tailed research hypothesis, age is the independent variable and turnover is the dependent variable. Age is measured at the ratio level of measurement and turnover is measured at the interval level.

Step 2: Set criteria for rejecting H_0.
Set alpha at .05 ($\alpha = .05$). Reject H_0 only if $p \leq .05$.

Step 3: Select the appropriate statistical test.

a. Data for both the independent variable (age) and the dependent variable (turnover) were collected from the same subjects at the same time. They are paired observations.

b. Both variables are measured at the interval level of measurement or higher.

c. Based on steps a and b, the data meet the basic assumptions for the bivariate correlation tests, Pearson correlation and Spearman rho. Which one is most suitable to examine the null hypothesis: To determine, examine the distributions of both variables.

d.   Evaluate normality: Figure 7.7.A displays the distribution for turnover. The shape of the distribution approximates the shape of a normal curve.

Figure 7.7.B displays the distribution for age. Unlike figure 7.7.A, it shows the shape of the distribution of age as severely skewed to the right (positive skewness), which violates the assumption of normality. In this case, transform age to the square root or another transformation method that may bring the shape of the distribution of age closer to a normal curve. However, for our discussion, assume it remains severely skewed and does not meet the assumption of normality.

e.   Sample size: As in the previous example, 218 social workers participated in this study.

f.   Data for both variables meet all the assumptions for the Pearson parametric test except the assumption of normality, as the independent variable is severely skewed. In this case, consider using the nonparametric Spearman rho correlation to examine the null hypothesis. Also run the parametric Pearson correlation to see whether the results of both tests are consistent.

Step 4: Compute the test statistic (Use SPSS).

To use SPSS to compute the Spearman rho and Pearson r correlation coefficients, follow the same SPSS methods as in the previous example and replace the variables **PROMOT** and **SATISFAC** with **D2** and **TURNOVER**.

Table 7.2.A displays the results of the nonparametric Spearman rho correlation and table 7.2.B displays the results of the alternative parametric Pearson correlation.

Table 7.2.A shows that the correlation coefficient between turnover and age is $-.25$ ($r_s = -.25$), the p value is .000 (Sig. = .000), and the sample size is 215 social workers (while 218 subjects participated in the study, 215 completed pair observations of age and turnover). This indicates a significant negative relationship between age and turnover.

The results of the Pearson correlation presented in table 7.2.B are similar to the results of Spearman rho presented in table 7.2.A: $r = -.23$, the p value is .000 (Sig. = .000), and the sample size is 215 subjects (N = 215). The correlation coefficient between turnover and age is significant.

Recommendation: When the results of both the parametric test and its corresponding nonparametric test are consistent, report the results of the parametric test and indicate that they are consistent with the results of the nonparametric test. In the above example, because the results of Pearson correlation and Spearman rho are both significant and both have similar coefficients ($r = -.23$ and $r_s = -.25$), it is recommended to report the results of the Pearson correlation.

Step 5: Decide whether to reject the null hypothesis.

The results of Spearman rho presented in table 7.2.A show a significant relationship between age and turnover ($p < .05$). Therefore, reject the null hypothesis.

Figure 7.7.A: Histogram for Turnover

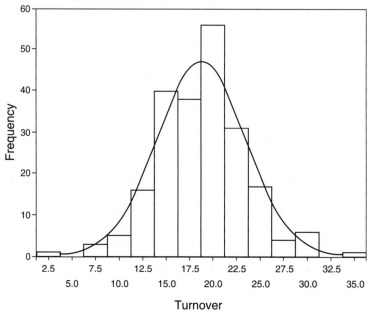

Figure 7.7.B: Histogram for Age

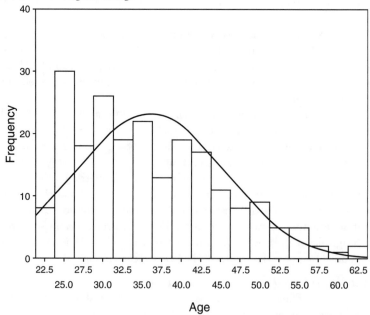

Table 7.2.A: Results of Spearman rho Correlation Coefficient

			TURNOVER	D2 (age)
Spearman rho	**TURNOVER**	Correlation coefficient	1.000	−.250**
		Sig. (1-tailed)	.	.000
		N	218	215
	D2 (age)	Correlation coefficient	−.250**	1.000
		Sig. (1-tailed)	.000	.
		N	215	215

**Correlation is significant at the 0.01 level.

Table 7.2.B: Results of Pearson Correlation Coefficient

		TURNOVER	D2 (age)
TURNOVER	Pearson correlation	1	−.233**
	Sig. (1-tailed)	.	.000
	N	218	215
D2 (age)	Pearson correlation	−.233**	1.000
	Sig. (1-tailed)	.000	.
	N	215	215

**Correlation is significant at the 0.01 level.

Writing the Results

To examine the relationship between turnover and age, we used the Spearman rho test. The results show a significant negative correlation between turnover and age ($r_s = -.25, p < .01$), so we rejected the null hypothesis. These results show that older social workers tend to experience lower levels of turnover than younger social workers; the older the social worker, the less the level of turnover. The results of the Pearson correlation coefficient support these results ($r = -.23, p < .01$).

These results, however, show that age explains only 5.4% [$r^2 = (-.233)^2 = 5.4\%$] of the variance in turnover. More than 94% of the variance in turnover is unaccounted for and could be explained by extraneous variables. In other words, the results show a significant, but weak, relationship between age and turnover. Figure 7.8 is a Venn diagram describing the relationship between turnover and age.

Figure 7.9 is a scatterplot for turnover and age. The plot shows a negative, but weak ($r^2 = 5.4\%$) linear relationship between the two variables; lower turnover is associated with older age.

Presentation of Results in Summary Tables

There are two types of correlation tables. The first presents the correlation coefficients between one dependent variable and a number of independent variables.

Figure 7.8:   Venn Diagram for Age and Turnover

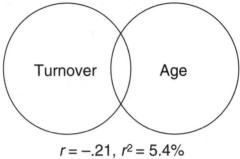

$$r = -.21, \ r^2 = 5.4\%$$

Figure 7.9:   Scatterplot for Turnover and Age

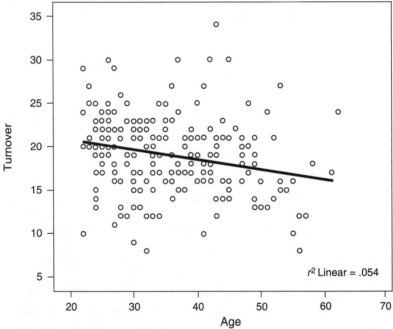

The limitation of this table is that the relationship between independent variables is not reported. The second type is a correlation matrix. A correlation matrix presents the correlation coefficients between each pair of variables and it flags with asterisk each correlation that is significant.

Tables 7.3.A and 7.3.B compare these two types. Table 7.3.A displays the correlation between job satisfaction (dependent variable) and a number of independent variables. (Although only the correlation between job satisfaction and promotion is computed here, assume that the correlation between job satisfaction and working with colleagues and quality of supervision has also been computed).

Table 7.3.A: Relationship Between Job Satisfaction and the Independent Variables
(N = 218)

Variable	r	r^2	p^+
Colleagues	.28	.08	>.010
Supervision	.32	.10	>.010
Promotion	.21	.04	>.010

+One-tailed p

Table 7.3.B: Correlation Matrix (N = 218)

Variable	Satisfaction	Promotion	Colleagues	Supervision
Satisfaction	1.00			
Promotion	.21**	1.00		
Colleagues	.28**	.45**	1.00	
Supervision	.32**	.30**	.43**	1.00

**One-tailed, $p < .01$

Table 7.3.C: Correlation Matrix (N = 218)

Variable	Satisfaction	Promotion	Colleagues	Supervision
Satisfaction	.82			
Promotion	.21**	.86		
Colleagues	.28**	.45**	.89	
Supervision	.32**	.30**	.43**	.90
Mean	66.16	30.20	54.72	18.01
SD	8.83	7.51	14.73	5.62
Range	39–85	12–48	2–79	4–35

**One-tailed, $p < .01$

Table 7.3.B is a correlation matrix. It displays the correlation between each pair of variables in the analysis. The "1.00" in the diagonal represents the correlation between each variable and itself. Because this is useless, many researchers prefer to report the reliability coefficients (Chronbach alpha) in the diagonal and the mean, standard deviation, and range for each scale, or subscale at the bottom of the table. Table 7.3.C, for example, is the same as table 7.3.B but it also reports the reliability coefficient for each scale (job satisfaction, promotion, colleagues, and supervision) and their mean, standard deviation, and range at the bottom of the table.

SUMMARY

Social work practitioners are interested to examine whether one social construct is related to another social construct such as life satisfaction and self-esteem, as this helps to develop a treatment plan. To verify that a relationship exists, practitioners carefully measure these constructs and then statistically examine whether the two variables are related.

This chapter introduced the Pearson product-moment correlation coefficient, the assumptions underlying the statistic, and introduced the alternative nonparametric Spearman rho test. The chapter then discussed the importance of the Venn diagram and scatterplot in evaluating and visualizing the direction and strength of the relationship between two variables.

Two social work research questions demonstrated how to state the hypothesis, evaluate the assumptions, choose the appropriate statistical test, and use SPSS to compute the correlation coefficient, interpret the output, and write and present results in summary tables.

Chapter 8 will introduce the independent *t*-test and Mann-Whitney U, the purpose of the two tests, and their assumptions. Two social work examples discuss how to compute the *t*-test and Mann-Whitney U statistics, interpret the output, and write and present the results.

PRACTICAL EXERCISE

Access the SPSS *Depression-Elderly* data file (appendix A). Use the variables life satisfaction (**SATISF**), emotional balance (**EB**), physical health (**PH**), and negative recent life events (**NRLEV**) and answer the following questions:

1. Develop three one-tailed research hypotheses predicting the relationship between life satisfaction and emotional balance, physical health, and negative recent life events.
2. For each hypothesis, also state the null hypothesis.
3. What test will you use to examine each hypothesis? Justify your answer.
4. Examine each hypothesis. Follow the steps in hypothesis testing. Discuss the direction and strength of the relationship.
5. Are there any differences between the results of the test you chose and its alternative test? If so, what are the differences?
6. Present the results in a correlation matrix table.
7. Present the results of one pair in a Venn diagram.
8. Create a scatterplot for each relationship.

CHAPTER 8

Group Comparisons: Two Group Means— Independent *t*-Test

LEARNING OBJECTIVES

1. Understand the purpose of the independent *t*-test
2. Understand the assumptions underlying the independent *t*-test
3. Understand the alternative nonparametric Mann-Whitney U test
4. Understand how to use SPSS to compute the statistics
5. Understand how to interpret and present the results of the tests

Data Set: *Job Satisfaction* (appendix A)

INTRODUCTION

One goal of a social work practitioner conducting a therapy group for battered women with low levels of self-esteem is to demonstrate that battered women who participate in a therapy (experiment group) significantly improve self-esteem while those who do not participate (control group) do not improve. In this case, the practitioner's interest is to demonstrate that therapy is significantly effective. To test this, the practitioner conduct a pretest posttest control group design.

A social work administrator may believe that the level of burnout among male social workers is higher than the level among females. The administrator asks all social workers in the agency to complete a self-administered survey consisting of demographic variables (gender, age, etc.) and a standardized burnout scale.

The practitioner and administrator are both interested in examining the difference between two groups with regard to one outcome. In the first case, the two groups consist of the experiment and control groups and the outcome is level of self-esteem. In the second case, the two groups consist of male and female social workers and the outcome is level of burnout. Figure 8.1 illustrates the two cases.

Figure 8.1:   Group Comparison

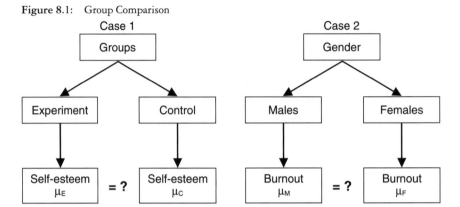

In both cases, the independent variables (groups and gender) are categorical variables that each consist of two levels, or attributes. This is also known as a dichotomous variable. The dependent variables (self-esteem and burnout) are continuous data. Which statistical test is suitable to examine the difference between each set of two groups with regard to the dependent variable?

This chapter presents the independent *t*-test, its purpose, and underlying assumptions. The alternative nonparametric Mann-Whitney U test is also presented. Two social work examples illustrate how to use SPSS to compute the statistics and their levels of significance, as well as how to interpret, write, and present the results.

STUDENT *t*-TEST

The student *t*-test is a group of three inferential statistical tests. The first is the one sample–one group *t*-test, also known as the single-sample *t*-test. It compares the sample's mean with a known, or estimated, population's mean. The assumption is that if the sample is representative of the population, then the sample's mean will not be statistically significant from the population's mean. The researcher's aim is to not reject the null hypothesis (that there is no significant difference between the sample's mean and the population's mean). The limitation of the single-sample *t*-test is that researchers rarely know the population's mean (parameter) and therefore it is rarely used in social work research and is not discussed in this book.[1] The second test is the independent *t*-test, the topic of this chapter; the third test is the dependent *t*-test, the topic of chapter 10.

---

[1]For more on the single-sample *t*-test, see Weinbach & Grinnell (2004) and Cronk (2004).

INDEPENDENT *t*-TEST

Purpose

The independent *t*-test is perhaps the most commonly used bivariate statistical test, and the most widely known among social sciences researchers. It is simple, easily interpreted, and easy to use—by hand and by statistical software.

The independent *t*-test, also known as independent samples *t*-test, is a bivariate parametric test, used to examine the difference between the means of two independent groups observed at the same time (one sample–two groups) and whether this difference is statistically significant. For example, in the research question "Is there a significant statistical difference between male and female social workers with regard to their levels of burnout?" the variable of gender consists of two groups: male and female. Gender is the independent variable and burnout is the dependent variable.

The independent *t*-test produces a test statistic called *t* that measures how far apart the means of the two groups are in standard error units. The larger the *t* is, the more likely that the difference between the two means is statistically significant.

Assumptions

Because the independent *t*-test is a parametric test, it is best utilized when parametric assumptions are met.

1. The dependent variable must be measured at the interval or ratio level of measurement.

2. The shape of the distribution of the dependent variable must approximate the shape of a normal curve.

3. The sample size should be large enough to compare two group means.[2] A sample size of 30 subjects or more is usually sufficient to utilize the independent *t*-test. Because the independent *t*-test compares the mean scores of two groups and not their frequencies, the two groups do not need to have equal frequencies.

    In addition to parametric assumptions, the following assumptions must also be met in order to run the independent *t*-test.

4. The independent variable must be dichotomous; it must consist of two groups, or attributes (e.g., Gender: males or females; Are you sick? Yes or No).

---

[2]Determining a sample size is not such an easy task as it may seem. It depends on a number of factors, including whether a hypothesis is one- or two-tailed, level of significance, statistical power, and effect size. For more on sample size for independent *t*-tests, see Munro (2005).

5.   Data for both groups must be collected at the same time (e.g., data on burnout for males and for females must be collected simultaneously).

6.   Variances of both groups on the dependent variable should be equal. This is known as the assumption of homogeneity of variances, or equality of variances.

MANN-WHITNEY U TEST

The Mann-Whitney U test is the nonparametric version of the independent *t*-test. It is the most popular among the four nonparametric tests that examine differences between two groups. In addition to the Mann-Whitney U, other nonparametric tests include the Kolmogorov-Simirnov Z, Moses extreme reactions, and Wald-Wolfowitz runs.

As with the Spearman rho correlation, the Mann-Whitney U ranks the scores of each group. Unlike Spearman rho, Mann-Whitney U then computes mean rank for each group and examines whether there is a significant difference between the two mean ranks.

The Mann-Whitney U test is appropriate to compare two groups when the dependent variable is measured at the ordinal level, or measured at the interval level that does not meet the assumption of normality. Mann-Whitney U still requires the sample to be representative of the population and the independent variable to be dichotomous.

PRACTICAL EXAMPLES

To practice the use of the independent *t*-test and the Mann-Whitney U, follow the steps in hypothesis testing discussed in chapter 6 and use SPSS to compute the *t* and *p* values for the independent *t*-test and the *z* and *p* values for the Mann-Whitney U test.

Example 1—Burnout by Gender

Use the SPSS *Job Satisfaction* data file (appendix A) to examine the difference between male and female social workers with regard to their levels of burnout; that is, to answer the following research question:

Is there a significant difference between male and female social workers (**D1**) with regard to their levels of burnout (**BURNOUT**)?

Step 1: State the null and alternative hypotheses.

H_o: There is no significant difference between male social workers (μ_M) and female social workers (μ_F) with regard to their levels of burnout.

$$\mu_M = \mu_F$$

H_a: Male social workers will have significantly higher levels of burnout than female social workers.

$$\mu_M > \mu_F$$

Figure 8.2:   Histogram for Burnout

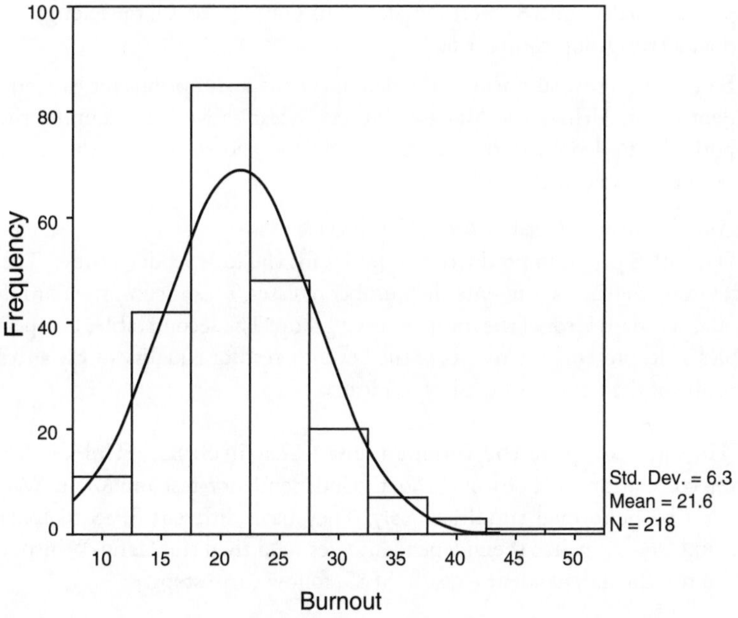

This is a one-tailed research hypothesis, where gender is the independent variable and burnout is the dependent variable.

Step 2: Set the criteria for rejecting H_0.
Set alpha at .05 ($\alpha = .05$). Reject H_0 only if $p \leq .05$.

Step 3: Select the appropriate statistical test.
To select an appropriate statistical test, first evaluate the data to be analyzed. Examine levels of measurement for the independent and dependent variables to assist in selecting a pair of bivariate tests. Then, evaluate the assumptions.

a. The independent variable in this hypothesis is gender and the dependent variable is burnout. Gender is a dichotomous variable (males and females) and burnout is continuous data (interval level of measurement). These are the two assumptions for the independent t-test and Mann-Whitney U.

b. To evaluate the assumption of normality, create a histogram with a normal curve for burnout. Figure 8.2 displays the distribution for burnout. Here, the distribution for burnout is positively skewed, but not severely.

c. To evaluate the assumption of homogeneity of variance, check the results of Levene's test of equality of variance. This test is performed simultaneously with the independent t-test. SPSS uses two formulas to compute the t value for the independent t-test; one assumes that the variances are equal, and the second assumes that the variances are significantly different (this is discussed in the next step).

d. Sample size: In this study, 218 social workers completed the survey. Of them, 36 were males and 182 were females. This sample size is large enough to conduct a two-group comparison.

e. Based on these assumptions, the data meet the assumptions for the independent *t*-test. Utilize the Mann-Whitney U test as well, to examine the hypothesis, to demonstrate how to use this test and to test whether results of both tests are consistent.

Step 4: Compute the test statistic (Use SPSS).

The SPSS program produces two tables for the independent *t*-test. The first table, Group Statistics, presents the number of cases, mean score, standard deviation, and standard error of the mean for each group. The second table, Independent Samples Test, presents the results of the Levene's test for equality of variances and the results of the *t*-test for Equality of Means.

How to Compute the Independent *t*-Test in SPSS.   Unlike with the Pearson correlation and Spearman rho, the independent *t*-test and Mann-Whitney U cannot be performed simultaneously. They have different SPSS toolbars and commands. First, utilize the independent *t*-test and then the Mann-Whitney U.

To run the independent *t*-test in SPSS, follow these steps:

Screen 8.1:   SPSS *Independent t-test* Toolbar

Screen 8.2: SPSS *Independent Samples t-Test* Dialog Box

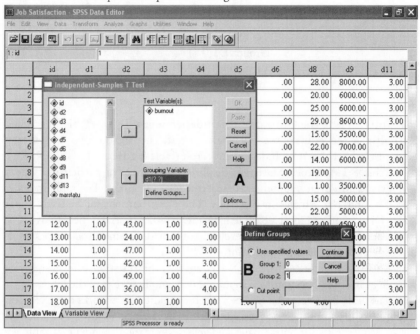

a. Open the SPSS *Job Satisfaction* data file.

b. Click on *Analyze* in the SPSS main toolbar.

c. Scroll down and click on *Compare Means* and click on *Independent-Samples t-Test* (screen 8.1).

d. A dialog box called *Independent Samples t-Test* will open (screen 8.2.A).

e. Scroll down in the variables list, click on **BURNOUT** (dependent variable), and click on the upper arrow button to move it in the *Test Variable(s)* box.

f. Scroll down in the variables list, click on **D1** (independent variable), and click on the lower arrow button to move it in the *Grouping Variable* box.

g. Click on *Define Groups.* A new dialog box called *Define Groups* will open (screen 8.2.B).

h. Type 0 for *Group 1* and type 1 for *Group 2* under *Use Specified Values.* Remember: these are the values for the variable **D1**: 0 = male and 1 = female. If you do not remember these values, click on *Cancel* to close *Define Groups,* point the mouse on **D1**, right-click, then click on *Variable Information.* A new box displaying the variable name and value labels for **D1** will open.

i. Click on *Continue* to close the *Define Groups* dialog box.

j. Click on *OK.*

SPSS syntax for the Independent *t*-Test:

T-TEST
Group=D1(0 1)
Variable=BURNOUT.

Interpreting the Output of the Independent *t*-Test.   Tables 8.1.A and 8.1.B display the results of the independent *t*-test. They include two parts: Group Statistics (table 8.1.A) and Independent *t*-Test (table 8.1.B).

Table 8.1.A, Group Statistics, displays the number of participants, mean score, standard deviation, and standard error for each group. The table includes 36 males and 182 females in the study. The mean burnout for males is 24.03 (SD = 7.19) compared to 21.08 for females (SD = 6.02). Based on these two means, it appears that males have higher levels of burnout than female social workers. Is this difference statistically significant?

The Independent *t*-Test, table 8.1.B, answers this question. However, before you can answer the question, you should understand how to read the table.

The table has two parts: Levene's test for equality of variances and the *t*-Test for Equality of Means. Levene's test for equality of variances examines whether the variances of the two groups (males and females) on the dependent variable are equal, or whether the assumption of homogeneity of variances is met.

Table 8.1.A: Group Statistics—Burnout by Gender

	D1 GENDER	N	Mean	Std. deviation	Std. error mean
BURNOUT	.00 male	36	24.0278	7.18922	1.19820
	1.00 female	182	21.0824	6.01828	.44610

Table 8.1.B: Results of Independent *t*-Test—Burnout by Gender

		Levene's test for equality of variances		*t*-test for Equality of Means					95% confidence interval of the difference	
		F	Sig.	*t*	df	Sig. (2-tailed)	Mean difference	Std. error difference	Lower	Upper
BURNOUT	Equal variances assumed	2.949	.087	2.595	216	.010	2.9454	1.13512	.70804	5.18268
	Equal variances not assumed			2.304	45.208	.026	2.9454	1.27855	.37055	5.52017

Table 8.1.B shows that the *F* value (second column) for Levene's test of equality of variances is 2.949 and the *p* value is .087 (Sig., third column). This *p* value is greater than *alpha* of .05, which indicates the two variances are not significantly different. The two variances are equal, which indicates that the data met the assumption of homogeneity of variances.

If the *p* value of Levene's test of equality of variances is greater than .05, then the two variances are not significantly different. The variances are approximately equal and, thus, the assumption of homogeneity of variances is met.

If the *p* value is less than or equal to .05, then the two variances are significantly different, so the assumption of homogeneity of variances is not met.

The second part of the table, *t*-test for Equality of Means, examines whether the two means are significantly different. Notice that there are two lines.

1. If the variances are equal, then read and report the results of the top line under *t*-test for Equality of Means (fourth column *t*; fifth column df; sixth column Sig. 2-tailed; seventh column Mean Difference).

2. If the variances are not equal, then read and report the results of the bottom line under *t*-test for equality of means.

In our case, read the top line because the variances are equal, which shows that the *t* statistic is 2.595; df[3] is 216; Sig. 2-tailed is .010 (*p* value); and the mean difference is 2.945 ($\overline{X}_m - \overline{X}_f$).

Remember: Unlike the Pearson correlation and Spearman rho, the independent *t*-test and Mann-Whitney U always produce a two-tailed statistic, even if the alternative hypothesis is one-tailed. Divide the *p* value by 2 only if you have a one-tailed research hypothesis.

Results of the Mann-Whitney U Test

Next, run and present the results of the Mann-Whitney U test. As with the independent *t*-test, SPSS produces two tables for the Mann-Whitney U. The first table, Ranks, reports the number of cases, mean rank, and sum of ranks for each group. The second table, Test Statistics, reports the Mann-Whitney U, Wilcoxon W, *z*, and *p* value (two-tailed).

How to Compute the Mann-Whitney U Test in SPSS.   The independent variable is gender (**D1**) and the dependent variable is burnout (**BURNOUT**).

---

[3]df (degrees of freedom) = N − 2.

Screen 8.3:   SPSS *Nonparametric Tests* Menu

To run the Mann-Whitney U in SPSS, follow these steps:

a.   Open the SPSS *Job Satisfaction* data file.

b.   Click on *Analyze* in the SPSS main tool bar.

c.   Scroll down and click on *Nonparametric Tests* and click on *2 Independent Samples* (screen 8.3).

d.   A dialog box called *Two-Independent-Samples Tests* will open (screen 8.4.A).

e.   Scroll down in the variables list, click on **BURNOUT** (dependent variable), and click on the upper arrow button to move it in the *Test Variable List* box.

f.   Scroll down in the variables list, click on **D1** (independent variable), and click on the lower arrow button to move it in the *Grouping Variable* box.

g.   Click on *Define Groups.* A new dialog box titled *Two Independent Samples: Defi* will open (screen 8.4.B).

h.   Type 0 for Group 1 and type 1 for Group 2 (values for the variable **D1**: 0 = male, 1 = female).

i.   Click on *Continue.*

j.   Click on *OK.*

Screen 8.4:   SPSS *Mann-Whitney U* Dialog Box

SPSS syntax for Mann-Whitney U:

NPAR TEST
/M-W=BURNOUT BY D1(0 1)
/MISSING ANALYSIS.

Interpreting the Output of the Mann-Whitney U.   The results of the Mann-Whitney U test are presented in tables 8.2.A and 8.2.B. Table 8.2.A shows that the study includes 36 males and 182 females. The mean rank for males is 132.38, compared to 104.98 for females. This indicates that males have higher levels of burnout than females. Is this difference statistically significant?

Table 8.2.B answers this question. The table shows that the z value (third line) is -2.386 with a significance level (fourth line, Asymp. Sig.) of .017 (two-tailed). As with the independent t-test, divide this p value by 2, because our research hypothesis is one-tailed. Thus, the p value is $.017/2 = .0085$, which indicates a significant difference between the two groups.

Step 5: Decide whether to reject the null hypothesis.
The results of the independent t-test presented in table 8.1.B show a signifi-

Table 8.2.A: Group Ranks—Burnout by Gender

	D1 (GENDER)	N	Mean Rank	Sum of Ranks
BURNOUT	.00 male	36	132.38	4765.50
	1.00 female	182	104.98	19105.50
	Total	218		

Table 8.2.B: Results of the Mann-Whitney U

	BURNOUT
Mann-Whitney U	2452.500
Wilcoxon W	19105.500
z	−2.386
Asymp. Sig. (2-tailed)	.017

Grouping variable: D1 (GENDER)

cant difference between male and female social workers with regard to levels of burnout ($p < .05$). Thus, reject the null hypothesis.

Writing the Results.   When writing the results of the independent *t*-test or Mann-Whitney U, present the *t* value, degrees of freedom (df), and the *p* value. Also present the mean score for each group and the overall mean difference. In the example, results of the independent *t*-test are summarized as follows:

The independent *t*-test examined levels of burnout based on gender. The results show a significant difference between male and female social workers ($t_{(df=216)} = 2.59; p < .05$).[4] In this study, male social workers reported significantly higher levels of burnout ($\overline{X} = 24.03$) than female social workers ($\overline{X} = 21.08$). The mean difference was 2.95. These results are supported by the results of the Mann-Whitney U, which also show a significant difference between male and female social workers with regard to burnout ($z = −2.39; p < .05$).

Example 2—Job Satisfaction by Levels of Education

Use the SPSS *Job Satisfaction* data file to examine the difference between undergraduate and graduate social workers with regard to job satisfaction. The following is the research question:

Is there a significant difference between undergraduate and graduate (EDUCAT) social workers with regard to levels of job satisfaction (SATISFAC)?

Step 1: State the null and alternative hypotheses.

---

[4]$p = .010/2 = .005$, which is less than .05.

Figure 8.3: Histogram for Job Satisfaction

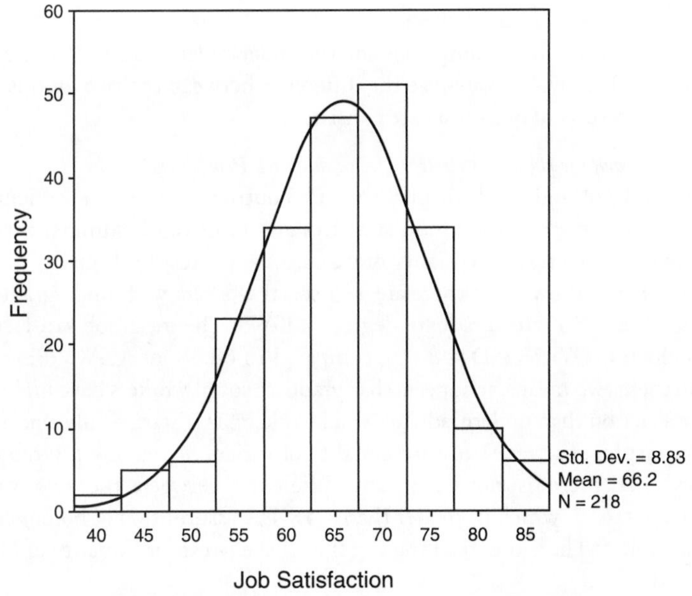

H_0: There is no significant difference between undergraduate (μ_U) and graduate (μ_G) social workers with regard to their levels of job satisfaction.

$$\mu_G = \mu_U$$

H_a: Graduate social workers will have significantly higher levels of job satisfaction than their undergraduate counterpart.

$$\mu_G > \mu_U$$

In this one-tailed research hypothesis, education is the independent variable and job satisfaction is the dependent variable.

Step 2: Set the criteria for rejecting H_0.
Set alpha at .05 ($\alpha = .05$). Reject H_0 only if $p \leq .05$.

Step 3: Select the appropriate statistical test.

a. In this hypothesis, the independent variable (levels of education) is dichotomous (undergraduate and graduate) and the dependent variable (job satisfaction) is interval level of measurement. This is the basic assumption for both the independent *t*-test and Mann-Whitney U.

b. To evaluate the assumption of normality, create and evaluate the distribution for job satisfaction. Figure 8.3 shows that the distribution for job satisfaction is negatively, but not severely, skewed.

c. To evaluate the assumption of homogeneity of variance, check the results of Levene's test of equality of variance (step 4).

d. Sample size: 218 social workers participated in the study; 33 were graduates and 185 were undergraduates.

e. The data meet the assumptions for the independent *t*-test. Use the Mann-Whitney U as well, to analyze the difference between the two groups and examine if results of both tests are consistent.

Step 4: Compute the test statistic (Use same SPSS Procedures).

Tables 8.3.A and 8.3.B display the SPSS output for the independent *t*-test. Table 8.3.A summarizes the group statistics and table 8.3.B summarizes the results of the Levene's test for equality of variances and *t*-test for Equality of Means.

Table 8.3.A shows that there are 185 social workers with undergraduate degrees (BSW) and 33 with graduate degrees (MSW). The mean job satisfaction for undergraduates is 65.73 (SD = 8.80), compared to 68.58 for MSWs (SD = 8.72). Based on these two means, it appears that graduate social workers have higher levels of job satisfaction than undergraduate social workers. Is it statistically significant?

The results of Levene's test for equality of variances presented in table 8.3.B indicates that there is no significant difference between the two variances ($F = .198, p = .657$, which is greater than .05). The assumption of homogeneity of variances is met. Therefore, read the top line of the *t*-test for Equality of Means in table 8.3.B.

The results of the *t*-test for Equality of Means show that the *t* is –1.714; df is 216; Sig. (2-tailed) is .088 (*p* value); and the mean difference is –2.846.

Table 8.3.A: Group Statistics—Job Satisfaction by Education

	EDUCAT (Level of Education)	N	Mean	Std. deviation	Std. error mean
SATISFAC	.00 Undergraduate	185	65.7297	8.79800	.64684
	1.00 Graduate	33	68.5758	8.71791	1.51759

Table 8.3.B: Results of Independent *t*-Test—Job Satisfaction by Education

		Levene's test for equality of variances		*t*-test for Equality of Means					95% confidence interval of the difference	
		F	Sig.	*t*	df	Sig. (2-tailed)	Mean difference	Std. error difference	Lower	Upper
SATISFAC	Equal variances assumed	.198	.657	–1.714	216	.088	–2.8460	1.66030	–6.11848	.42643
	Equal variances not assumed			–1.726	44.428	.091	–2.8460	1.64969	–8.16986	.47781

Because this *p* value is two-tailed and the research hypothesis is one-tailed, divide the *p* value by 2. If not divided by 2, the decision will be to not reject the null hypothesis (*p* = .088, which is greater than .05). However, dividing the *p* value by 2 produces a *p* value less than .05 (.088/2 = .044).

> The decision whether to state a one-tailed or two-tailed hypothesis must precede the statistical analysis.

Results of the Mann-Whitney U Test

Next, present the results of the Mann-Whitney U. Tables 8.4.A and 8.4.B display the SPSS output for the Mann-Whitney U. As with the independent *t*-test, table 8.4.A shows that there are 185 undergraduate social workers and 33 graduate social workers. The mean rank for graduate social workers is higher than for undergraduates (127 and 106.38).

Table 8.4.B shows that the *z* value is −1.732 with a significance level of .083 (two-tailed). As with the independent *t*-test, divide the *p* value by 2 because this is a one-tailed research hypothesis; the *p* value is .083/2 = .041, which indicates a significant difference between the two groups.

Step 5: Decide whether to reject the null hypothesis.

The results of the independent *t*-test presented in table 8.3.B show a significant difference between undergraduate and graduate social workers with regard to levels of job satisfaction (*p* < .05). Thus, reject the null hypothesis.

Table 8.4.A: Group Ranks—Job Satisfaction by Education

	EDUCAT (Level of Education)	N	Mean Rank	Sum of ranks
SATISFAC	.00 Undergraduate	185	106.38	19680.00
	1.00 Graduate	33	127.00	4191.00
	Total	218		

Table 8.4.B: Results of the Mann-Whitney U

	SATISFAC
Mann-Whitney U	2475.000
Wilcoxon W	19680.000
z	−1.732
Asymp. Sig. (2-tailed)	.083

Grouping variable: EDUCAT

Table 8.5:   Results of the Independent *t*-Test—Summary Table

Variable	N	$\overline{X}$	SD	*t*	*p*[+]
Burnout					
Males	36	24.03	7.09	2.59	.005
Females	182	21.08	6.02		
Job Satisfaction					
Undergraduate	185	65.73	8.80	−1.71	.044
Graduate	33	68.56	8.72		

[+]One-tailed *p*; N = 218

Writing the Results

The independent *t*-test examines the difference between undergraduate and graduate social workers with regard to levels of job satisfaction. The results of this test show a significant difference between the two groups ($t_{(df=216)}=-1.71; p<.05$).[5] In this study, graduate social workers have significantly higher levels of job satisfaction ($\overline{X}=68.58$) than undergraduates ($\overline{X}=65.73$). The mean difference is 2.85. These results are supported by results of the Mann-Whitney U, which also show a significant difference between graduate and undergraduate social workers: Graduates are more satisfied with their jobs than undergraduate social workers ($z=-1.73; p<.05$).

Presentation of Results in Summary Table

The results of the independent *t*-test are easily presented in a summary table that includes results of the two SPSS tables, the Group Statistics and the independent *t*-test. The table should report the number of cases for each group, the means and standard deviations, overall test statistic, and *p* value. Table 8.5 presents results of the independent *t*-test for burnout by gender and job satisfaction by education.

SUMMARY

One primary goal of social work practitioners is to ensure that their practice meets the expectations of their clients. The group therapist's goal is to show that participation in therapy significantly improves the lives of clients. To accomplish this goal, social work therapists will observe clients who participate versus clients who do not participate, then examine differences between the two groups. Other therapists may observe changes before and after therapy is administered (see chapter 10).

This chapter introduced two statistical techniques that allow practitioners

---

[5]Remember to report the results of the one-tailed *p* value ($p=.088/2=.044$, which is less than .05).

and therapists to make such comparisons, along with the purpose and assumptions for the independent *t*-test and the Mann-Whitney U. Two social work examples illustrated how to evaluate the data, use the SPSS to compute the statistics and *p* values for both tests, and how to interpret, write, and present the results.

Chapter 9 introduces another pair of bivariate statistical tests, suitable to examine differences between three or more groups with regard to one dependent variable. The chapter presents one-way analysis of variance and the Kruskal-Wallis H test. The chapter discusses assumptions underlying the one-way ANOVA and Kruskal-Wallis H test and the importance of post hoc tests in group comparison. How to compute the statistics, interpret the output, and write and present results are also presented.

PRACTICAL EXERCISES

I.   Access the SPSS *Depression-Elderly* data file (appendix A). Use the variables race (**RACE**), sick (**SICK**), emotional balance (**EB**), Cognitive Status (**CS**), and depression (**CES_D**), and answer the following questions.

1.   Develop two one-tailed research hypotheses where the first hypothesis examines emotional balance by race and the second hypothesis examines depression by sickness.

2.   For each hypothesis, also state the null hypothesis.

3.   Which test will you utilize to examine each hypothesis? Justify your answer.

4.   Use SPSS to examine each hypothesis. Follow the steps in hypothesis testing.

5.   What is the alternative test? Use this test to examine each hypothesis.

6.   Are there any differences between the results of the test you chose and its alternative test? If so, what are these differences?

7.   Present the results in a summary table.

II.   Access the SPSS *Self-Esteem* data you entered in chapter 2. Use the variables of gender and self-esteem to answer the following questions.

1.   Develop a one-tailed research hypothesis that examines self-esteem by gender.

2.   What is the null hypothesis?

3.   What test will you use to examine this hypothesis? Justify your answer.

4.   Run your analysis. Follow the steps in hypothesis testing.

5.   What is the alternative test? Run the analysis for this test.

6.   Are there any differences between the results of the test you chose and its alternative test? If so, what are these differences?

7.   Present the results in a summary table.

CHAPTER 9

Group Comparisons:
K Group Means—One-Way
Analysis of Variance

LEARNING OBJECTIVES

1. Understand the purpose of the one-way ANOVA
2. Understand the assumptions underlying the one-way ANOVA
3. Understand the post hoc tests
4. Understand the alternative nonparametric Kruskal-Wallis H test
5. Understand how to use SPSS to compute the statistics
6. Understand how to interpret, write, and present results of the tests

Data Sets: *Job Satisfaction, Group Design* (appendix A)

INTRODUCTION

Chapter 8 presented the independent *t*-test and Mann-Whitney U, which are utilized to compare the means of two groups on one continuous dependent variable. Sometimes, however, researchers are interested in comparing the means of multiple groups. For example, in the *Job Satisfaction* study (appendix A), one of the researcher's aims is to determine if there are significant differences in levels of turnover among social workers based on marital status. The researcher hypothesizes significant differences in levels of turnover among married, single, and divorced social workers. Figure 9.1 illustrates these comparisons. In statistical terms, the researcher hypothesizes the following:

$$\mu_1 \neq \mu_2 \neq \mu_3$$

In this example, the researcher is interested in three pairs of comparisons: married (μ_1) vs. single (μ_2), married (μ_1) vs. divorced (μ_3), and single (μ_2) vs. divorced (μ_3).

Figure 9.1:   Levels of Turnover by Marital Status

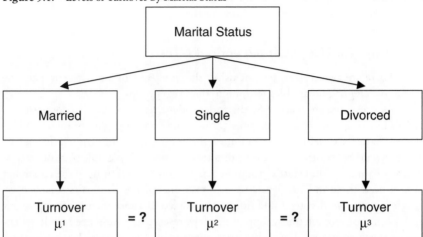

Table 9.1:   Solomon Four-Group Design

Group	Pretest	Treatment	Posttest
Experiment 1	μ_1	Yes	μ_2
Control 1	μ_3	No	μ_4
Experiment 2		Yes	μ_5
Control 2		No	μ_6

The Solomon Four-Group Design is another possibility for multiple comparisons. This combines classical pretest-posttest control group design with posttest-only control group design. Table 9.1 illustrates the Solomon Four-Group Design utilized in the *Group Design* study (appendix A).

The researcher hypothesizes a significant difference between pretest and posttest depression scores of the experiment 1 group and no significant difference between pretest and posttest depression scores of the control 1 group (see next chapter).

The researcher also hypothesizes a significant difference between the posttest depression scores of the experiment groups and the posttest depression scores of the control groups ($\mu_2 \neq \mu_4$, $\mu_2 \neq \mu_6$, $\mu_4 \neq \mu_5$, and $\mu_5 \neq \mu_6$). At the same time, there will be no significant difference between the posttest depression scores of the two experiment groups ($\mu_2 = \mu_5$) and no significant difference between the posttest depression scores of the two control groups ($\mu_4 = \mu_6$). The researcher is interested in six pairs of comparisons: $\mu_2 \neq \mu_4$, $\mu_2 \neq \mu_6$, $\mu_4 \neq \mu_5$, $\mu_5 \neq \mu_6$, $\mu_2 = \mu_5$, and $\mu_4 = \mu_6$.

In the above examples, the independent variables, marital status and posttest groups, are categorical variables. Each consists of more than two groups (marital status = married, single, divorced; posttest groups = experiment 1, control 1, experiment 2, control 2). The dependent variables, levels of turnover and levels of depression, are continuous data. What statistical test(s) are most suitable to examine differences between the mean scores of these groups?

Why Not Use the Independent *t*-Test?

There are two reasons for not using the independent *t*-test to compare the means of categorical variables with more than two groups.

As presented in chapter 8, the independent *t*-test is used to compare the means of two groups (e.g., experiment group and control group, or males and females). When a variable consists of more than two groups, multiple independent *t*-tests would be required to examine differences among all possible pairs of groups. There are three marital status groups in this *Job Satisfaction* study, so the researcher would need three independent *t*-tests to examine all possible pairs: married vs. single, married vs. divorced, and single vs. divorced. Because there are four posttest groups in the Solomon four-group design, the researcher would need six independent *t*-tests to examine all possible pairs: experiment 1 vs. control 1, experiment 1 vs. experiment 2, experiment 1 vs. control 2, control 1 vs. experiment 2, control 1 vs. control 2, and experiment 2 vs. control 2.

The number of comparisons depends on the number of groups (levels) in a variable; the more groups, the more independent *t*-tests are required to compare all possible pairs. Mathematically, the number of independent *t*-tests needed to compare all pairs is as follows:

$$\text{Number of independent } t\text{-tests} = \frac{K(K-1)}{2}$$

$$K = \text{Number of groups}$$

For example, if a researcher wants to examine the impact of race (White, African American, Native American, Hispanic, and Other; that is, 5 groups) on levels of burnout among child welfare workers, then the number of independent *t*-tests needed to compare all possible pairs of races will be as follows:

$$\text{Number of independent } t\text{-tests} = \frac{5(5-1)}{2} = \frac{5(4)}{2} = 10 \text{ tests}$$

The second reason for not using the independent *t*-test is derived from the first one. By using multiple independent *t*-tests, the probability of making type I error (*alpha*) is higher. If alpha is set up at, say, .05 with one independent *t*-test, alpha will be greater if multiple independent *t*-tests are used. In other words, the more tests are used, the greater the likelihood of making type I error.

When multiple independent *t*-tests are used, it is necessary to adjust alpha to a higher level to avoid making type I error. To adjust alpha, first compute the number of independent *t*-tests needed to compare all possible pairs and then use the following formula to compute the adjusted alpha for multiple independent *t*-tests:

$$\text{Type I error} = 1 - (1 - \alpha)^K$$
α = Level of significance (e.g., .05)
K = Number of independent t-tests

For example, in the Solomon four-group design, which requires six independent t-tests, alpha will be significantly increased, to .26 instead of .05. That is,

$$\text{Type I error} = 1 - (1 - .05)^6 = 1 - (.95)^6 = 1 - .74 = .26$$

If the researcher decides to undertake six independent t-tests to compare all possible pairs, then set alpha at .26 instead of .05.

With this in mind, R. A. Fisher (1915) developed what has become known as the analysis of variance (ANOVA), which is an extension version of the independent t-test. ANOVA allows researchers to compare the means of K independent samples selected from a normal population without affecting the level of significance.

This chapter presents the one-way ANOVA, its purpose, and the assumptions underlying the test. Its alternative, the nonparametric Kruskal-Wallis H test is discussed, as well as different post hoc tests and when they should be utilized. The chapter also offers two social work examples illustrating how to use SPSS to compute the statistics and their levels of significance, and how to interpret, write, and present the results.

ONE-WAY ANOVA

Analysis of variance (ANOVA) is a group of statistical tests that examines one or more categorical variables on one or more dependent variables. These tests include the one-way ANOVA, two-way ANOVA, factorial ANOVA, and multivariate ANOVA.

1. When one categorical variable is examined on one continuous dependent variable, use one-way ANOVA.

2. When two categorical variables are examined on one continuous dependent variable, use two-way ANOVA.

3. When three or more categorical variables are examined on one continuous dependent variable, use factorial ANOVA.

4. When multiple categorical variables are examined on multiple continuous dependent variables, use multivariate ANOVA.

This chapter focuses on the one-way analysis of variance. Like the independent t-test and Pearson correlation, one-way ANOVA is a bivariate parametric test that examines the relationship between one independent variable and one dependent variable.

Purpose

The purpose of one-way ANOVA is to examine differences between the mean scores of three or more groups (one independent variable, three or more groups) and whether these differences are statistically significant. For example, one-way ANOVA can help determine whether there are significant statistical differences in levels of turnover among social workers based on marital status or if there are significant statistical differences in levels of depression among the four groups in the Solomon Four-Group Design study.

The one-way ANOVA produces a test statistic called the F ratio. Like the t value in the independent t-test, the F ratio measures how far apart the means of the groups are in standard error units. The larger the F ratio is, the more likely that the difference between the group means is statistically significant. Mathematically, F is the square of t; $(F = t^2)$.

Sources of Variation

The one-way ANOVA evaluates whether all groups under investigation come from the same population. Are the sample group's observed scores similar to scores in the population? To evaluate this, one-way ANOVA examines two sources of variability: *within-group variability* and *between-group variability*. Within-group variability refers to variations in the scores of subjects within each group (e.g., different levels of turnover among married social workers). Between-group variability refers to variations in the scores between groups (e.g., different levels of turnover among married vs. single, married vs. divorced, and single vs. divorced social workers). The sum of the within-group variance and the between-group variance is the *total variance*.

One-way ANOVA computes the variance for each group separately (e.g., variance for married, variance for single, and variance for divorced social workers). Next, all group variances are summed and averaged to compose the between-group variance. In the next step, one-way ANOVA computes the variance for all participants in the study, regardless of their group affiliation, to compose the within-group variance. If the within-group variance and between-group variance are equal, then the means of the groups are said to be equal. The logic is that if the total variance is the sum of within-group variance and between-group variance and if the within-group variance and the total variance are equal, then the between-group variance should equal zero. If the within-group variance is much greater than the between-group variance, then the means of the separate groups are said to be significantly different.

Assumptions

Because one-way ANOVA is a parametric test and an extension version of the independent t-test, most of its assumptions are similar to assumptions for the independent t-test.

1. The dependent variable must be continuous and measured at the interval level of measurement or higher.

2. The shape of the distribution of the dependent variable must approximate the shape of a normal curve.

3. The sample size for one-way ANOVA is the same as for the independent t-test. That is, a sample size of 30 subjects or more is usually sufficient to undertake one-way ANOVA. While it is preferred to have groups with equal frequencies, this is not a requirement.

4. The independent variable must be nominal; however, unlike the independent t-test, it should consist of three or more groups (e.g., race = White, African American, Native American, Hispanic, Other; marital status = single, married, divorced, widowed, other).

5. Data for all groups must be collected at the same time (e.g., data on levels of turnover from married, single, and divorced social workers collected simultaneously).

6. The variances of all groups on the dependent variable should be equal. This is the assumption of *homogeneity of variances* or *equality of variances*.

KRUSKAL-WALLIS H TEST

The Kruskal-Wallis H test is the nonparametric version of the one-way ANOVA. Like the Mann-Whitney U, Kruskal-Wallis H first ranks scores for each group, computes mean rank for each group, and then determines whether there is a significant difference between at least two mean ranks.

The Kruskal-Wallis H test is appropriate to compare three or more groups when the dependent variable is either measured at the ordinal level, measured at an interval level that does not meet the assumption of normality, or when the variances of the groups are not equal. As with one-way ANOVA, Kruskal-Wallis H requires the sample to be representative of the population and the independent variable to be nominal with three or more levels.

POST HOC TESTS

Unlike the independent t-test and Mann-Whitney U, the one-way ANOVA and Kruskal-Wallis H examine whether there is an overall significant difference between three or more groups. Yet, when a significant difference *is* detected, neither the one-way ANOVA nor the Kruskal-Wallis H tests pinpoint which groups are significantly different. Further statistical tests are needed to precisely detect which groups are significantly different with regard to the dependent variable. These tests are known as *post hoc* tests.

Like the independent t-test and Mann-Whitney U, post hoc tests examine whether there is a statistical significant difference between the means of each possible pair of groups. The SPSS program is equipped with 18 post hoc tests; 14 of them are appropriate when data meet the assumption of homogeneity of variances and four are appropriate when this assumption is not met; that is, the variances are not equal.

The four most frequently reported post hoc tests when equality of variances is assumed include the *LSD* (least significant difference); *Bonferroni* (also known as *Bonferroni correction*); *Scheffe;* and *Tukey.* The *Tamahane's T2* is another post hoc test that is based on the independent *t*-test. It is most appropriately utilized when equality of variances is not assumed.

Each post hoc test uses different statistical methods to examine the difference between the means of each possible pair of groups. All these tests, except the LSD, adjust the level of significance (*alpha*) based on the number of comparisons.

PRACTICAL EXAMPLES

To demonstrate use of the one-way ANOVA and the Kruskal-Wallis H tests, follow the steps for hypothesis testing. Use SPSS to compute the *F* and *p* values for the one-way ANOVA and the chi-square (χ^2) and *p* values for the Kruskal-Wallis H test. Two examples are presented. First, we will examine if there are significant differences in levels of turnover among single, married, and divorced social workers. Second, we will examine if there are significant differences in the levels of posttest levels of depression between the four groups in the Solomon four-group design.

Example 1—Turnover by Marital Status

Use the SPSS *Job Satisfaction* data file (appendix A) to examine the following research question:

Are there significant differences in the levels of turnover (**TURNOVER**) between single, married, and divorced social workers (**D3**)?

Step 1: State the null and alternative hypotheses.

H_0: There are no significant differences in the levels of turnover among single, married, and divorced social workers.

$$\mu_1 = \mu_2 = \mu_3$$

H_a: Married social workers will have significantly higher levels of turnover than single and divorced social workers. Also, single social workers will have significantly higher levels of turnover than divorced social workers.[1]

$$\mu_1 > \mu_2; \mu_1 > \mu_3; \mu_2 > \mu_3$$

---

[1]Two-tailed hypothesis: There are significant differences in the levels of turnover among married, single, and divorced social workers; that is, $\mu_1 \neq \mu_2 \neq \mu_3$.

Figure 9.2:   Histogram for Levels of Turnover

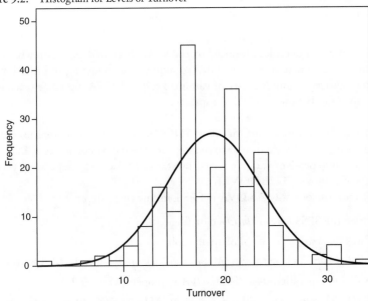

In this one-tailed research hypothesis, marital status is the independent variable and turnover is the dependent variable.

Step 2: Set the criteria for rejecting the null hypothesis.
Set alpha at .05 ($\alpha = .05$). Reject H_0 only if $p \leq .05$.

Step 3: Select the appropriate statistical test.

a. The independent variable (marital status) is nominal with three groups (single, married, divorced) and the dependent variable (turnover) is continuous data and measured at the interval level of measurement. These are the basic requirements for both the one-way ANOVA and Kruskal-Wallis H test.

b. Normality of distribution: To evaluate the assumption of normality, create a histogram with a normal curve for levels of turnover. Figure 9.2 displays a histogram for turnover. The shape of the distribution of turnover approaches the shape of a normal curve.

c. Homogeneity of variances: To evaluate this assumption, check the results of Levene's test of equality of variance. This test is performed simultaneously with the one-way ANOVA. We return to this assumption when we discuss the results of the one-way ANOVA.

d. Sample size: 218 social workers participated in the *Job Satisfaction* study. 141 were married, 47 were single, 30 were divorced. This sample size is large enough to conduct a one-way ANOVA.

e. The data appear to meet assumptions for the one-way ANOVA. We will also use the Kruskal-Wallis H test to demonstrate how to use this test and to examine whether results of both tests are consistent.

Step 4: Compute the test statistic (Use SPSS).

The number of tables produced by the SPSS program depends on what information we request. It is recommended to request the following information: descriptive statistics, homogeneity of variances test, ANOVA, post hoc tests, and a plot displaying the means of all groups.

How to Compute the One-Way ANOVA in SPSS.   The steps used to run the one-way ANOVA are similar to the steps for the independent *t*-test. In this example, the independent variable is marital status (**D3**) and the dependent variable is levels of turnover (**TURNOVER**).

To run the one-way ANOVA in SPSS, follow these steps:

a.   Open the SPSS *Job Satisfaction* data file.

b.   Click on *Analyze* in the SPSS main toolbar.

c.   Scroll down, click on *Compare Means,* and click on *One-Way ANOVA* (screen 9.1).

d.   A dialog box called *One-Way ANOVA* will open (screen 9.2.A).

e.   Scroll down in the variables list, click on **TURNOVER** (dependent variable),

Screen 9.1:   SPSS *One-Way ANOVA* Menu

Screen 9.2:   SPSS *One-Way ANOVA* Dialog Box

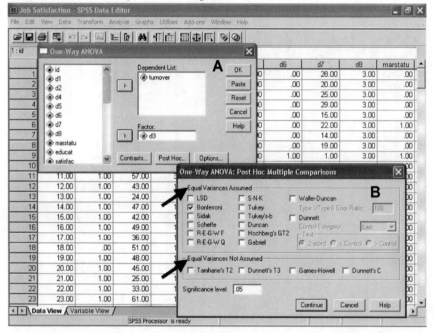

and click on the upper arrow button to move **TURNOVER** in the *Dependent List* box.

f.   Scroll down in the variables list, click on **D3** (independent variable), and click on the lower arrow button to move **D3** in the *Factor* box.

g.   Click on *Post Hoc* at the bottom of the *One-Way ANOVA* dialog box (screen 9.2.A) to request one or more post hoc tests. A new dialog box called *One-Way ANOVA: Post Hoc Multiple Comparisons* will open (screen 9.2.B). These tests are organized in two groups: *Equal Variances Assumed* and *Equal Variances Not Assumed.*

h.   Check the box corresponding with *Bonferroni* (you may also select *LSD, Scheffe,* etc.).

i.   Click on *Continue.*

j.   Click on *Options* in the *One-Way ANOVA* dialog box (screen 9.3.A). A new dialog box called *One-Way ANOVA: Options* will open (screen 9.3.B).

k.   Check the boxes corresponding with *Descriptive* (this generates descriptive statistics for each group), *Homogeneity of variance test* (this is the Levene's test of equality of variances), and *Means plot* (this creates a plot comparing the means of all groups).

l.   Click on *Continue* and click on *OK.*

Screen 9.3:   SPSS *One-Way ANOVA* Dialog Box

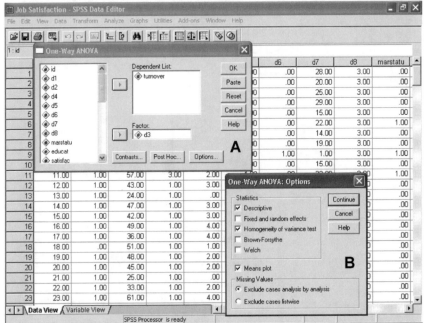

SPSS syntax for one-way ANOVA:

ONEWAY TURNOVER BY D3
/STATISTICS DESCRIPTIVES HOMOGENEITY
/PLOT MEANS
/POSTHOC=BONFERRONI ALPHA (.05).

To request a different post hoc test, change *Bonferroni* with the desired test (*Scheffe, Tukey, T2,* etc.).

Interpreting the Output of the One-Way ANOVA.   Table 9.2 (A through D) and figure 9.3 present the results of the one-way ANOVA generated by SPSS. These results include descriptive statistics, the Levene's test of equality of variance, ANOVA, and means plot.

Table 9.2.A displays the number of participants (N), mean, standard deviation, standard error, 95% confidence interval, and minimum and maximum scores for each marital status in the independent variable and for the sample as a whole. The table shows that of 218 participants, 141 are married, 47 are single, and 30 are divorced. The table shows that single social workers have the highest level of turnover ($\overline{X} = 19.87$), followed by married ($\overline{X} = 19.29$), then divorced ($\overline{X} = 15.00$). Are the differences between these means statistically significant?

Table 9.2.A: Descriptive Statistics

					95% confidence interval for mean			
	TURNOVER							
	N	Mean	Std. deviation	Std. error	Lower bound	Upper bound	Minimum	Maximum
Married	141	19.29	4.38592	.36936	18.561	20.0210	8.00	34.00
Single	47	19.87	4.41153	.64349	18.577	21.1676	10.00	29.00
Divorced	30	15.00	4.17711	.76283	13.440	16.5598	2.00	27.00
Total	218	18.83	4.61183	.31235	18.210	19.4413	2.00	34.00

Table 9.2.B: Levene's Test of Homogeneity of Variance

TURNOVER			
Levene statistic	df_1	df_2	Sig.
1.830	2	215	.163

Table 9.2.C: Results of One-Way ANOVA

TURNOVER					
	Sum of squares (SS)	df	Mean square	*F*	Sig.
Between groups	521.064	2	260.532	13.681	.000
Within groups	4094.312	215	19.043		
Total	4615.376	217			

Table 9.2.D: Post Hoc Bonferroni—Turnover by Marital Status

Dependent variable: **TURNOVER**					95% confidence interval	
(I) Marital status	(J) Marital status	Mean difference (I–J)	Std. error	Sig.	Lower bound	Upper bound
Married	Single	–.58156	.7350	1.000	–2.3550	1.1919
	Divorced	4.29078*	.8774	.000	2.1737	6.4078
Single	Married	.58156	.7350	1.000	–1.1919	2.3550
	Divorced	4.87234*	1.020	.000	2.4118	7.3329
Divorced	Married	–4.29078*	.8774	.000	–6.4078	–2.1737
	Single	–4.87234*	1.020	.000	–7.3329	–2.4118

*The mean difference is significant at the .05 level.

Table 9.2.B displays results of the Levene's test of homogeneity of variance. The Sig. value represents the *p* value. As with Levene's test of homogeneity of variance in the independent *t*-test, a *p* value greater than .05 indicates equality of variances. In this example, Levene's test shows that the variances of the three groups (single, married, divorced) are equal (*p* = .163 > .05). This indicates that the data met the assumption of homogeneity of variance.

Table 9.2.C displays results of the overall one-way ANOVA test. The table shows the sum of square deviations (SS), the degrees of freedom[2] (df), and the mean square deviations for both between groups (MS_B) and within groups (MS_W). The table also shows the *F* ratio and the level of significance (Sig., or *p* value). Mathematically, the *F* ratio is simply the mean square between groups (MS_B) divided by the mean square within groups (MS_W); that is, $F = MS_B/MS_W$.

The table shows that the *p* value (two-tailed) is .000. As with the independent *t*-test, if the research hypothesis is one-tailed (as in this case), divide the *p* value by 2. However, because this *p* value is smaller than .05, dividing it by 2 is unnecessary. In other words, the results indicate a significant difference between at least two groups. Which groups are significantly different? To find out, examine results of the Bonferroni post hoc test.

Table 9.2.D displays the results of multiple comparisons for all possible pairs. These pairs are shown in the first column (**D3, Marital status**). The table also displays the mean difference for each pair (second column), standard error (third column), the Sig., or *p* value (fourth column), and the 95% confidence interval (last two columns).

The first row compares married vs. single (first line), and married vs. divorced (second line) with regard to levels of turnover. The table shows the mean difference between married and single as –.58 with a standard error of .74. This difference is not significant at the .05 level (Sig. = 1.000). The first row also shows that the mean difference between married and divorced is 4.29 with a standard error of .88. This mean difference is significant at the .05 level[3] (Sig. = .000). Recall from table 9.2.A that the mean score for married is 19.29 and the mean score for divorced is 15.00 (mean difference = 19.29 – 15.00 = 4.29). In other words, married social workers scored significantly higher than divorced social workers in the turnover scale.

The second row compares single vs. married (first line). This line is redundant of the first line in the first row. The second row also compares single vs. divorced (second line). The table shows the mean difference between the two groups as 4.87 with a standard error of 1.02 and a *p* value (Sig.) of .000. This *p* value indicates a significant difference between the two groups. The third row compares divorced vs. married, and divorced vs. single. These results are redundant of the first two rows.

---

[2]One-way ANOVA has two parts of degrees of freedom; one is between groups and the other is within groups. They are (K – 1) and (N – K), respectively. K = number of groups and N = sample size. In this case, df = K – 1 and N – K = 3 – 1 and 218 – 3 = 2 and 215.

[3]By default, results that are significant at .05 or less are marked by a single asterisk.

Figure 9.3: Mean Plot—Turnover by Marital Status

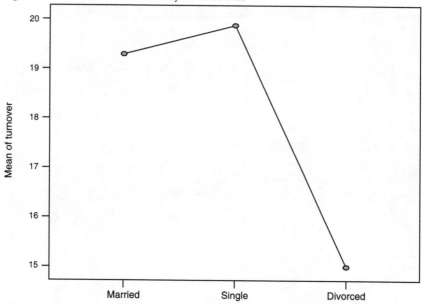

The last part of the output is a line graph displaying the mean scores for all groups in the study. Figure 9.3 shows that the mean score for divorced social workers is significantly lower than the mean scores of single and married social workers. The graph also shows that the mean score for married is slightly lower than the mean score for single social workers.

Results of the Kruskal-Wallis H Test

SPSS produces two tables for the Kruskal-Wallis H test. The first table, Ranks, reports number of cases, mean rank, and sum of ranks for each group. The second table, Test Statistics, reports the results of the Kruskal-Wallis H and the *p* value (two-tailed).

How to Compute the Kruskal-Wallis H Test in SPSS.   Like with the Mann-Whitney U test, you need to know the numeric value associated with the first group and the numeric value associated with the last group in the independent variable. In this example, marital status (**D3**) is coded as 1 = married, 2 = single, 3 = divorced. The range of values for the independent variable is 1 to 3. The dependent variable is turnover (**TURNOVER**).

To run the Kruskal-Wallis H in SPSS, follow these steps:

a.   Open the SPSS *Job Satisfaction* data file.

b.   Click on *Analyze* in the SPSS main toolbar.

Screen 9.4: SPSS *Nonparametric* Tests Main Menu

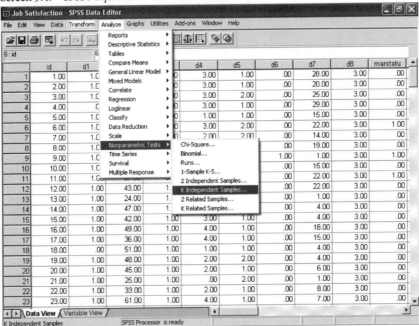

c.   Scroll down, click on *Nonparametric Tests,* and click on *K Independent Samples* (screen 9.4).

d.   A dialog box called *Tests for Several Independent Samples* will open (screen 9.5.A).

e.   Scroll down in the variables list, click on **TURNOVER** (dependent variable), and click on the upper arrow button to move **TURNOVER** in the *Test Variable List* box.

f.   Scroll down in the variables list, click on **D3** (independent variable), and click on the lower arrow button to move **D3** in the *Grouping Variable* box.

g.   Click on *Define Range.* A new dialog box called *Several Independent Samples: Define* will open (screen 9.5.B).

h.   Type 1 for *Minimum* and type 3 for *Maximum* (the range of values for **D3**).

i.   Click on *Continue* and click on *OK.*

SPSS syntax for the Kruskal-Wallis H:

NPAR TESTS
/*K*–W=TURNOVER BY D3 (1 3).

Screen 9.5:   SPSS *Kruskal-Wallis H Test* Dialog Box

Interpreting the Output of the Kruskal-Wallis H.   Tables 9.3.A and 9.3.B display the results of the Kruskal-Wallis H test generated by SPSS. These tables include descriptive statistics (mean rank) for levels of turnover by marital status and the results of the test statistics.

Table 9.3.A displays the number of participants in each group and the total number of participants in the sample. The mean rank for married social workers is 116.18, compared to 126.83 for single and 50.97 for divorced social workers. Are the differences between these mean ranks statistically significant?

Table 9.3.B displays the results of the Kruskal-Wallis H test. The chi-square (χ^2) is 31.137 with two degrees of freedom.[4] The level of significance (Sig.) is .000 (two-tailed). As with the one-way ANOVA, divide this p value by 2 because our research hypothesis is one-tailed. Overall, the results show a significant difference among the three means. Which groups are significantly different?

Because the results of the nonparametric Kruskal-Wallis H test are significant, a post hoc test is needed to determine which groups are significantly different. For this purpose, use the post hoc Tamahane T2 to examine which pairs are significantly different. Use this test when data do not meet the assumption of equality of variance.

---

[4]df = K − 1, where K = number of groups. In this case, df = K − 1 = 3 − 1 = 2.

Table 9.3.A: Mean Rank—Turnover by Marital Status

	Marital status	N	Mean rank
TURNOVER	Married	141	116.18
	Single	47	126.83
	Divorced	30	50.97
	Total	218	

Table 9.3.B: Results of Kruskal-Wallis H

Test Statistics[a,b]

	TURNOVER
chi-square	31.137
df	2
asymp. Sig.	.000

[a]Kruskal-Wallis test
[b]Grouping variable: Marital status

Table 9.4:   Post Hoc Tamahane T2—Turnover by Marital Status

Dependent variable: **TURNOVER**

(I) Marital status	(J) Marital status	Mean difference (I–J)	Std. error	Sig.	95% confidence interval Lower bound	Upper bound
Married	Single	−.58156	.74196	.820	−2.3918	1.2286
	Divorced	4.29078*	.84737	.000	2.1870	6.3946
Single	Married	.58156	.74196	.820	−1.2286	2.3918
	Divorced	4.87234*	.99784	.000	2.4262	7.3185
Divorced	Married	−4.29078*	.84737	.000	−6.3946	−2.1870
	Single	−4.87234*	.99784	.000	−7.3185	−2.4262

*The mean difference is significant at the .05 level.

To use SPSS to run the Tamahane T2 test, repeat the steps outlined under one-way ANOVA. Instead of requesting Bonferroni, check box *Tamahane T2*. Do not request *Descriptive, Homogeneity of Variance test*, or *Means Plot*. You already have them under ANOVA. Table 9.4 displays the results of the Tamahane T2 test.

The results of the Tamahane T2 presented in table 9.4 are similar to results for the Bonferroni presented in table 9.2.D. Table 9.4 shows that married and single social workers have similar (not significant) levels of turnover (first line, first row; Sig. = .820). The table also shows that married social workers have significantly higher levels of turnover than divorced social workers (second line, first row;

Sig. = .000), and that single social workers have significantly higher levels of turnover than divorced social workers (second line, second row; Sig. = .000).

Step 5: Decide whether to reject the null hypothesis.

The results of the one-way ANOVA presented in table 9.2.C show an overall significant difference in levels of turnover among married, single, and divorced social workers ($p < .05$). Therefore, reject the null hypothesis.

Writing the Results

When writing the results of the one-way ANOVA, present the F ratio, degrees of freedom (df), and the p value. If significant results are revealed, report which post hoc tests were utilized along with their results, and the means for each group in the study. The following presents the results of the one-away ANOVA for the *Job Satisfaction* example:

The one-way ANOVA was utilized to examine a null hypothesis which claims no significant differences among married, single, and divorced social workers with regard to levels of turnover. The results show an overall significant difference in mean scores of turnover between at least two marital status groups ($F_{(df=2,215)} = 13.68, p < .05$).

The Bonferroni post hoc test was run to determine which marital status groups were significantly different. The results of the Bonferroni test show that divorced social workers reported significantly lower levels of turnover than married social workers (mean difference = 4.29) or single social workers (mean difference = 4.87), and no significant difference between single and married social workers with regard to levels of turnover (mean difference = .58).

Overall, the results of the one-way ANOVA and the Bonferroni post hoc tests indicate that divorced social workers experienced significantly less levels of turnover ($\overline{X} = 15.00$) than married social workers ($\overline{X} = 19.29$) or single social workers ($\overline{X} = 19.87$). Married and single social workers experienced similar levels of turnover. These results are supported by the results of the Kruskal-Wallis H and the Tamahane T2 tests.

Example 2—Solomon Four-Group Design

Use the SPSS *Group Design* data file (appendix A) to examine the following research question:

Are there significant posttest differences in the levels of depression (**DEPRESS2**) between experiment group 1, control group 1, experiment group 2, and control group 2 (**GROUP**)?

Step 1: State the null and alternative hypotheses.

H_0: There are no significant posttest differences in levels of depression between experiment 1, control 1, experiment 2, and group 2. That is,

$$\mu_2 = \mu_4 = \mu_5 = \mu_6$$

Figure 9.4:   Histogram for Posttest Depression

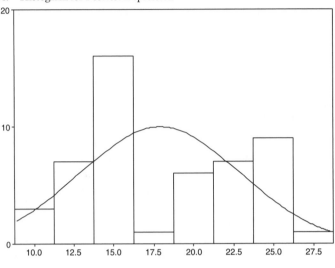

Posttest Depression

H_a: Experiment group 1 and experiment group 2 will have significantly lower levels of depression than control group 1 and control group 2.[5] That is,

$$\mu_2 < \mu_4; \, \mu_2 < \mu_6; \, \mu_5 < \mu_6; \, \mu_5 < \mu_2$$

In this one-tailed research hypothesis, group is the independent variable and depression (posttest depression) is the dependent variable.

Step 2: Set the criteria for rejecting the null hypothesis.
Set alpha at .05 ($\alpha = .05$). Reject H_0 only if $p \leq .05$.

Step 3: Select the appropriate statistical test.

a.   The independent variable (group) is nominal with four levels (experiment 1, control 1, experiment 2, and control 2) and the dependent variable (depression) is continuous data, measured at the interval level. These are the basic requirements for both the one-way ANOVA and Kruskal-Wallis H test.

b.   Normality of distribution: To evaluate the assumption of normality, create a histogram with a normal curve for depression. Figure 9.4 displays the distribution of levels of depression. Here, the shape of the distribution of depression is not severely skewed and appears to approach the shape of a normal curve.

c.   Homogeneity of variance: To evaluate the assumption of homogeneity of variance, look at Levene's test of equality of variance. This test is performed along

[5]Two-tailed hypothesis: There will be significant differences in the levels of posttest depression between the experiment groups and the control groups: $\mu_2 \neq \mu_4; \, \mu_2 \neq \mu_6, \, \mu_5 \neq \mu_6; \, \mu_5 \neq \mu_2$).

with the one-way ANOVA. The results (table 9.5.B) indicate that the variances are not significantly different, therefore the assumption is met.

d. Sample size: 50 subjects participated in the study, which is greater than a sample size of 30 needed for ANOVA.

e. The data meet the assumptions of the one-way ANOVA. Utilize the one-way ANOVA to examine the differences among the groups. Use the Kruskal-Wallis H test to find whether the results of both tests are consistent.

Step 4: Compute the test statistic (Use SPSS steps above).

Table 9.5 (A through D) and figure 9.5 display the results of the parametric one-way ANOVA generated by SPSS.

Table 9.5.A shows that 50 subjects participated in the study. Of them, 15 subjects participated in experiment 1, 15 in control 1, 10 in experiment 2, and 10 in control 2. In addition, the table displays the mean depression score, standard

Table 9.5.A: Descriptive Statistics

					95% confidence interval for mean			
	N	Mean	Std. deviation	Std. error	Lower bound	Upper bound	Minimum	Maximum
1.00 experiment 1	15	13.60000	1.95667	.5052	12.5164	14.68	9.00	16.00
2.00 control 1	15	22.2000	2.95683	.7635	20.5626	23.84	16.00	27.00
3.00 experiment 2	10	13.4000	1.77639	.5617	12.1292	14.67	10.00	16.00
4.00 control 2	10	22.4000	2.45855	.7775	20.6413	24.16	19.00	26.00
Total	50	17.9000	4.98672	.7052	16.4828	19.32	9.00	27.00

DEPRESS2 (Depression after Treatment)

Table 9.5.B: Levene's Test of Homogeneity of Variance

DEPRESS2 (Depression after Treatment)

Levene Statistic	df_1	df_2	Sig.
1.371	3	46	.263

Table 9.5.C: Results of One-Way ANOVA

DEPRESS2 (Depression after Treatment)

	Sum of Squares	df	Mean Square	F	Sig.
Between groups	959.700	3	319.900	56.860	.000
Within groups	258.800	46	5.626		
Total	1218.500	49			

Table 9.5.D: Post Hoc LSD—Posttest Depression by Group

Dependent variable: **DEPRESS2** (Depression after Treatment)						
					95% confidence interval	
(I) Group	(J) Group	Mean difference (I–J)	Std. error	Sig.	Lower bound	Upper bound
1.00 experiment 1	2.00 control 1	–8.6000*	.86611	.000	–10.3434	–6.8566
	3.00 experiment 2	.2000	.96834	.837	–1.7492	2.1492
	4.00 control 2	–8.8000*	.96834	.000	–10.7492	–6.8508
2.00 control 1	1.00 experiment 1	8.6000*	.86611	.000	6.8566	10.3434
	3.00 experiment 2	8.8000*	.96834	.000	6.8508	10.7492
	4.00 control 2	–.2000	.96834	.837	–2.1492	1.7492
3.00 experiment 2	1.00 experiment 1	–.2000	.96834	.837	–2.1492	1.7492
	2.00 control 1	–8.8000*	.96834	.000	–10.7492	–6.8508
	4.00 control 2	–9.0000*	1.06076	.000	–11.1352	–6.8648
4.00 control 2	1.00 experiment 1	8.8000*	.96834	.000	6.8508	10.7492
	2.00 control 1	.2000	.96834	.837	–1.7492	2.1492
	3.00 experiment 2	9.0000*	1.06076	.000	6.8648	11.1352

*The mean difference is significant at the .05 level.

Figure 9.5: Mean Plot—Posttest Levels of Depression by Group

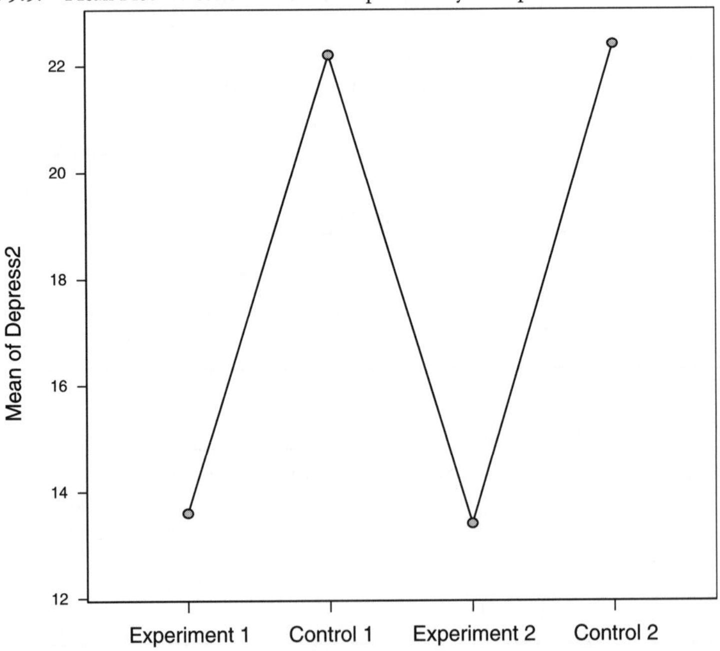

deviation, standard error, 95% confidence interval, and the range of the depression scores for each group and for the sample as a whole. The means of the experiment groups are lower than the means of the control groups: experiment 1 = 13.60; experiment 2 = 13.40; control 1 = 22.2; control 2 = 22.40.

Table 9.5.B displays the results of Levene test of homogeneity of variance. The variances of the four groups are not significantly different ($p = .263 > .05$). The data met the assumption of homogeneity of variance.

Table 9.5.C presents the results of the one-way ANOVA test. The p value (Sig.) is .000, which indicates a significant difference between at least two means. A post hoc test is needed to determine which groups are significantly different.

To introduce another post hoc test, we will use the LSD, to compare all possible pairs. To run it, follow the same steps as for the Bonferroni test and check the corresponding box for LSD. Table 9.5.D presents the results.

Each row in table 9.5.D displays three group comparisons. The first row compares experiment 1 and control 1, experiment 1 and experiment 2, and experiment 1 and control 2 with regard to posttest levels of depression.

The first line in the first row shows that the mean difference between experiment 1 and control 1 is −8.6 ($\overline{X}$ experiment 1 − $\overline{X}$ control 1 = −8.60) with a standard error of .87 and a significance level (Sig.) of .000 ($p < .05$).

The second line in the first row shows that the mean difference between experiment 1 and experiment 2 is .20 ($\overline{X}$ experiment 1 − $\overline{X}$ experiment 2 = .20) with a standard error of .97 and a significance level of .837 ($p > .05$).

The third line in the first row shows that the mean difference between experiment 1 and control 2 is −8.8 ($\overline{X}$ experiment 1 − $\overline{X}$ control 2 = −8.80) with a standard error of .97 and a significance level of .000 ($p < .05$).

The second line in the second row shows that the mean difference between control 1 and experiment 2 is 8.8 ($\overline{X}$ control 1 − $\overline{X}$ experiment 2 = 8.80) with a standard error of .97 and a significance level of .000 ($p < .05$).

The third line in the second row shows that the mean difference between control 1 and control 2 is −.20 ($\overline{X}$ control 1 − $\overline{X}$ control 2 = −.20) with a standard error of .97 and a significance level of .837 ($p > .05$).

The third line in the third row shows that the mean difference between control 2 and experiment 2 is 9.00 ($\overline{X}$ control 2 − $\overline{X}$ experiment 2 = 9.00) with a standard error of 1.06 and a significance level of .000 ($p < .05$).

Figure 9.5 shows a line graph for the posttest levels of depression for all groups. The mean scores of the two experiment groups are lower than the mean scores of the two control groups. The figure also shows that the mean scores of both experiment groups are similar to one another and so are the mean scores of the control groups.

Results of the Kruskal-Wallis H Test

Tables 9.6.A and 9.6.B display the results of the Kruskal-Wallis H test generated by SPSS.

Table 9.6.A: Mean Rank—Posttest Depression by Group

DEPRESS2 (Depression after Treatment)		
Group	N	Mean rank
1.00 experiment 1	15	13.63
2.00 control 1	15	37.83
3.00 experiment 2	10	12.15
4.00 control 2	10	38.15
Total	50	

Table 9.6.B: Kruskal-Wallis H test—Posttest Depression by Group

Test Statistics[a,b]	
DEPRESS2 (Depression after Treatment)	
Chi-square	36.866
df	3
Asymp. Sig.	.000

[a]Kruskal Wallis H Test
[b]Grouping variable: Group

Table 9.6.A shows the number of participants and the mean rank for each group. Control group 1 and control group 2 have higher mean ranks (37.83 and 38.15) than experiment group 1 and experiment group 2 (13.63 and 12.15).

Table 9.6.B displays the results of the Kruskal-Wallis H test. The χ^2 value is 36.87 (df = 3) with a significance level of .000 (two-tailed). This indicates a significant difference between at least two mean ranks.

The Kruskal-Wallis H test shows significant results, so a post hoc test is needed to determine which groups are significantly different. In the previous example the post hoc Tamahane T2 was used for data that did not meet the assumption of equality of variance. In this example we demonstrate use of the Mann-Whitney U nonparametric test (see chapter 8) as a post hoc test for group comparisons when the Kruskal-Wallis H test detects significant differences between the groups.

Because the results of the Kruskal-Wallis H are significant and there are four groups in the independent variable, conduct six group comparisons: experiment 1 vs. control 1; experiment 1 vs. experiment 2; experiment 1 vs. control 2; control 1 vs. experiment 2; control 1 vs. control 2; experiment 2 vs. control 2. (Chapter 8 describes how to use SPSS to compute the Mann-Whitney U and read its output.)

Tables 9.7.A to 9.12.B present the results of the six possible pair comparisons. Each pair of tables (A and B) compares the means of two groups.

The results presented in these tables are consistent with the results of the LSD

Table 9.7.A: Mean Ranks—Experiment 1 vs. Control 1

DEPRESS2 (Depression after Treatment)			
Group	N	Mean rank	Sum of ranks
1.00 experiment 1	15	8.03	120.50
2.00 control 1	15	22.97	344.50
Total	30		

Table 9.7.B: Mann-Whitney U—Experiment 1 vs. Control 1

Test Statistics[b]	
	DEPRESS2 (Depression after Treatment)
Mann-Whitney U	.500
Wilcoxon W	120.500
z	−4.666
Asymp. Sig. (2-tailed)	.000
Exact Sig. [2[b] (1-tailed Sig.)]	.000[a]

[a]Not corrected for ties.
[b]Grouping variable: Group

Table 9.8.A: Mean Ranks—Experiment 1 vs. Experiment 2

	Group	N	Mean rank	Sum of ranks
DEPRESS2 (Depression after Treatment	1.00 experiment 1	15	13.60	204.00
	3.00 experiment 2	10	12.10	121.00
	Total	25		

Table 9.8.B: Mann-Whitney U—Experiment 1 vs. Experiment 2

Test Statistics[b]	
	DEPRESS2 (Depression after Treatment)
Mann-Whitney U	66.000
Wilcoxon W	121.000
z	−.510
Asymp. Sig. (2-tailed)	.610
Exact Sig. [2[b] (1-tailed Sig.)]	.643[a]

[a]Not corrected for ties.
[b]Grouping variable: Group

Table 9.9.A: Mean Ranks—Experiment 1 vs. Control 2

	Group	N	Mean rank	Sum of ranks
DEPRESS2 (Depression after treatment)	1.00 experiment 1	15	8.00	120.00
	4.00 control 2	10	20.50	205.00
	Total	25		

Table 9.9.B: Mann-Whitney U—Experiment 1 vs. Control 2

Test Statistics[b]	
	DEPRESS2 (Depression after Treatment)
Mann-Whitney U	.000
Wilcoxon W	120.000
z	−4.188
Asymp. Sig. (2-tailed)	.000
Exact Sig. [2* (1-tailed Sig.)]	.000[a]

[a]Not corrected for ties.
[b]Grouping variable: Group

Table 9.10.A: Mean Ranks—Control 1 vs. Experiment 2

	Group	N	Mean rank	Sum of ranks
DEPRESS2 (Depression after Treatment)	2.00 control 1	15	17.97	269.50
	3.00 experiment 2	10	5.55	55.50
	Total	25		

Table 9.10.B: Mann-Whitney U—Control 1 vs. Experiment 2

Test Statistics[b]	
	DEPRESS2 (Depression after Treatment)
Mann-Whitney U	.500
Wilcoxon W	55.500
z	−4.142
Asymp. Sig. (2-tailed)	.000
Exact Sig. [2* (1-tailed Sig)]	.000[a]

[a]Not corrected for ties.
[b]Grouping variable: Group

post hoc test, which show a significant difference between experiment 1 and control 1 (table 9.7.B), experiment 1 and control 2 (table 9.9.B), experiment 2 and control 1 (table 9.10.B), and experiment 2 and control 2 (table 9.12.B). No significant difference exists between control 1 and control 2 (table 9.11.B) or between experiment 1 and experiment 2 (table 9.8.B).

Table 9.11.A: Mean Ranks—Control 1 vs. Control 2

	Group	N	Mean rank	Sum of ranks
DEPRESS2 (Depression	2.00 control 1	15	12.90	193.50
after Treatment)	4.00 control 2	10	13.15	131.50
	Total	25		

Table 9.11.B: Mann-Whitney U—Control 1 vs. Control 2

Test Statistics[b]	
	DEPRESS2 (Depression after Treatment)
Mann-Whitney U	73.500
Wilcoxon W	193.500
z	−.084
Asymp. Sig. (2-tailed)	.933
Exact Sig. [2* (1-tailed Sig.)]	.935[a]

[a]Not corrected for ties.
[b]Grouping variable: Group

Table 9.12.A: Mean Ranks—Experiment 2 vs. Control 2

	Group	N	Mean rank	Sum of ranks
DEPRESS2 (Depression	3.00 experiment 2	10	5.50	55.00
after Treatment)	4.00 control 2	10	15.50	155.00
	Total	20		

Table 9.12.B: Mann-Whitney U—Experiment 2 vs. Control 2

Test Statistics[b]	
	DEPRESS2 (Depression after treatment)
Mann-Whitney U	.000
Wilcoxon W	55.000
z	−3.790
Asymp. Sig. (2-tailed)	.000
Exact Sig. [2* (1-tailed Sig.)]	.000[a]

[a]Not corrected for ties.
[b]Grouping variable: Group

Step 5: Decide whether to reject the null hypothesis.

The results of the one-way ANOVA presented in table 9.5.C show an overall significant difference in the posttest levels of depression among the four groups ($p < .05$). Reject the null hypothesis.

Writing the Results

The one-way ANOVA was conducted to examine the posttest depression scores among all groups. The results of the one-way ANOVA show an overall significant difference between the posttest depression scores among the groups $(F_{(df=3,46)} = 56.86, p < .05)$.

Because overall significant results were found, the LSD post hoc test was run to determine which groups were significantly different. The results show that the first experiment group $(\overline{X} = 13.60)$ and the second experiment group $(\overline{X} = 13.40)$ have significantly lower levels of depression than the first control group $(\overline{X} = 22.20)$ and the second control group $(\overline{X} = 22.40)$. These results show no significant differences between the two experiment groups or between the two control groups. The results of Kruskal-Wallis H and the post hoc Mann-Whitney U tests confirm these findings.

The results of the one-way ANOVA and the LSD post hoc tests indicate that the levels of depression of subjects who participated in therapy are significantly lower than the levels of depression of subjects who did not participate in therapy. These results provide statistical evidence that therapy is effective in reducing the levels of depression of clinically depressed subjects.

Presentation of Results in a Summary Table

As with the independent *t*-test, the results of the one-way ANOVA should be displayed in a readable table. Present the number of cases in each group, mean score, standard deviation, overall test statistic (*F* ratio), and the *p* value. Table 9.13 presents results of the one-way ANOVA for both practical examples.

Table 9.13:   Results of One-Way ANOVA

Variable	N	$\overline{X}$	SD	F	p
Levels of Turnover	218	18.83	4.61	13.68	.000+
married	141	19.87	4.41		
single	47	19.87	4.41		
divorced	30	15.00	4.17		
Levels of Depression	50	17.90	4.99	56.88	.000++
experiment 1	15	13.60	1.96		
control 1	15	22.20	2.96		
experiment 2	10	13.40	1.78		
control 2	10	22.40	2.46		

+1-tailed *p* (df = 2, 215)
++1-tailed *p* (df = 3, 46)

SUMMARY

This chapter presented new statistical techniques to help social work practitioners and researchers to statistically compare a number of groups on one dependent variable. This is especially helpful for practitioners who conduct therapy for more than two groups simultaneously (for example, experiment, control, and placebo groups).

The chapter discussed the purpose and assumptions of the one-way analysis of variance (ANOVA) and its corresponding nonparametric Kruskal-Wallis H test. These two powerful statistical techniques are extended versions of the independent *t*-test and the Mann-Whitney U test. They allow researchers to compare three or more groups on one dependent variable without adjusting the level of significance.

The chapter demonstrated how to use the one-way ANOVA and the Kruskal-Wallis H tests in group comparisons, as well as a number of post hoc tests, including the Bonferroni, LSD, Tamahane T2, and Mann-Whitney U.

Two practical examples illustrated how to compute the one-way ANOVA, Kruskal-Wallis H, and post hoc tests and how to interpret, write, and present the results.

Chapter 10 introduces the dependent *t*-test and the Wilcoxon sign ranks test. The purpose and assumptions of these tests are described, along with how to compute the statistics, interpret the output, and write and present the results.

PRACTICAL EXERCISES

I.   Use the variables marital status (**MSTATUS**) and emotional balance (**EB**) from the SPSS *Depression-Elderly* data file.

II. Use the variables region (**D8**) and job satisfaction (**SATISFAC**) from the SPSS *Job Satisfaction* data file.

For each pair of variables, answer the following questions:

1. Develop a one-tailed research hypothesis.
2. State the null hypothesis.
3. What test will you use to examine the hypothesis? Justify your answer.
4. Use SPSS to examine each hypothesis.
5. What is the alternative test? Run the analysis.
6. Are there any differences between the results of the test you chose and its alternative test? If so, what are these differences?
7. Construct a mean plot displaying the means of all groups.
8. Present the results of both hypotheses in one summary table.

Two Repeated Measures– Two Matched Samples: Dependent *t*-Test

LEARNING OBJECTIVES

1. Understand the purpose of the dependent *t*-test
2. Understand the assumptions underlying the dependent *t*-test
3. Understand the alternative nonparametric Wilcoxon signed ranks test
4. Understand how to use SPSS to compute the statistics
5. Understand how to interpret and present the results of the tests

Data Sets: *Pretest-Posttest, Research Final* (appendix A)

INTRODUCTION

Recall from chapter 9 the Solomon Four-Group Design that combines the classic pretest-posttest control group design with the posttest-only control group design. In that chapter we examined the differences between groups only at the posttest level. Social work practitioners are not interested only in the differences between groups but also in the differences within groups. Consider the following two cases:

Case 1: In the *Pretest-Posttest* study (appendix A), a social work practitioner utilizes the classic pretest-posttest control group design with individuals who are considered clinically depressed as measured by the CES-D. The practitioner's aims in this study are to examine if the levels of depression of individuals who participate in the therapy (experiment group) will significantly decrease after they complete the therapy and to examine if the posttest depression scores of individuals who do not participate in the therapy (control group) will remain the same as in the pretest. If these two aims are confirmed, then the practitioner may conclude that therapy is effective and could be replicated with similar individuals who have

Table 10.1:   Classic Pretest-Posttest Control Group Design

Group	Pretest	Therapy	Posttest
Experiment	μ_1	Yes	μ_2
Control	μ_3	No	μ_4

μ (mu) = mean

Table 10.2:   Two Matched Samples

Group	Previous grades	Current grades
First sample	μ_S	—
Second sample	—	μ_F

similar depression symptoms. Table 10.1 illustrates the classic pretest-posttest control group design.

Statistically, the practitioner hypothesizes that $\mu_2 < \mu_1$ (posttest levels of depression of the experiment group are less than their pretest levels of depression); and $\mu_3 = \mu_4$ (posttest levels of depression of the control group are similar to their pretest levels of depression).

Case 2: A social work research faculty has recently implemented a new teaching technique for current graduate students. The faculty claims that the new teaching technique significantly improves final grades of graduate students enrolled in the Research Methods course. To test this claim, the faculty compares final grades of current graduate students who took the course under the new teaching technique with final grades of previous students who took the course under the old technique. Table 10.2 describes this comparison (final grades of previous students vs. final grades of current students).

In the first example, each group (experiment and control) is tested twice: once before administering the therapy, then again after the therapy is completed. In the second example, two similar (matched) samples (graduate social work students) are measured on the same variable (final grades in Research Methods) at two different times. In both cases one variable is measured at two different periods, before and after an intervention is conducted. What statistical test(s) is(are) most suitable to examine if a significant change occurs between the two time periods?

This chapter presents the dependent *t*-test for two repeated measures or two matched samples, its purpose, and underlying assumptions. The alternative non-parametric Wilcoxon signed ranks test is then presented, along with two practical examples illustrating how to use SPSS to compute the statistics and levels of significance, and how to interpret, write, and present the results.

DEPENDENT *t*-TEST

Purpose

The dependent *t*-test is also known as the *paired-samples t-test, t-test for pairs, t-test for matched samples,* and *t-test for related samples.* It is a parametric statistical test, used to compare the means of two repeated measures of the same sample, or the means of two matched samples.

Example research question for two repeated measures: Is there a significant difference between the pretest and posttest levels of depression among participants in the experiment group? Here, the same subjects are measured at the pretest and again at the posttest.

Example research question for two matched samples: Is there a significant difference between the final grades in Research Methods for current graduate students and final grades of students from the previous year? Here, data from two similar groups (graduate students who took the same test at two different times) are matched to form one data set. The first sample includes students from the previous year and the second sample includes current students. The two samples are measured on the same variable (final grades in Research Methods).

Like the independent *t*-test, the dependent *t*-test produces a test statistic called *t,* which measures how far apart the two means are in standard error units. The larger the difference between the two means (also known as mean difference), the more likely it is statistically significant. In the first example, the greater the difference between the posttest depression mean score and pretest depression mean score, the more likely this mean difference is significant $(\mu_2 - \mu_1)$. In the second example, the greater the mean difference between the two sets of final grades, the more likely this mean difference is significant $(\mu_F - \mu_S)$.

Assumptions

The assumptions of the dependent *t*-test are similar to the assumptions of the Pearson correlation coefficient.

1. The dependent and independent variables (the two measures) must be continuous variables, measured at the interval level of measurement or higher. In reality, only one variable is measured twice: depression at Time 1 (pretest) and depression at Time 2 (posttest), and final grades at Time 1 (previous year) and final grades at Time 2 (current year).

2. The two measures must be either repeated measures for the same set of subjects or objects (Time 1 and Time 2) or two matched samples measured on the same variable.

3. The shape of the distributions of the two measures must approximate the shape of a normal curve.

4. As with the independent *t*-test, a sample size of 30 subjects or more is usually

needed to examine the mean difference between two repeated measures or two matched samples.

It is highly recommended that the variable at both times be measured using the same scale, or instrument. For example, if the CES-D is used to measure levels of depression at the pretest, it should also be used to measure levels of depression at the posttest. However, if the CES-D is used to measure depression at the pretest and a different scale is used to measure depression at the posttest, the raw scores of both measures should be transformed into standard scores (z scores) before any statistical analysis is conducted (see chapter 5).

Wilcoxon Signed Ranks Test

The Wilcoxon signed ranks test, also known as the Wilcoxon matched-pairs signed ranks test, is the nonparametric version of the dependent *t*-test. Like Spearman rho, the Wilcoxon signed ranks test ranks each pair of raw scores for the two measures, or the two samples. The test computes the difference within each pair and gives more weight to pairs that show a large difference than pairs that show a small difference. The Wilcoxon signed ranks test is based on the distribution of the z score. Thus, it produces a z value that is compared with a pre-established z score. A z value above +1.96 or below −1.96 (for a two-tailed hypothesis) will be significant at .05 *alpha* (see chapter 5).

Like the Spearman rho, the Wilcoxon signed ranks test is most appropriate to examine the difference between the mean ranks of two repeated measures or two matched samples when either variable (e.g., scores of pretest or posttest, previous or current final grades) is measured at the ordinal level of measurement, or measured at the interval level of measurement that does not meet the assumption of normality. As with the dependent *t*-test, the Wilcoxon signed ranks test requires that the sample be representative of the population, and that the two measures be repeated measures of the same subjects or matched samples measured on the same variable.

PRACTICAL EXAMPLES

We will use SPSS to compute the mean difference, *t,* and *p* values for the dependent *t*-test and the *z* and *p* values for the Wilcoxon signed ranks test. Two examples are presented; the first demonstrates two repeated measures and the second demonstrates two matched samples.

Example 1—Two Repeated Measures

To demonstrate the use of the dependent *t*-test and Wilcoxon signed ranks test, use the classical pretest-posttest control group design data from the *Pretest-Posttest* SPSS data file (appendix A) to examine the following research questions (see table 10.1):

Is there a significant difference between the pretest depression scores and the posttest depression scores of participants in the experiment group?

Is there a significant difference between the pretest depression scores and the posttest depression scores of participants in the control group?

Step 1: State the null and alternative hypotheses.

H_{0_1}: There is *no significant* difference between the levels of depression at the pretest and the levels of depression at the posttest of participants in the experiment group.

$$\mu_1 = \mu_2$$

H_{a_1}: Posttest levels of depression of participants in the experiment group will be *significantly lower* than their pretest levels of depression.

$$\mu_1 > \mu_2$$

H_{0_2}: There is *no significant* difference between the levels of depression at the pretest and the levels of depression at the posttest of participants in the control group.

$$\mu_3 = \mu_4$$

H_{a_2}: Posttest levels of depression of participants in the control group will be *significantly different* than their pretest levels of depression.

$$\mu_3 \neq \mu_4$$

The first research hypothesis (H_{a_1}) is a one-tailed hypothesis because the practitioner's interest is to show that participants who attend and complete the therapy significantly reduce their levels of depression. In other words, the practitioner would like to show that the therapy is effective. In this hypothesis the two measures are the pretest depression scores (**CESD1**) and the posttest depression scores (**CESD2**).

The second research hypothesis (H_{a_2}) is a two-tailed hypothesis. In this case the practitioner is interested to show that there will be no changes over time in the levels of depression of participants who do not participate in the therapy, or that the posttest levels of depression of participants in the control group will significantly increase due to lack of therapy. If either situation occurs, this will strengthen the practitioner's claim that the therapy is effective. However, if a significant decrease in the posttest depression scores of participants who do not participate in therapy occurs, this could indicate that extraneous factors other than therapy are responsible for the improvement in levels of depression, which is a threat to the interval validity of the study. In this hypothesis, the two measures are also the pretest depression scores (**CESD1**) and the posttest depression scores (**CESD2**) of the control group.

Step 2: Set the criteria for rejecting the null hypothesis.
Set alpha at .05 ($\alpha = .05$). Reject H_0 only if $p \leq .05$.

Step 3: Select the appropriate statistical test.

a.   Pretest levels of depression and posttest levels of depression are two repeated measures of the same subjects. The CES-D scale was used to collect data at the two times. Levels of depression at each time are continuous data, measured at the interval level of measurement. These are the two basic assumptions (two repeated measures and continuous data) needed to utilize the dependent *t*-test or the Wilcoxon signed ranks test.

b. Normality of distribution: To evaluate the assumption of normality, create a histogram with a normal curve for the pretest levels of depression and another histogram for posttest levels of depression for the experiment group. Since we have two research hypotheses, create two histograms for the control group as well.

c. To use SPSS to create separate histograms for each group, first instruct SPSS to Split the data file by *Group* (only if you want to create separate output for each group, one for the experiment group and another for the control group). Remember, this will not determine if there is a significant difference between the two groups (see chapters 8 and 9 for group comparisons). The Split command separates the data file by groups and generates output for each group independently. To split a data file by groups, follow these steps:

1. Open the SPSS *Pretest-Posttest* data file.

2. Click on *Data* in the SPSS main toolbar and click on *Split File*. A new dialog box called *Split File* will open (screen 10.1).

3. Check the box associated with *Organize output by groups*.

Screen 10.1:   SPSS *Split File* Dialog Box

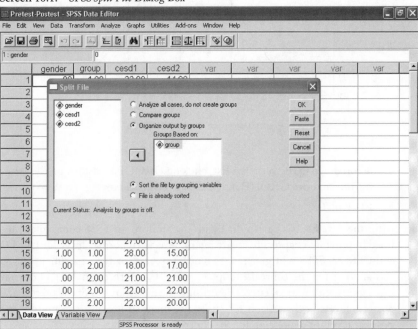

Figure 10.1.A: Histogram of Pretest Depression—Experiment Group

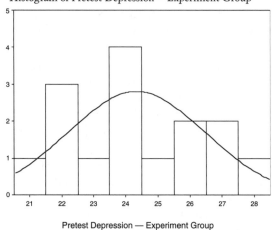

Pretest Depression — Experiment Group

Figure 10.1.B: Histogram of Posttest Depression—Experiment Group

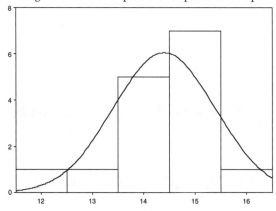

Posttest Depression — Experiment Group

4. Scroll down in the variables list, click on **GROUP,** and click on the arrow button to move **GROUP** in the *Groups Based on* box.

5. Click on *OK.*

d. After the data file has been split by groups, follow the SPSS commands outlined in previous chapters to create histograms with normal curve for **CESD1** and **CESD2.** SPSS will generate two outputs, one for the experiment group and another for the control group. Figures 10.1.A through 10.1.D display histograms with normal curves describing the distributions of the pretest and posttest levels of depression for the experiment group and the pretest and posttest levels of depression for the control group.

Figure 10.1.C: Histogram of Pretest Depression—Control Group

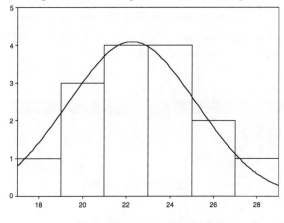

Pretest Depression — Control Group

Figure 10.1.D: Histogram of Posttest Depression—Control Group

Posttest Depression — Control Group

e.   Figures 10.1.A and 10.1.B show that the histograms of the experiment group at both times are not severely skewed (although posttest has minor negative skewness). The shapes of both distributions approach the shape of a normal curve. The shapes of the distributions of the control group also approach the shape of a normal curve.

Because the scores are repeated measures, at interval levels of measurement, and approach the shape of a normal curve, utilize the dependent *t*-test to examine the research hypotheses. We will also utilize the Wilcoxon signed ranks test to demonstrate how to use the test and to examine whether the results of both parametric and nonparametric tests are consistent.

Step 4: Compute the test statistic (Use SPSS).

SPSS produces three tables for the dependent *t*-test. The first table is called Paired Samples Statistics, the second is Paired Samples Correlations, and the third table is Paired Samples Test. These tables present measures of central tendency and variability for each time, the Pearson correlation coefficients between both times, and the level of significance of the mean difference, respectively.

How to Compute the Dependent *t*-Test in SPSS.   In this example, the independent variable is pretest levels of depression (**CESD1**) and the dependent variable is posttest levels of depression (**CESD2**).

To run the dependent *t*-test in SPSS, follow these steps:

a. Open the SPSS *Pretest-Posttest* data file.

b. Click on *Analyze* in the SPSS main toolbar. (Remember to split the data file if you are interested in separate outputs for the experiment and for the control groups).

c. Scroll down and click on *Compare Means,* then click on *Paired-Samples t-Test* (screen 10.2).

d. A new dialog box called *Paired-Samples t-Test* will open (screen 10.3).

e. Scroll down in the variables list and click on **CESD1. CESD1** will appear under *Current Selection* next to *Variable 1.*

Screen 10.2:   SPSS *Dependent t-Test* Main Toolbar

Screen 10.3:   SPSS *Dependent t-Test* Dialog Box

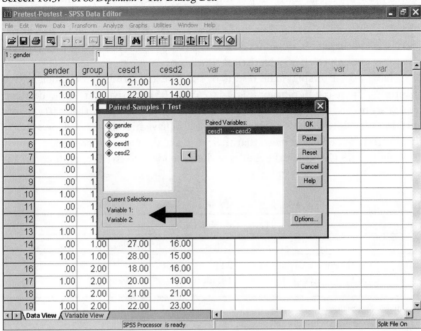

f.   Scroll down in the variables list and click on **CESD2. CESD2** will appear under *Current Selection* next to *Variable 2.*

g.   Click on the arrow button to move this pair in the *Paired Variables* box.

h.   Click on *OK.*

SPSS syntax to split file by group:

SPLIT FILE SEPARATE BY GROUP.

SPSS syntax for the dependent *t*-test:

T-TEST PAIRS=CESD1 WITH CESD2 (PAIRED).

Interpreting the Output of the Dependent *t*-Test.   The following tables describe the results of the dependent *t*-test generated by SPSS. Tables 10.3.A through 10.3.C display the output for the experiment group.

Table 10.3.A displays the mean, number of cases, standard deviation, and standard error of the mean for levels of depression at the pretest and posttest for the experiment group. The table shows that the number of cases at pretest and posttest is (and must be) equal. Each subject must have two scores: one at Time 1 and another at Time 2.

The mean of the pretest levels of depression is 24.33 compared to 14.4 at the posttest, a decrease of 9.93 points on average (24.33 – 14.40). Is this mean difference large enough to claim a statistical significance?

Table 10.3.B displays the results of the Pearson correlation coefficient (see chapter 7). There is a significant (Sig. = .024; $p < .05$) positive correlation between pretest scores and posttest scores ($r = .58$). This simply indicates that participants with high levels of depression at the pretest also have high levels of depression at the posttest, but does not mean that their levels of depression increased.

Table 10.3.C displays the results of the dependent *t*-test. This table compares

Table 10.3.A: Descriptive Statistics—Experiment Group

	Paired Samples Statistics[a]				
		Mean	N	Std. deviation	Std. error mean
Pair 1	**CESD1** (Pretest Depression)	24.3333	15	2.12692	.54917
	CESD2 (Posttest Depression)	14.4000	15	.98561	.25448

[a]Group = 1.00 experiment

Table 10.3.B: Pearson Correlation—Experiment Group

	Paired Samples Correlations[a]			
		N	Correlation	Sig.
Pair 1	**CESD1** (Pretest Depression & **CESD2** (Posttest Depression)	15	.579	.024

[a]Group = 1.00 experiment

Table 10.3.C: Dependent *t*-Test—Experiment Group

	Paired Samples Test[a]								
		Paired differences							
					95% confidence interval of the difference				
		Mean	Std. deviation	Std. error mean	Lower	Upper	*t*	df	Sig. (2-tailed)
Pair 1	**CESD1** (Pretest Depression – **CESD2** (Posttest Depression)	9.93	1.75119	.4522	8.9636	10.903	21.97	14	.000

[a]Group = 1.00 experiment

the mean score of levels of depression at the pretest with the mean score of levels of depression at the posttest. The first column displays the pairs being compared (Pretest – Posttest). The second column displays the mean difference (Pretest – Posttest = 9.93). The table also displays the standard deviation, standard error of the mean difference, and the 95% confidence interval of the mean difference, respectively.

The last three columns include the values for the dependent t-test: the t value, degrees of freedom,[1] and the level of significance (two-tailed hypothesis).[2] The t value is 21.97 with 14 degrees of freedom and a p value (Sig.) of .000. Because the hypothesis is one-tailed, divide this two-tailed p value by 2. However, because this p value is significant at *alpha* of .05, dividing it by 2 is not necessary.[3] These results show a significant decrease in the levels of depression of the experiment group from pretest to posttest.

Tables 10.4.A through 10.4.C display the results of the dependent t-test for the control group.

Table 10.4.A shows that the mean of the pretest levels of depression for the control group is 22.73 and the mean of the posttest is 22.27, a decrease of only .46 points on average (22.73 – 22.27). Is this mean difference significant?

Table 10.4.B shows that there is a significant (Sig. = .000) positive correlation between the pretest scores and the posttest scores (r = .91). This indicates that participants with high levels of depression at the pretest also have high levels of depression at the posttest. Again, this does not mean their levels of depression increased.

Table 10.4.C presents the results of the dependent t-test for the control group. The t value is 1.5 (df = 14), which is not significant at .05 alpha (p = .169). Remember, because the second research hypothesis is two-tailed, there is no need to divide the p value by 2. This p value indicates no significant change in the levels of depression of the control group.

Results of the Wilcoxon Signed Ranks Test

As with the dependent t-test, SPSS produces three tables for the Wilcoxon signed ranks test. The first table is called Descriptive Statistics (unlike with the dependent t-test, in this case we need to instruct SPSS to produce this table), the second is Ranks, and the third one is Test Statistics. These tables display measures of central tendency and variability for each time, ranks of scores, and the level of significance for the mean rank difference, respectively.

---

[1] df = N − 1; N = sample size.

[2] By default, except with the Pearson r, SPSS always produces a two-tailed p value. Thus, for a one-tailed hypothesis, simply divide the p value by 2.

[3] Sometimes, dividing a p value that is not significant (e.g., p = .08) by 2 produces a significant p value (.08/2 = .04, which is significant at alpha of .05).

Table 10.4.A: Descriptive Statistics—Control Group

	Paired Samples Statistics[a]				
		Mean	N	Std. deviation	Std. error mean
Pair 1	**CESD1** (Pretest Depression)	22.7333	15	2.28244	.58932
	CESD2 (Posttest Depression)	22.2667	15	2.91466	.75256

[a]Group = 2.00 control

Table 10.4.B: Pearson Correlation—Control Group

	Paired Samples Correlations[a]			
		N	Correlation	Sig.
Pair 1	**CESD1** (Pretest Depression) & **CESD2** (Posttest Depression)	15	.913	.000

[a]Group = 2.00 control

Table 10.4.C: Dependent *t*-Test—Control Group

		Paired Samples Test[a]							
		Paired differences							
					95% confidence interval of the difference				
		Mean	Std. deviation	Std. error mean	Lower	Upper	*t*	df	Sig. (2-tailed)
Pair 1	**CESD1** (Pretest Depression) & **CESD2** (Posttest Depression)	.4667	1.24595	.32170	−.2233	1.1566	1.5	14	.169

[a]Group = 2.00 control

How to Compute the Wilcoxon Signed Ranks Test in SPSS.   The independent variable is pretest levels of depression (**CESD1**) and the dependent variable is posttest levels of depression (**CESD2**).

To run the Wilcoxon signed ranks test in SPSS, follow these steps:

a.   Open the SPSS *Pretest-Posttest* data file. (Remember to split the file if you wish to run separate analysis for each group).

b.   Click on *Analyze* in the SPSS main toolbar, scroll down, click on *Nonparametric Tests,* and click on *2 Related Samples* (screen 10.4).

c.   A dialog box called *Two-Related-Samples Tests* will open (screen 10.5.A).

d.   Scroll down in the variables list and click on **CESD1** and then click on **CESD2**.

Screen 10.4:   SPSS *Wilcoxon Signed Ranks Test* Main Menu

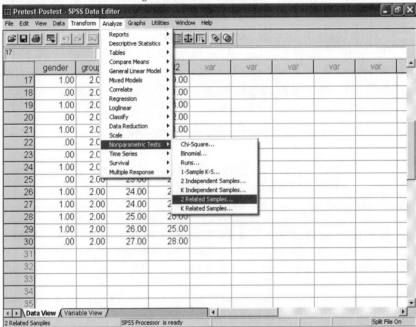

Screen 10.5:   SPSS *Wilcoxon Signed Ranks Test* Dialog Box

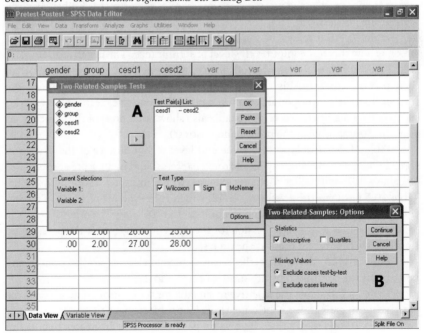

e. Click on the arrow button to move this pair in the *Test Pair(s) List* box.

f. Make sure that *Wilcoxon* is checked (SPSS default).

g. Click on *Options* (to request Descriptive Statistics). A new dialog box entitled *Two-Related-Samples Tests: Options* will open (screen 10.5.B).

h. Check the box associated with *Descriptive.*

i. Click on *Continue,* then click on *OK.*

SPSS syntax for the Wilcoxon signed ranks test:

NPAR TEST
/WILCOXON=CESD1 WITH CESD2 (PAIRED)
/STATISTICS DESCRIPTIVES.

Interpreting the Output of the Wilcoxon Signed Ranks Test.   Tables 10.5.A through 10.5.C display the results of the Wilcoxon signed ranks test for the experiment group and Tables 10.6.A through 10.6.C display results for the control group.

Table 10.5.A displays the number of participants at each measure (pretest and posttest), the mean score, standard deviation, and range of scores of depression for the experiment group. This table is similar to table 10.3.A of the dependent *t*-test, except the dependent *t*-test table does not report the minimum and maximum scores. It appears that the mean depression score at the pretest is higher than the score at the posttest.

Table 10.5.B displays the sum of the negative, positive, and ties mean ranks, which is how this test computes the level of significance. The negative mean rank is 15. This indicates the number of subjects whose posttest score is smaller than their pretest score. (In this experiment, N = 15; that is, all posttest scores are smaller than their corresponding pretest scores.) The positive mean rank is zero (all subjects have a negative score). The table also shows that none of the subjects has a tie score (same score at the pretest and posttest).

Table 10.5.C displays the *z* value and level of significance of the Wilcoxon signed ranks test. As you may recall from chapters 5 and 6, a *z* score above +1.96 or below −1.96 will fall at the rejection area, which indicates a significant value. Table 10.5.C shows the *z* value as −3.42, which is beyond a *z* of −1.96. The Sig. (2-tailed) confirms that this value is significant at .05 *alpha.* In other words, the results show that levels of depression for the experiment group at the posttest are significantly lower than those at the pretest.

Table 10.6.A shows that the mean depression scores at the pretest and posttest for the control group are similar (22.73 and 22.27).

Table 10.6.B shows the negative mean rank for the control group as 7 and the positive mean rank as 4. At the same time, four subjects have tie scores.

Table 10.6.C shows that the *z* value is −1.39, which is greater than a *z* of

Table 10.5.A: Descriptive Statistics—Experiment Group

Descriptive Statistics[a]					
	N	Mean	Std. deviation	Minimum	Maximum
CESD1 (Pretest Depression)	15	24.3333	2.12692	21.00	28.00
CESD2 (Posttest Depression)	15	14.4000	.98561	12.00	16.00

[a]Group = 1.00 experiment

Table 10.5.B: Mean Ranks of Depression—Experiment Group

Ranks[d]				
		N	Mean rank	Sum of ranks
CESD2 (Posttest	Negative ranks	15[a]	8.00	120.00
Depression) &	Positive ranks	0[b]	.00	.00
CESD1 (Pretest	Ties	0[c]		
Depression)	Total	15		

[a]CESD2 (Posttest Depression) < CESD1 (Pretest Depression)
[b]CESD2 (Posttest Depression) > CESD1 (Pretest Depression)
[c]CESD2 (Posttest Depression) = CESD1 (Pretest Depression)
[d]Group = 1.00 experiment

Table 10.5.C: Results of the Wilcoxon Test—Experiment Group

Test Statistics[b,c]	
	CESD2 (Posttest Depression) & CESD1 (Pretest Depression)
z	−3.417[a]
Asymp. Sig. (2-tailed)	.001

[a]Based on positive ranks
[b]Wilcoxon signed ranks test
[c]Group = 1.00 experiment

−1.96 and smaller than a z of +1.96. A z of −1.39 falls at the *Do Not Reject Area* (see chapter 6). The Sig. (2-tailed) confirms that this value is not significant at .05 *alpha.* These results indicate that levels of depression for participants in the control group at the posttest are not significantly different than their levels of depression at the pretest.

Step 5: Decide whether to reject the null hypothesis.

The results of the dependent t-test presented in table 10.3.C show a significant change in levels of depression among participants in the experiment group ($p < .05$) and, therefore, reject the first null hypothesis. The results of the dependent t-test presented in table 10.4.C show no change in levels of depression

Table 10.6.A: Descriptive Statistics—Control Group

Descriptive Statistics[a]					
	N	Mean	Std. deviation	Minimum	Maximum
CESD1 (Pretest Depression)	15	22.7333	2.28244	18.00	27.00
CESD2 (Posttest Depression)	15	22.2667	2.91466	17.00	28.00

[a]Group = 2.00 control

Table 10.6.B: Mean Ranks of Depression—Control Group

Ranks[d]				
		N	Mean rank	Sum of ranks
CESD2 (Posttest	Negative ranks	7[a]	6.86	48.00
Depression) &	Positive ranks	4[b]	4.50	18.00
CESD1 (Pretest	Ties	4[c]		
Depression)	Total	15		

[a]CESD2 (Posttest Depression) < CESD1 (Pretest Depression)
[b]CESD2 (Posttest Depression) > CESD1 (Pretest Depression)
[c]CESD2 (Posttest Depression) = CESD1 (Pretest Depression)
[d]Group = 2.00 control

Table 10.6.C: Results of the Wilcoxon Test—Control Group

Test Statistics[b,c]	
	CESD2 (Posttest Depression) & CESD1 (Pretest Depression)
z	−1.393[a]
Asymp. Sig. (2-tailed)	.163

[a]Based on positive ranks
[b]Wilcoxon signed ranks test
[c]Group = 2.00 control

among participants in the control group ($p > .05$); do not reject the second null hypothesis.

Writing the Results

As with the previous test, when writing the results report the *t*, df, and *p* values for the dependent *t*-test, and the *z* and *p* values for the Wilcoxon. Report mean score for each time along with the mean difference. In our example, the results are as follows:

The dependent *t*-test shows a significant change in levels of depression among participants in the experiment group, who significantly decreased their levels of depression, from 24.33 points at the pretest to 14.40 points at the posttest

$(t_{(df=14)} = 21.97; p < .05)$, a decrease of 9.93 points on average. The Wilcoxon signed ranks test confirms these results $(z = -3.42; p < .05)$.

On the other hand, the results of the dependent t-test show no significant difference $(t_{(df=14)} = 1.45; p > .05)$ between the pretest levels of depression $(\overline{X} = 22.73)$ and posttest levels of depression $(\overline{X} = 22.27)$ for participants who did not receive therapy. In this study, the mean difference is only .47 on average. The results of the Wilcoxon signed ranks test confirm these results $(z = -1.39; p > .05)$.

To conclude, the results of the dependent t-test and the Wilcoxon signed ranks test show that individuals who participated in the therapy significantly decreased their levels of depression while individuals who did not participate did not decrease their levels of depression. The findings provide statistical evidence that the therapy is effective.

Example 2—Two Matched Samples

To demonstrate the use of the dependent t-test and the Wilcoxon signed ranks test with two matched samples, use the SPSS *Research Final* data file (appendix A) to examine the following research question:

Is there a significant difference between the final grades in Research Methods for current graduate social work students and the final grades of graduate social work students from the previous year?

Step 1: State the null and alternative hypotheses.

H_0: There is *no significant* difference between the final grades in Research Methods for current graduate social work students and final grades of graduate social work students from the previous year.

$$\mu_F = \mu_S$$

H_a: Final grades in Research Methods for current graduate social work students will be *significantly higher* than the final grades of graduate social work students from the previous year.

$$\mu_F > \mu_S$$

This is a one-tailed research hypothesis in which two samples are matched. The first sample was measured in the previous year and the second sample was measured in the current year. The two samples were measured on the same variable. Final grades in Research Methods are measured at the ratio level (possible grades 0 to 100).

Step 2: Set the criteria for rejecting the null hypothesis.
Set alpha at .05 ($\alpha = .05$). Reject H_0 only if $p \leq .05$.

Step 3: Select the appropriate statistical test.

a.   Final grades in Research Methods for graduate social work students from two different years (previous grades and current grades) were matched to form one data set. Both grades are continuous data. These are the basic assumptions needed to utilize the dependent *t*-test or the Wilcoxon signed ranks test.

b. Normality of distribution: To evaluate the assumption of normality, create histograms for both previous and current final grades in Research Methods.[4] Figures 10.2.A and 10.2.B display both distributions. Neither distribution has severe skewness. Both approach the shape of a normal curve.

c. Because the two samples are matched and measured on the same variable, both scores are interval or higher level of measurement (in this case ratio), and their distributions approach the shape of a normal curve, utilize the dependent *t*-test to examine the hypothesis. In addition, use the Wilcoxon signed ranks test to determine whether the results of both tests are consistent.

Step 4: Compute the test statistic (Use SPSS).

Tables 10.7.A through 10.7.C display the results of the dependent *t*-test generated by SPSS.

Table 10.7.A displays mean scores for previous and current final grades in Research Methods. The mean score for previous grades is 65.37, compared to 76.90 for current grades, an increase of 11.5 points on average. Is this increase significant?

Table 10.7.B shows that there is a significant (Sig. = .000) positive correlation between the final grades of the two groups ($r = .75$). As discussed in chapter 7, the Pearson correlation is appropriate when the independent and dependent variables are paired observations for the same subjects. Because the measures here were not paired observations and not collected from the same subjects, this correlation coefficient is useless.

Table 10.7.C shows that the mean difference between the two final grades is –11.5 (previous grades – current grades = –11.5). The *t* value is –7.63 with 29 degrees of freedom ($30 – 1 = 29$). This *t* value is significant at the .05 *alpha* ($p = .000$). In other words, the results show a significant increase in the final grades in Research Methods.

Results of the Wilcoxon Signed Ranks Test

Tables 10.8.A through 10.8.C display the results of the Wilcoxon signed ranks test generated by SPSS.

Table 10.8.A displays the descriptive statistics for previous and current final grades. It is similar to table 10.7.A of the dependent *t*-test.

Table 10.8.B shows that there is only one negative rank (one current grade is smaller than one previous grade). There are 28 positive ranks (28 current grades are greater than 28 previous grades), and one grade is tied (one current grade is equal to one previous grade).

Table 10.8.C shows that the *z* value is –4.57 and the level of significance

---

[4]Unlike in the previous example, here there is no need to split the SPSS data file because only one data set (two matched samples) is being analyzed; no groups are being compared.

Figure 10.2.A: Histogram for Previous Final Grades

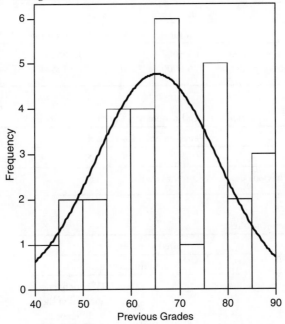

Figure 10.2.B: Histogram for Current Final Grades

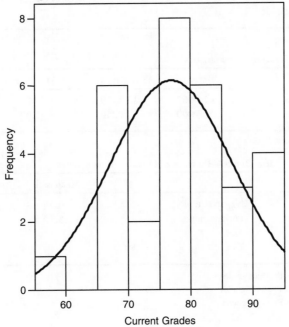

Table 10.7.A: Descriptive Statistics

		Mean	N	Std. deviation	Std. error mean

Paired Samples Statistics					
		Mean	N	Std. deviation	Std. error mean
Pair 1	Previous grades	65.3667	30	12.55192	2.29166
	Current grades	76.9000	30	9.72501	1.77554

Table 10.7.B: Correlation between Previous and Current Final Grades

Paired Samples Correlations				
		N	Correlation	Sig.
Pair 1	Previous Grades & Current Grades	30	.752	.000

Table 10.7.C: Dependent *t*-Test

Paired Samples Test								
	Paired differences							
				95% confidence interval of the difference				Sig.
	Mean	Std. deviation	Std. error mean	Lower	Upper	t	df	(2-tailed)
Pair 1 Previous Grades & Current Grades	−11.5	8.27849	1.511	−14.62	−8.442	−7.631	29	.000

Table 10.8.A: Descriptive Statistics

	N	Mean	Std. deviation	Minimum	Maximum
Previous grades	30	65.3667	12.55192	40.00	88.00
Current grades	30	76.9000	9.72501	55.00	95.00

Table 10.8.B: Mean Ranks—Previous and Current Final Grades

		N	Mean rank	Sum of ranks
Current grades	Negative ranks	1[a]	6.50	6.50
Previous grades	Positive ranks	28[b]	15.30	428.50
	Ties	1[c]		
	Total	30		

[a]Current grades < Previous grades
[b]Current grades > Previous grades
[c]Current grades = Previous grades

Table 10.8.C: Results of the Wilcoxon Test

Test Statistics[b]	
	Current grades & Previous grades
z	−4.573[a]
Asymp. Sig. (2-tailed)	.000

[a]Based on negative ranks
[b]Wilcoxon signed ranks test

(Sig.) is .000. This indicates a significant change in the mean score between the previous and current final grades.

Step 5: Decide whether to reject the null hypothesis.

The results of the dependent *t*-test presented in table 10.7.C show a significant change in the final grades of graduate social work students over time ($p < .05$). Therefore, we will reject the null hypothesis.

Writing the Results

The results of the dependent *t*-test show a significant difference ($t_{(df=29)} = -7.63; p < .05$) between the current final grades ($\overline{X} = 76.90$) and the previous final grades in Research Methods ($\overline{X} = 65.37$). Graduate social work students who took Research Methods under the new teaching technique (current grades) scored 11.5 points higher on average than graduate students who took Research Methods under the old teaching technique (previous grades). These results are consistent with the results of the Wilcoxon test ($z = -4.57; p < .05$). These results may provide statistical support that the new teaching technique is effective.

Presentation of Results in a Summary Table

As with the independent *t*-test, the results of the dependent *t*-test should be presented in a readable table that includes the number of participants each time, mean score, standard deviation, overall test statistic (*t*), and the *p* value. The table should also present the degrees of freedom and whether the *p* value is a one-tailed

Table 10.9:   Dependent *t*-Test—Pretest-Posttest Levels of Depression

Levels of Depression	N	$\overline{X}$	SD	t	p^+
Experiment					
Pretest	15	24.33	2.13	21.97	.000
Posttest	15	14.40	.99		
Control					
Pretest	15	22.73	2.28	1.45	.085
Posttest	15	22.27	2.91		

+One-tailed *p*, df = 14

Table 10.10:   Results of the Dependent *t*-Test—Research Methods' Final Grades

Variable	N	$\overline{X}$	SD	*t*	*p*[+]
Final grades					
Previous grades	30	65.37	12.55	−7.63	.000
Current grades	30	76.90	9.73		

[+]One-tailed *p*, df = 29

or two-tailed hypothesis. Tables 10.9 and 10.10 present results of the dependent *t*-test for both examples.

SUMMARY

This chapter introduced the dependent *t*-test and the Wilcoxon signed ranks test. These tests provide another statistical way for social work practitioners to evaluate their practice and the effectiveness of their group therapy. These tests are most suitable to examine changes in subjects' behavior over time (e.g., before and after a treatment or a therapy is completed).

The chapter presented and discussed the purpose and assumptions of the dependent *t*-test and its corresponding nonparametric Wilcoxon signed ranks test. The chapter then presented two research examples illustrating the use of the dependent *t*-test and the Wilcoxon signed ranks test. The first illustrated use of these tests with two repeated measures (pretest and posttest); the second illustrated use of the tests with two matched samples. The chapter also discussed how to use SPSS to compute the dependent *t*-test and the Wilcoxon signed ranks test. We ended with two practical examples describing how to interpret the results of the dependent *t*-test and Wilcoxon signed ranks test and how to write and present results in a summary table.

The next chapter introduces the contingency table and the chi-square test. The chapter will define the contingency table, the difference between observed and expected frequencies, and discuss the purpose of the chi-square test. The type of data to use with the chi-square test, assumptions underlying the test, and the difference between the phi and Cramer's V coefficients are presented. The chapter will also discuss how to compute the statistics, interpret the output, and write and present the results of the chi-square.

PRACTICAL EXERCISES

A social work clinician claims that his newly developed psychosocial therapy helps individuals to reduce their anxiety levels. To examine this claim, the clinician randomly selects 30 battered women from local area shelters. All women completed a standardized anxiety scale prior to the therapy (baseline), then participated in a 12-week group therapy session aimed to decrease their levels of anxiety. After the therapy was completed, all women completed the anxiety scale (after 3 months).

As a followup, the women were again asked to complete the anxiety scale three months after the therapy was completed (after 6 months). The scores range between 30 and 120, with high scores indicating higher levels of anxiety.

The following are the women's scores on the anxiety scale at the baseline, after 3 months, and after 6 months.

Baseline	After 3 months	After 6 months
69	64	56
89	91	79
81	77	68
71	69	59
75	77	64
86	88	74
86	85	73
69	64	47
100	98	78
85	77	61
93	86	68
87	77	64
76	67	53
95	85	71
97	79	61
89	77	57
83	65	49
100	93	71
94	83	61
92	75	58
92	74	58
75	65	60
80	64	55
86	68	38
88	75	65
76	56	45
89	80	70
70	60	55
91	75	65
95	80	60

Enter these data in an SPSS data file, then answer the following two research questions:

I.   Is there a significant decrease in women's levels of anxiety after 3 months?

II. Is there a significant decrease in women's levels of anxiety after 6 months?

For each research question, answer the following:

1. State a one-tailed research hypothesis.

2. Set the criteria for rejecting the null hypothesis.

3. Select the appropriate statistical test.

    a. State your rationale for selecting this test.

    b. What is the alternative test?

4. Use SPSS to run the analysis.

5. Based on the analysis, what is your conclusion?

6. Is the therapy effective? Why?

7. Present the results in an APA-style summary table.

CHAPTER 11

Association between
Two Categorical Variables:
Chi-Square Test of Association

LEARNING OBJECTIVES

1. Understand the contingency table
2. Understand the purpose of the chi-square test
3. Understand the difference between observed and expected frequencies
4. Understand the assumptions underlying the chi-square test
5. Understand the phi and Cramer's V coefficients
6. Understand how to use SPSS to create a contingency table and compute the statistics and levels of significance
7. Understand how to interpret and present the results the test

Data Sets: *Depression-Welfare, Job Satisfaction* (appendix A)

INTRODUCTION

So far in this book we have presented four bivariate parametric and four nonparametric tests that examine the relationships between one independent variable and one dependent variable. Tests such as the independent *t*-test, Mann-Whitney U, one-way ANOVA, and Kruskal-Wallis require a categorical independent variable (nominal), while others such as the Pearson *r*, Spearman rho, dependent *t*-test, and Wilcoxon test require a continuous independent variable (ordinal or higher). All these tests require that the dependent variable is continuous data, measured at the ordinal level of measurement or higher. None of these tests is appropriate when the dependent variable consists of categorical data; that is, nominal variables.

Sometimes, however, social workers may be interested to examine the relationship between categorical variables, for example, a social work administrator who wishes to examine the relationship between social workers' race and their level of education. The administrator mailed self-addressed and stamped surveys to 1500 social workers in five states. Among the questions in the survey, the administrator asked social workers to indicate their race (Are you: 1 = White; 2 = African American; 3 = Hispanic; 4 = Other) and whether they have undergraduate, graduate, or PhD degrees in social work (Do you have: 1 = BSW; 2 = MSW, 3 = PhD?). How would the administrator analyze the responses and test the hypothesis of the relationship between race and levels of education?

This chapter defines the contingency table and the difference between observed and expected frequencies. The chapter presents the chi-square test of association, its purpose, and underlying assumptions, as well as the phi and Cramer's V coefficients and the difference between them. Two practical examples illustrate how to create a contingency table and compute chi-square statistics and levels of significance in SPSS. The chapter also discusses how to interpret, write, and present the results of a contingency table and chi-square test.

CONTINGENCY TABLE

A contingency table, also called a cross-tabs table, cross-tabulation, or a chi-square table, is a frequency table that presents the observed frequencies of one categorical variable (dependent variable) as a function of another categorical variable (independent variable). A contingency table presents the frequencies of two categorical variables simultaneously (e.g., levels of education by race).

How to Construct a Contingency Table

To construct a contingency table, first list all the values (groups) in the first variable in the rows of the table (also called row variable) and the values (groups) in the second variable in the columns (also called column variable). Second, find the frequency for each cell (intersection). Third, sum all cell frequencies for each row and place it in the corresponding row margin. Fourth, sum all cell frequencies for each column and place it in the corresponding column margin. Fifth, sum all row margins as well as all column margins. The sum of all row margins and the sum of all column margins each should equal the number of all cases in the sample size (N).

Example: Table 11.1 displays the frequencies for levels of education by race. Education is defined as BSW, MSW, and PhD, and race is defined as W (White), AFA (African American), HS (Hispanic), and OT (Others).

Levels of education are placed in three rows and levels of race are placed in four columns. The fourth row in table 11.1 displays the total column margins (C_1, C_2, C_3, and C_4) and the fifth column displays the total row margins (R_1, R_2, and R_3). The joint cell of both Totals (N) displays the total number of cases in the study, the sample size.

Table 11.1:   Contingency Table—Levels of Education by Race

	W	AFA	HS	OT	Total
BSW	O_1	O_2	O_3	O_4	$R_1 = N_{BSW}$
MSW	O_5	O_6	O_7	O_8	$R_2 = N_{MSW}$
PhD	O_9	O_{10}	O_{11}	O_{12}	$R_3 = N_{PhD}$
Total	$C_1 = N_W$	$C_2 = N_{AFA}$	$C_3 = N_{HS}$	$C_4 = N_{OT}$	N

O = observed frequency; R = row margin; C = column margin; N = sample size

Each joint cell in table 11.1 displays the frequency for only one level of education by only one race. For example, the joint cell of W and BSW displays the number of Whites who have a BSW (O_1), and the joint cell of HS and PhD displays the number of Hispanics who have a PhD (O_{11}).

Number of Cells

The number of cells in a contingency table is determined by multiplying the number of levels (groups) in the first variable (number of rows) by the number of levels (groups) in the second variable (number of columns). In our example, because education has 3 levels and race has 4 levels, the number of cells is 12 cells ($3 \times 4 = 12$). The number of rows and columns is used to label a contingency table; in this example, a 3×4 table.

Row and Column Margins

Each *row margin* represents the total number of cases within a particular row. For example, R_1 (N_{BSW}) represents the first row margin; the number of all participants who have a BSW ($R_1 = O_1 + O_2 + O_3 + O_4$). R_2 (N_{MSW}) represents the second row margin; the number of all participants who have a MSW ($R_2 = O_5 + O_6 + O_7 + O_8$), and R_3 (N_{PhD}) represents the third row margin; the number of all participants who have a PhD ($R_3 = O_9 + O_{10} + O_{11} + O_{12}$). The sum of R_1, R_2, and R_3 is equal to the number of all cases in the study (N).

The same explanation applies to columns. Each *column margin* represents the total number of cases within a particular column. For example, C_1 (N_W) represents the first column margin; the number of all participants who are White ($C_1 = O_1 + O_5 + O_9$), C_2 (N_{AFA}) represents the second column margin; the number of all participants who are African American ($C_2 = O_2 + O_6 + O_{10}$), and so on. The sum of C_1, C_2, C_3, and C_4 is equal to the number of all cases in the study (N).

Row, Column, and Total Percentages

Sometimes, along with the observed frequencies, it is useful to present the row, column, and total percentages for each cell. Table 11.2 is an extension of table 11.1. In table 11.2, O stands for the observed frequency, RP stands for row per-

Table 11.2:   Contingency Table—Levels of Education by Race

	W	AFA	HS	OT	Total
BSW	O_1	O_2	O_3	O_4	O_{BSW}
	RP_1	RP_2	RP_3	RP_4	RP_{BSW}
	CP_1	CP_2	CP_3	CP_4	CP_{BSW}
	TP_1	TP_2	TP_3	TP_4	TP_{BSW}
MSW	O_5	O_6	O_7	O_8	O_{MSW}
	RP_5	RP_6	RP_7	RP_8	RP_{MSW}
	CP_5	CP_6	CP_7	CP_8	CP_{MSW}
	TP_5	TP_6	TP_7	TP_8	TP_{MSW}
PhD	O_9	O_{10}	O_{11}	O_{12}	O_{PhD}
	RP_9	RP_{10}	RP_{11}	RP_{12}	RP_{PhD}
	CP_9	CP_{10}	CP_{11}	CP_{12}	CP_{PhD}
	TP_9	TP_{10}	TP_{11}	TP_{12}	TP_{PhD}
Total	O_W	N_{AFA}	N_{HS}	N_{OT}	N
	RP_W	RP_{AFA}	RP_{HS}	RP_{OT}	RP_N
	CP_W	CP_{AFA}	CP_{HS}	CP_{OT}	CP_N
	TP_W	TP_{AFA}	TP_{HS}	TP_{OT}	TP_N

centage, CP stands for column percentage, TP stands for total percentage, and N stands for the overall number of cases in the study.

The row percentage (RP) conveys the percentage of cases in a particular cell within the corresponding row (row margin). For example, in table 11.2 RP_1 conveys the percentage of participants with a BSW who are White, RP_7 conveys the percentage of participants with a MSW who are Hispanic, and RP_{12} conveys the percentage of participants with a PhD who are Other.

> To compute the row percentage, divide the number of cases in a particular cell by the corresponding row margin and multiply it by 100%.

The column percentage (CP) conveys the percentage of cases in a particular cell within the corresponding column (column margin). For example, CP_2 in table 11.2 conveys the percentage of African-Americans who have a BSW, CP_5 conveys the percentage of Whites who have a MSW, and CP_{11} conveys the percentage of Hispanics who have a PhD.

> To compute the column percentage, divide the number of cases in a particular cell by the corresponding column margin and multiply it by 100%.

The total percentage (TP) conveys the percentage of cases in a particular cell of the total number of cases in the study (N). For example, TP_3 in table 11.2 conveys the overall percentage of Hispanics with a BSW, TP_6 conveys the overall percentage of African-Americans with a MSW, and TP_9 conveys the overall percentage of Whites with a PhD.

> To compute the total percentage, divide the number of cases in a particular cell by the sample size (N) and multiply it by 100%.

Example: To illustrate the observed frequency, row, column, and total percentages, use the variables levels of education and depression from the *Depression-Welfare* study (appendix A). In this study, education was classified as less than high school or high school or higher (two levels); depression was categorized as Depressed or Not Depressed (two levels).

Table 11.3 displays the frequencies and percentages of levels of education by depression. In this table, two rows correspond with the two levels of education and two columns correspond with the two levels of depression, forming a 2×2 table (4 cells).

Each row in table 11.3 has four lines. The first line *Count* represents the observed frequency (O) for the particular cell. For example, the frequency of the first joint cell, Less than high school and Not depressed, is 4. Of the 107 participants in the study, 4 have less than high school education and are not depressed, while 10 participants have less than high school education and are depressed according to the second joint cell, Less than high school and Depressed. The third joint cell, High school or higher and Not depressed, shows that 59 participants have high school or higher education and are not depressed, compared to 34 participants who have high school or higher education and are depressed according to the fourth joint cell, High school or higher and Depressed.

Table 11.3: Contingency Table—Levels of Education by Depression

		Depression		
		Not depressed	Depressed	Total
Less than high school	Count	4	10	14
	% within Education	28.6%	71.4%	100.0%
	% within Depression	6.3%	22.7%	13.1%
	% of Total	3.7%	9.3%	13.1%
High school or higher	Count	59	34	93
	% within Education	63.4%	36.6%	100.0%
	% within Depression	93.7%	77.3%	86.9%
	% of Total	55.1%	31.8%	86.9%
Total	Count	63	44	107
	% within Education	58.9%	41.1%	100.0%
	% within Depression	100.0%	100.0%	100.0%
	% of Total	58.9%	41.1%	100.0%

The second line % *within Education* represents the row percentage. This conveys the percentage of cases in a particular cell within the corresponding level of education. For example, the second line in the second joint cell, Less than high school and Depressed, indicates that 71.4% of all participants who have less than high school education are depressed. That is:

$$\text{row percentage} = \frac{10}{14} \times 100\% = .714 \times 100\% = 71.4\%$$

The third line % *within Depression* represents the column percentage. This conveys the percentage of cases in a particular cell within the corresponding level of depression. For example, the third line in the third joint cell, High school or higher and Not depressed, indicates that 93.7% of all participants who are not depressed have high school or higher education. That is:

$$\text{column percentage} = \frac{59}{63} \times 100\% = .937 \times 100\% = 93.7\%$$

The fourth line % *of Total* represents the total percentage. This conveys the percentage of cases in a particular cell of the total number of cases (N = 107). For example, the fourth line in the fourth joint cell, High school or higher and Depressed indicates that 31.8% of all participants have high school or higher education and are depressed. That is:

$$\text{total percentage} = \frac{34}{107} \times 100\% = .318 \times 100\% = 31.8\%$$

The table also displays the total count and percentages for the rows and the total count and percentages for the columns. The joint cell, Less than high school and Total (third column), shows that, overall, 14 (14/107 = 13.1%) of participants have less than high school education. The joint cell, High school or higher and Total, shows that, overall, 93 (93/107 = 86.9%) of participants have high school or higher education.

The joint cell, Not depressed and Total (third row), shows that, overall, 63 (63/107 = 58.9%) of participants are not depressed and the joint cell, Depressed and Total row, shows that, overall, 44 (44/107 = 41.1%) of participants are depressed.

Observed and Expected Frequencies

Observed frequencies (O) are the actual number of cases in each cell obtained by direct observation of a sample presumed to represent the population from which it is selected.

Expected frequencies (E) are the frequencies or number of cases in each cell that the researcher would expect if the row and column variables were unrelated. That is, they are the frequencies the researcher expects if the null hypothesis is correct.

Unlike observed frequencies, expected frequencies are hypothetical numbers, estimated by using the actual row and column margins and the total sample size from a contingency table.

To illustrate computation of expected frequencies (E), use the observed frequencies of levels of education and depression from table 11.3. Table 11.4 is similar to table 11.3; it displays the observed O frequencies, but does not present row, column, and total percentages.

The expected frequency for each cell is computed simply by multiplying the corresponding row margin by the corresponding column margin for each cell and dividing the product by the total number of cases (N). The formula for the expected frequency is as follows:

$$\text{Formula: } E_i = \frac{R_i \times C_i}{N}$$

E_i = expected frequency for a particular cell
R_i = row margin for the corresponding cell
C_i = column margin for the corresponding cell
N = sample size

Computing the expected frequencies for table 11.4:

$$E_1 = \frac{R_1 \times C_1}{N} = \frac{14 \times 63}{107} = 8.2 \qquad E_2 = \frac{R_1 \times C_2}{N} = \frac{14 \times 44}{107} = 5.8$$

$$E_3 = \frac{R_2 \times C_1}{N} = \frac{93 \times 63}{107} = 54.8 \qquad E_4 = \frac{R_2 \times C_2}{N} = \frac{93 \times 44}{107} = 38.2$$

Table 11.4:   Observed Frequencies—Levels of Education by Depression

	Not depressed	Depressed	Total
Less than high school	$O_1 = 4$	$O_2 = 10$	$R_1 = 14$
High school or higher	$O_3 = 59$	$O_4 = 34$	$R_2 = 93$
Total	$C_1 = 63$	$C_2 = 44$	$N = 107$

Table 11.5:   Expected Frequencies—Levels of Education by Depression

	Not depressed	Depressed	Total
Less than high school	$E_1 = 8.2$	$E_2 = 5.8$	$R_1 = 14$
High school or higher	$E_3 = 54.8$	$E_4 = 38.2$	$R_2 = 93$
Total	$C_1 = 63$	$C_2 = 44$	$N = 107$

Table 11.5 displays the expected frequencies for levels of education and depression. Comparing these frequencies to the observed frequencies presented in table 11.4 shows differences between the observed and expected frequencies. Are they statistically significant? The chi-square test of association addresses this question.

CHI-SQUARE TEST

Purpose

The chi-square (pronounced "kai") test is a bivariate test and probably the most used nonparametric test in social work research. It is symbolized by the Greek letter χ^2. It is used to examine whether the observed frequencies of a contingency table of a sample are similar to those expected in the population from which the sample is selected. It compares the observed frequency in each cell with its corresponding expected frequency. The larger the difference between the observed and expected frequencies, the larger the chi-square value and the smaller the level of significance.

The chi-square test can be used to examine if the observed joint frequencies of levels of education and levels of depression in the previous example are significantly different from the expected frequencies of these variables in the population from which the sample was drawn. Is there a significant statistical association between levels of education and levels of depression?

The chi-square test is an alternative test to the Anderson-Darling and the Kolmogorov-Simirnov goodness of fit tests (not covered in this book), which are used with continuous distributions.

Assumptions

As stated earlier, chi-square is a nonparametric test. Thus, it does not follow the assumptions for parametric tests. Data need not be continuous nor approach the shape of a normal curve. The chi-square test requires the following assumptions:

1. All statistical tests, whether parametric and nonparametric, require that the sample be representative of the population from which it is selected and to which generalizations will be made.

2. The dependent and independent variables must be measured at the nominal level. Each variable must have at least two mutually exclusive and exhaustive levels, or groups (each subject or case must be in only one cell).

3. The two variables must be independent one from another; that is, a response to one variable has nothing to do with a response to the other variable.

4. Unlike the previous tests, data analyzed by a chi-square test must be frequencies (number of cases for each joint cell), not scores. As you may recall, all previous tests examine the relationship between means (parametric tests) or mean ranks (nonparametric tests).

5. As a rule of thumb, no more than 20% of cells should have expected frequencies of less than 5 cases per cell. For example, in a 3×5 table (15 cells) no more than 3 cells (15 × 20%) should have expected frequencies less than 5 cases. All other cells (12 cells) should have a minimum of 5 cases per cell. In a 2×2 table, however, all cells must have expected frequencies of 5 cases or more per cell; that is, a sample size of at least 20 cases is needed to analyze a 2×2 table.

Because there is no alternative test to the chi-square, it is recommended to collapse small cells together when more than 20% of cells have expected frequencies less than 5 cases per cell. It is also recommended to use the Fisher exact test to examine the association between two dichotomous variables (2×2 tables). Fisher exact test is most appropriate with a small sample size and small expected frequencies.

Measures of Association

Like the Pearson correlation test, when the chi-square test reveals significant results, it is necessary to examine the strength of the association, or relationship between the independent and dependent variables; in other words, the variance in the dependent variable that is accounted for by the independent variable.

Two measures of association are produced simultaneously with chi-square test statistics. These are the phi and Cramer's V coefficients, which are both interpreted in the same way as the Pearson correlation coefficient (see chapter 7). Both coefficients convey the simple correlation between the independent and dependent variables. Squaring the phi or Cramer's V coefficients is interpreted in the same way as the coefficient of determination (r^2).

(phi)^2 or (Cramer's V)^2 = percentage of variance in the dependent variable that is accounted for by the independent variable

---

The difference between the phi and Cramer's V is simple. Phi is used to convey the correlation between two dichotomous variables, where each variable has only two groups: a 2×2 table. The Cramer's V is used with all other contingency tables such as 2×3, 2×4, 3×3, 3×4 tables, and so on. Report the phi or the Cramer's V only if the results of the chi-square test are significant.

PRACTICAL EXAMPLES

Use SPSS to generate a contingency table that displays the observed and expected frequencies, row, column, and total percentages, chi-square and p values, and measures of association. Two examples will be presented: the first example will present a chi-square analysis for a 2×2 table (the association between levels of education and depression from the previous example). The second example will present a chi-square analysis for a 2×3 table (the association between region of employment and ethnicity from the *Job Satisfaction* SPSS data file).

Example 1—A 2×2 Table

Use the data from the SPSS *Depression-Welfare* data file (appendix A) to examine the following research question:

> Is there a significant association between levels of education and levels of depression among welfare recipients?

Step 1: State the null and alternative hypotheses.

H_0: There is no significant association between levels of education and levels of depression among welfare recipients (in other words, the two variables are independent in the population).

H_a: There is a significant association between levels of education and levels of depression among welfare recipients (in other words, the two variables are dependent, or related, in the population).

This is a two-tailed research hypothesis in which depression (**DEPRESS**) is the dependent variable and education (**EDUCAT**) is the independent variable.

Step 2: Set the criteria for rejecting the null hypothesis.
Set alpha at .05 ($\alpha = .05$). Reject H_0 only if $p \le .05$.

Step 3: Select the appropriate statistical test.
Before beginning the statistical analysis, examine the type of data:

a.   The independent variable (levels of education) and the dependent variable (levels of depression) are nominal levels of measurement.

b.   The dependent variable has two levels (0 = Not depressed; 1 = Depressed). The independent variable also has two levels (0 = Less than high school; 1 = High school or higher). The two variables thus form a 2×2 table or 4 joint cells.

c.   A sample size of at least 20 cases is needed to utilize the chi-square test to analyze a 2×2 table. In our example, the sample size is 107 subjects, which is large enough to conduct any bivariate statistics.

d.   The data under analysis are the frequencies for levels of depression by levels of education.

e.   It appears that the data meet all assumptions for the chi-square test. Utilize it to examine the association between the two nominal variables. Because this is a 2×2 table, use the phi measure of association to examine the strength of the relationship between the two variables only if the chi-square test reveals significant results.

Step 4: Compute the test statistic (Use SPSS).

Depending on what SPSS commands are requested, instruct SPSS to generate four tables for the chi-square test. The first table is Case Processing Summary, the second is Cross-Tabulation, the third is Chi-Square Tests, and the fourth is Symmetric Measures. These tables present the number of valid and missing cases, the contingency table, the chi-square and levels of significance, and the phi and Cramer's V measures of association. The chi-square table also evaluates whether the data meet the assumption of expected frequencies.

How to Produce a Contingency Table and Chi-Square Test in SPSS. In our example, the independent variable is levels of education (**EDUCAT**) and the dependent variable is levels of depression (**DEPRESS**).

To run a contingency table and a chi-square test in SPSS, follow these steps:

a.   Open the SPSS *Depression-Welfare* data file.

b.   Click on *Analyze* in the SPSS main toolbar, click on *Descriptive Statistics,* and click on *Crosstabs* (screen 11.1).

Screen 11.1:   SPSS *Crosstabs* Main Menu

Screen 11.2:   SPSS *Crosstabs: Statistics* Dialog box

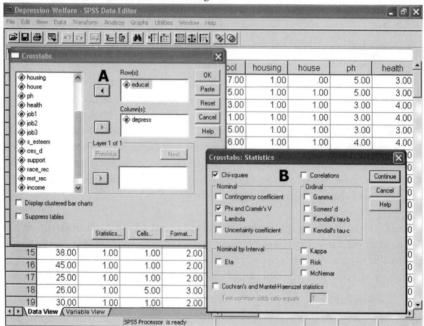

c.   A dialog box called *Crosstabs* will open (screen 11.2.A).

d.   Scroll down in the variables list, click on **EDUCAT,** and click on the upper arrow button to move it in the *Row(s)* box.

e.   Scroll down in the variables list, click on **DEPRESS,** and click on the middle arrow button to move it in the *Column(s)* box.

f.   Click on *Statistics.* A new dialog box called *Crosstabs: Statistics* will open (screen 11.2.B).

g.   Check *chi-square.*

h.   Check *phi* and *Cramer's V* under *Nominal.*

i.   Click on *Continue.*

j.   Click on *Cells.* A new dialog box called *Crosstabs: Cell Display* will open (screen 11.3.B).

k.   Check *Expected* under *Counts* (*Observed* is checked by default. If not checked, do so).

l.   Check *Row, Column, and Total* under *Percentages.*

m.   Click on *Continue* and click on *OK.*

Screen 11.3:   SPSS *Crosstabs: Cell Display* Dialog Box

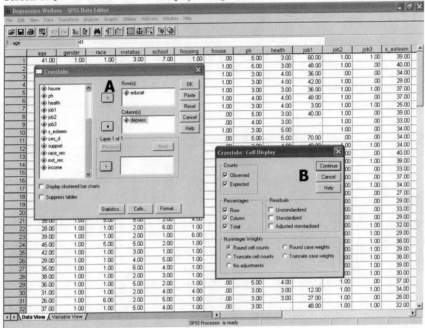

SPSS syntax for contingency table and chi-square:

CROSSTABS
/TABLES=EDUCAT BY DEPRESS
/FORMAT=AVALUE TABLES
/STATISTIC=CHISQ CC
/CELLS=COUNT EXPECTED ROW COLUMN TOTAL.

Interpreting the Output.   The following output presents the results of the chi-square analysis generated by SPSS. They include four tables (table 11.6, 11.7, 11.8, and 11.9).

Table 11.6 displays the number of valid, missing, and total cases and their respective percentages. The valid number is the number of cases included in the analysis. The missing number is the number of cases excluded from the analysis due to missing data in one or both variables. The total number is the number of all participants in the study. As the table shows, there are 107 cases in this analysis, none of which has missing data. Thus, all cases are included in the analysis (N = 107).

Table 11.7 is a 2×2 contingency table. It has two rows and two columns. Each row has 5 lines in which each line provides valuable information.

Table 11.6:   Case Processing Summary

	Cases					
	Valid		Missing		Total	
	N	Percent	N	Percent	N	Percent
EDUCAT (Level of Education)* depress	107	100%	0	.0%	107	100%

Table 11.7:   A 2×2 Contingency Table—Depression by Education

			DEPRESS (Depression)		
			.00 Not depressed	1.00 Depressed	Total
EDUCAT (Level of Education)	.00 Less than high school	Count	4	10	14
		Expected count	8.2	5.8	14.0
		% within EDUCAT (Level of Education)	28.6%	71.4%	100%
		% within DEPRESS (Depression)	6.3%	22.7%	13.1%
		% of Total	3.7%	9.3%	13.1%
	1.00 High school or higher	Count	59	34	93
		Expected count	54.8	38.2	93.0
		% within EDUCAT (Level of Education)	63.4%	36.6%	100.0%
		% within DEPRESS (Depression)	93.7%	77.3%	86.9%
		% of Total	55.1%	31.8%	86.9%
Total		Count	63	44	107
		Expected count	63.0	44.0	107.0
		% within EDUCAT (Level of Education)	58.9%	41.1%	100%
		% within DEPRESS (Depression)	100%	100%	100%
		% of Total	58.9%	41.1%	100%

The **first line**, *Count,* displays the observed frequencies. These are the same frequencies discussed in table 11.4.

The **second line**, *Expected count,* displays the expected frequencies. These are the same expected frequencies computed and presented in table 11.5.

The **third line**, *% within EDUCAT (Level of Education)*, displays the row percentage. The table shows that 28.6% of all participants who have less than high school education (14 participants) are not depressed (joint cell of Less than high school and Not depressed). On the other hand, 71.4% of all participants who have less than high school education are depressed. The table also shows that 63.4% of all participants who have high school or higher education are not depressed (joint cell of High school or higher and Depressed), compared to 36.6% of all participants who have high school or higher education and are depressed.

The **fourth line,** % *within* **DEPRESS** *(Depression),* displays the column percentage. The table shows that only 6.3% of all participants who are not depressed (63 participants) have less than high school education (joint cell of Less than high school and Not depressed). On the other hand, 93.7% of all participants who are not depressed have high school or higher education. The table also shows that 22.7% of all participants who are depressed (44 participants) have less than high school education (joint cell of Less than high school and Depressed), compared to 77.3% of all participants who are depressed that have high school or higher education.

The **fifth line,** % *of Total,* displays the total percentage. The table shows that only 3.7% of all participants (N = 107) have less than high school education and are not depressed (joint cell of Less than high school and Not depressed), compared to 9.3% of all participants who have less than high school education and are depressed. On the other hand, 55.1% of all participants have high school education and are not depressed, compared to 31.8% who are depressed and have high school or higher education.

Overall, 58.9% of all participants are not depressed (% *of Total* for joint cell of Not depressed and first Total column), compared to 41.1% of all participants who are depressed. Also, overall, 13.1% of all participants have less than high school education (% *of Total* for joint cell of Less than high school and first Total row), compared to 86.9% of all participants who have high school or higher education.

Table 11.8 displays the results of the chi-square test. This table examines whether there is a significant statistical difference between the observed frequencies and the expected frequencies. Table 11.8 has 6 rows. The number of rows will be smaller for tables that are greater than 2×2; see practical example 2).

Table 11.8: Results of Chi-Square Test

	Value	df	Asymp. Sig. (2-sided)	Exact Sig. (2-sided)	Exact Sig. (1-sided)
Pearson chi-square	6.111[b]	1	.013		
Continuity correction[a]	4.755	1	.029		
Likelihood ratio	6.069	1	.014		
Fisher exact test				.019	.015
Linear-by-linear association	6.054	1	.014		
N of valid cases	107				

[a]Computed only for a 2×2 table

[b]0 cells (.0%) have expected count less than 5. The minimum expected count is 5.76.

The **first row**, *Pearson chi-square*, displays the value (χ^2), degrees of freedom (df), and the level of significance (*p* value) for the chi-square test. The chi-square value is 6.11 with one degree of freedom[1] and a *p* value of .013 (two-tailed *p*), which is smaller than alpha of .05. The footnote "b" at the lower left side of the chi-square table shows that 0 cells (0%) have an expected count (frequency) of less than 5. The minimum expected count is 5.76. The data met the assumption of sample size; 5 cases per cell for a 2×2 table.

The **second row**, *Continuity correction*, displays the value, degrees of freedom, and level of significance for the continuity correction formula (not covered in this book). This is only computed for a 2×2 table to improve the approximation of the chi-square test. The corrected chi-square value is always smaller than the uncorrected chi-square value. In this case, the corrected chi-square value is 4.76, with 1 degree of freedom and a *p* value of .029 ($p < .05$).

The **third row**, *Likelihood ratio*, displays the value, degrees of freedom, and level of significance for the likelihood ratio test (not covered in this book). This test is similar to the chi-square test. It is useful for smaller sample sizes. The likelihood ratio and chi-square tests are equivalent when used with large sample sizes. The table shows that the likelihood value is 6.069 with 1 degree of freedom and a *p* value of .014 ($p < .05$).

The **fourth row**, *Fisher exact test*, only displays one-tailed and two-tailed levels of significance for the Fisher exact test. This test is only appropriate for 2×2 tables and with small sample sizes. The table shows that the two-tailed *p* value (fifth column, *Exact Sig. 2-sided*) is .019 ($p < .05$).

The **fifth row**, *Linear-by-linear association*, displays the value, degrees of freedom, and levels of significance for a linear-by-linear association (not covered in this book). This test is also known as the Mantel-Haenszel chi-square test. It is not appropriate for use with nominal variables.

The **sixth row**, N *of valid cases*, displays the number of valid cases in the analysis. In this case, the sample includes 107 cases.

To conclude, Table 11.8 provides the results of various statistical techniques. While all results in this table show significant association between the two variables under analysis ($p < .05$), we are only interested in the results of the chi-square test, the first row.

Because the results of the chi-square test presented in table 11.8 show a significant association between levels of education and levels of depression ($p < .05$), it is recommended to examine the strength of this association. Table 11.9 presents the results of phi and Cramer's V measures of association. It has three rows, phi, Cramer's V, and N.

In this case, because this is a 2×2 table, examine the phi coefficient. Table 11.9 shows that the correlation coefficient between levels of education and levels

---

[1]Degrees of freedom for a chi-square test = (number of rows − 1) × (number of columns − 1). In our example, there are two rows and two columns: df = (2 − 1) × (2 − 1) = 1.

Table 11.9:   Measures of Association

	Symmetric Measures		
		Value	Approx. Sig.
Nominal by nominal	phi	−.239	.013
	Cramer's V	.239	.013
	N of valid cases	107	

[a]Not assuming the null hypothesis
[b]Using the asymptotic standard error assuming the null hypothesis

of depression is −.24 (phi = −.239). The minus sign indicates that the two variables have a negative correlation; that is, the higher the level of education (0 = Less than high school; 1 = High school or higher), the lower the level of depression (1 = Depressed; 0 = Not depressed). This value is significant at alpha of .05 ($p = .013$).

Squaring the phi coefficient produces the variance in levels of depression that is accounted for by levels of education. That is, $(phi)^2 = (−.24)^2 = .0576 = 5.76\%$, which is considered a weak relationship (see chapter 7).

Step 5: Decide whether to reject the null hypothesis.
The results of the chi-square presented in table 11.8 show a significant association between levels of education and levels of depression ($p < .05$). Therefore, reject the null hypothesis.

Writing the Results

As with all other tests, when writing the results of the chi-square test, report the test statistic (χ^2), degrees of freedom, and the p value. If the results of the chi-square are significant, then report the results of the phi or Cramer's V and the frequencies of cells that appear to be significantly different. In our example, the results are as follows:

The chi-square test of association was run to examine the association between levels of education and levels of depression. The results show a *significant association* between the two variables ($\chi^2_{(df=1)} = 6.11; p < .05$). In other words, these results indicate that levels of education and levels of depression are related in the population.

The results of the contingency table show that the number of participants with less than high school education who are not depressed (n = 4) is less than expected (n = 8.2). It also shows that the number of participants with high school or higher education who are not depressed (n = 59) is higher than expected (n = 54.8). On the other hand, the number of participants with less than high school education who are depressed (n = 10) is higher than expected (n = 5.8), while the number of participants with high school or higher education who are depressed (n = 34) is less than expected (n = 38.2).

The phi coefficient indicates that levels of education explain only 5.76% of the variance in levels of depression, which indicates that the two variables have a weak relationship. In other words, more than 94% of the variance in depression is unaccounted for.

Example 2—A 2×3 Table

Use the data from the SPSS *Job Satisfaction* data file (appendix A) to examine the following research question:

Is there a significant association between social workers' ethnicity (Jews vs. Arabs) and their region of employment (North, Center, South Region)?

Step 1: State the null and alternative hypotheses.

H_o: There is no significant association between social workers' ethnicity and their region of employment.

H_a: There is a significant association between social workers' ethnicity and their region of employment.

In this two-tailed research hypothesis, region of employment (**D8**) is the dependent variable and ethnicity (**D6**) is the independent variable.

Step 2: Set the criteria for rejecting the null hypothesis.
Set alpha at .05 ($\alpha = .05$). Reject H_0 only if $p \leq .05$.

Step 3: Select the appropriate statistical test.

a.   The independent variable (ethnicity) and the dependent variable (region) are measured at the nominal level of measurement (categorical data).

b.   The dependent variable has three levels (1 = North, 2 = Center, 3 = South). The independent variable has two levels (0 = Jews; 1 = Arabs). The two variables form a 2×3 table, or 6 joint cells.

c.   To undertake a chi-square test, no more than 1 cell (6 cells × 20% = 1.2) should have an expected frequency of less than 5. In other words, 5 cells should have an expected frequency of at least 5 cases. The sample should have a minimum of 25 cases (5 cells × 5 cases). In this example, the sample size is 218 cases, which is large enough to conduct the chi-square test.

d.   The data to be analyzed are the frequencies for region of employment by ethnicity.

e.   It appears the data meet all assumptions for the chi-square test. Therefore, utilize the chi-square test to examine the association between the two nominal variables. Because this is a 2×3 table, use the Cramer's V measure of association to examine the strength of the relationship between the two variables, only if the chi-square test finds significant results.

Step 4: Compute the test statistic (Use SPSS).
Use SPSS to create a contingency table and compute the expected frequen-

Table 11.10:   Case Processing Summary

	Cases					
	Valid		Missing		Total	
	N	Percent	N	Percent	N	Percent
D8 (Region); D6 (Ethnicity)	217	99.5%	1	.5%	218	100%

cies, chi-square value, level of significance, and the Cramer's V coefficient. These results are presented in tables 11.10 through 11.13.

Table 11.10 shows that 218 subjects participated in the study (*Total*). Of them, only 1 subject is considered missing. This means that 1 subject did not indicate ethnicity, region, or both. Thus, 217 cases are valid (N = 217).

Table 11.11 is a 2×3 contingency table. It has three rows (North, Center, and South) and two columns (Jews and Arabs). As with table 11.7, each row has 5 lines.

To explain this table, we will only discuss two joint cells. The joint cell, *North* and *Jews,* shows that 19 Jewish social workers are employed in the Northern region, which is smaller than expected (n = 34.7; second line). This represents

Table 11.11:   A 2×3 Contingency Table—Region of Employment by Ethnicity

			D6 (Ethnicity)		
			.00 Jews	1.00 Arabs	Total
D8 (Region)	1.00 North	Count	19	33	52
		Expected count	34.7	17.3	52.0
		% within D8 (Region)	36.5%	63.5%	100.0%
		% within D6 (Ethnicity)	13.1%	45.8%	24.0%
		% of Total	8.8%	15.2%	24.0%
	2.00 Center	Count	40	21	61
		Expected count	40.8	20.2	61.0
		% within D8 (Region)	65.6%	34.4%	100.0%
		% within D6 (Ethnicity)	27.6%	29.2%	28.1%
		% of Total	18.4%	9.7%	28.1%
	3.00 South	Count	86	18	104
		Expected count	69.5	34.5	104.0
		% within D8 (Region)	82.7%	17.3%	100.0%
		% within D6 (Ethnicity)	59.3%	25.0%	47.9%
		% of Total	39.6%	8.3%	47.9%
Total		Count	145	72	217
		Expected count	145.0	72.0	217.0
		% within D8 (Region)	66.8%	33.2%	100.0%
		% within D6 (Ethnicity)	100.0%	100.0%	100.0%
		% of Total	66.8%	33.2%	100.0%

Table 11.12: Results of Chi-Square Test

	Value	df	Asymp. Sig. (2-sided)
Pearson chi-square	33.367[a]	2	.000
Likelihood ratio	33.133	2	.000
Linear-by-linear association	32.538	1	.000
N of valid cases	217		

[a]0 cells (.0%) have expected count less than 5. The minimum expected count is 17.25.

36.5% (row percentage; third line) of the total social workers employed in the Northern region (n = 52). This also represents 13.1% (column percentage; fourth line) of all Jewish social workers (n = 145), and 8.8% (total percentage; fifth line) of all social workers in the study (N = 217).

The joint cell, *South* and *Arabs,* shows that 18 Arab social workers are employed in the Southern region, which is also smaller than expected (n = 34.5). This represents only 17.3% of the total social workers employed in the Southern region (n = 104). This also represents 25% of all Arab social workers (n = 72), and 8.3% of all social workers in the study (N = 217).

Table 11.12 presents the results of the chi-square test. Unlike table 11.8, this table has only four rows. Notice that the continuity correction and Fisher exact tests are not presented in this table, even though we used the same SPSS commands. These two measures are produced only for 2×2 tables. All four other rows are similar to the ones presented in table 11.8. The table shows that no cell has an expected frequency of less than 5.

From this table we are only interested in the results of the chi-square, the first row (first line). The chi-square value is 33.367 ($\chi^2 = 33.37$), two degrees of freedom [(2 – 1) × (3 – 1) = 1 × 2 = 2], and a level of significance of .000 ($p = .000$).

Because the results of the chi-square are significant at alpha of .05, examine the strength of the relationship between the two variables. To do so, look at the Cramer's V, because this is not a 2×2 table but a 2×3 table.

The table shows that the correlation coefficient between region of employment and ethnicity is .24 (Cramer's V = .239). The sign (+ or –) indicates the direction of the relationship. In this case, it indicates that the two variables have a positive relationship; the higher the value in ethnicity (0 = Jews; 1 = Arabs), the

Table 11.13: Measures of Association

Symmetric Measures			
		Value	Approx. Sig.
Nominal by nominal	phi	−.239	.013
	Cramer's V	.239	.013
N of valid cases		107	

[a]Not assuming the null hypothesis.
[b]Using the asymptotic standard error assuming the null hypothesis.

higher the value in region (1 = North; 2 = Center; 3 = South). This value is significant at alpha of .05 (Approx. Sig. = .000).

Squaring the Cramer's V coefficient indicates that only 5.76% of the variance in region is accounted for by ethnicity; that is, (Cramer's V)^2 = (.24)^2 = .0576 = 5.76%.

Step 5: Decide whether to reject the null hypothesis.

The results of the chi-square presented in table 11.12 show a significant association between social workers' ethnicity and their region of employment ($p < .05$). Therefore, reject the null hypothesis.

Writing the Results

The chi-square test of association was utilized to examine the relationship between ethnicity and region of employment. The results show a *significant association* between social workers' ethnicity and region of employment ($\chi^2_{(df=2)}$ = 33.37, $p < .05$). The two variables are related in the population.

The results of the contingency table (table 11.11) show that the number of Jewish social workers employed in the North (n = 19) is less than expected (n = 34.7), while the number of Arab social workers employed in the North (n = 33) is higher than expected (n = 17.3). The table also shows that the number of Jewish social workers employed in the South (n = 86) is higher than expected (n = 69.5), while the number of Arab social workers employed in the South (n = 18) is less than expected (n = 34.5). On the other hand, the contingency table shows that the number of Jewish and Arab social workers employed in the center region is as expected (Jewish: O = 40, E = 40.8; Arabs: O = 21, E = 20.2).

The Cramer's V coefficient, however, indicates that ethnicity explains only 5.76% of the variance in region; thus, more than 94% of the variance in region is unaccounted for.

Presentation of Results in a Summary Table

When presenting the results of the chi-square test of association in a summary table, report the observed frequency for each level in the dependent variable by each level in the independent variable; that is, the frequency for each joint cell. In addition, while researchers may have different preferences for presenting either the row percentages or the column percentages, it is recommended to present the total percentages. Report the chi-square value and the level of significance for each analysis as well.

Table 11.14 presents the results of the chi-square for the first practical example (depression by education). It shows the observed frequency and total percentage for each cell. The sum of the total percentages of all cells must equal 100%.

Table 11.15 presents results for the second practical example (region of employment by ethnicity). It also shows the observed frequency for each cell. However, unlike table 11.14, table 11.15 presents the column percentages instead of

Table 11.14:   Results of Chi-Square—Depression by Education

Variable	Not depressed		Depressed		Total		χ^2	p
	N	%	N	%	N	%		
Education								
Less than high school	4	3.7	10	9.3	14	13.1	6.11	.013
High school or higher	59	55.2	34	31.8	93	86.9		
Total	63	58.9	44	41.1	107	100.0		

Table 11.15:   Results of Chi-Square—Region of Employment by Ethnicity

Variable	Jewish		Arab		Total		χ^2	p
	N	%	N	%	N	%		
Region of Employment								
North	19	13.1	33	45.8	52	24.0	33.37	.000
Center	40	27.6	21	29.2	61	28.1		
South	86	59.3	18	25.0	104	47.9		
Total	145	100.0	72	100.0	217	100.0		

the total percentages. In this format, the sum of all column percentages within each level of column (ethnicity) must equal 100%.

SUMMARY

Unlike previous bivariate tests which examine scores, this chapter introduced another statistical test that examines the frequency observed in the sample and whether it is different than the expected frequency in the population from which the sample is selected. This is especially important for social work practitioners and researchers who are more favorable of categorical data rather than continuous data.

This chapter presented the chi-square test of association and discussed the contingency table, defined its elements, how to construct it, and how to compute the expected frequencies. The chapter then discussed the assumptions underlying the chi-square test and the type of data. Two measures of association appropriate for use once significant results are detected by the chi-square were presented: the phi and Cramer's V coefficients. Two practical examples illustrated how to use the chi-square test and how to use SPSS to create a contingency table and compute the chi-square value and level of significance. Finally, the chapter discussed how to interpret the SPSS output, write, and present the results of the contingency table and the chi-square in two different summary tables.

The final chapter in this book will introduce multiple regression analysis, an advanced statistical technique widely used among social workers to predict outcomes. The chapter will discuss the purpose of multiple regression analysis, the regression equation, and the coefficients produced by this analysis, as well as the assumptions underlying multiple regression analysis and the process in selecting variables to be entered in the analysis. The chapter will also discuss differences among forward, stepwise, and backward regression methods and how to produce the coefficients in SPSS, how to interpret the output, and how to write and present the results of multiple regression analysis.

PRACTICAL EXERCISES

I. Access the SPSS *Job Satisfaction* data file (appendix A) and use the variables Gender (**D1**) and Ethnicity (**D6**) to answer the following questions:

    1. Follow the steps of hypothesis testing to examine the null hypothesis. That is, state the null and alternative hypotheses, set the criteria for rejecting the null hypothesis, select the test statistic (why), run the analysis, and discuss your decision.

    2. Discuss the strength of the relationship between the two variables.

    3. Present the results in a summary table. Present the total percentages.

II. Access the SPSS *Depression-Elderly* data file (appendix A) and use the variables sick (**SICK**) and levels of education (**EDUCAT**) to answer the following questions:

    1. Follow the steps of hypothesis testing to examine the null hypothesis. That is, state the null and alternative hypotheses, set the criteria for rejecting the null hypothesis, select the test statistic (why), run the analysis, and discuss your decision.

    2. Discuss the strength of the relationship between the two variables.

    3. Present the results in a summary table. Present the column percentages.

    4. What percentages of participants who have some business school/college consider themselves sick?

    5. What percentages of participants who consider themselves not sick have less than high school education?

    6. What percentages of participants have high school education and considered themselves sick?

CHAPTER 12

Multiple Regression Analysis

LEARNING OBJECTIVES

1. Understand the purpose of multiple regression analysis
2. Understand the regression equation
3. Understand the coefficients of multiple regression
4. Understand the assumptions underlying multiple regression
5. Understand how to select the variables to be entered in multiple regression
6. Understand forward, stepwise, and backward regression methods
7. Understand how to use SPSS to compute the coefficients of multiple regression
8. Understand how to interpret and present the results of the test

Data Set: *Job Satisfaction* (appendix A)

INTRODUCTION

The previous six chapters presented statistical techniques that examine the overall relationship between *one* dependent variable and *one* independent variable. These techniques are known as bivariate statistics. For instance, by using the Pearson correlation coefficient or the chi-square test, researchers may determine whether independent and dependent variables are significantly correlated and how much of the variance (r^2, phi, Cramer's V, etc.) in the dependent variable can be explained by the independent variable.

However, researchers may wish to know more than whether two variables are significantly correlated. By learning certain conditions or characteristics (independent variables) in the population, researchers might be able to predict a specific outcome (dependent variable). For example, a director of a graduate school admissions office wants to predict prospective graduate students' GPA based on their undergraduate GPA, GRE score (verbal and analytical), and letters of recommendation. Prospective students with the highest predicted graduate GPA will be admitted. A social work researcher wants to predict levels of depression among welfare recipients based on their age, education, social support, and physical health. Welfare recipients with the highest predicted levels of depression will be considered for intervention. A social work administrator wants to predict levels of burnout among social work employees based on their gender, age, salary, physical environment, and workload. Social workers with the highest predicted levels of burnout will be referred for intervention.

In these three examples, the purpose is to predict a single outcome (graduate GPA, depression, or burnout) based on multiple conditions (independent variables). An early prediction of the outcome can help social work professionals and others to plan treatment or intervention strategies in advance. In such cases, bivariate statistics are no longer appropriate because the relationship among multiple independent variables and one dependent variable is being examined. Multivariate statistics will be more useful.

Multivariate statistics examine the relationship among multiple independent variables and one dependent variable, or among multiple independent variables and multiple dependent variables. Various multivariate statistical techniques exist, such as multiple regression analysis, logistic regression, multivariate analysis of variance, multivariate analysis of covariance, canonical correlation, factor analysis, and others. This book will only introduce multiple regression analysis because of its wide use among social work researchers.

This chapter discusses the purpose of multiple regression analysis and the regression equation; coefficients produced by multiple regression analysis and the underlying assumptions; and how to select variables to enter in multiple regression. The chapter describes three regression methods of data entry: forward, stepwise, and backward. How to use SPSS to compute the coefficients of multiple regression analysis, and how to interpret, write, and present the results in a summary table are also presented.

MULTIPLE REGRESSION ANALYSIS

Purpose

Multiple regression analysis is a multivariate statistical technique, an extension of the simple correlation coefficient (Pearson product-moment correlation coefficient), first used by Pearson in 1908. It is widely used in social sciences research and perhaps the most used multivariate statistical technique in social work research.

Its purpose is to examine the effect of multiple independent variables (two or more) on one dependent variable. In multiple regression analysis, the dependent variable is referred to as a *criterion* and the independent variable is referred to as a *factor* or *predictor*. The criterion is symbolized by a capital letter Y and each predictor is symbolized by a capital letter X, with a subscript that represents the number of each factor; for example, X_1 represents the first factor, X_2 represents the second factor, and X_i represents the ith factor.

Generally, multiple regression analysis estimates a model of multiple factors that best predicts the criterion. Thus, it allows researchers to answer the following general research question:

> Which set of the following factors best predicts Y: X_1, X_2, X_3, . . . X_i?
>
> Y = criterion
> X_1 = first factor; X_2 = second factor; X_3 = third factor; X_i = i^{th} factor

Example: What set of the following factors best predicts levels of depression among welfare recipients: age, marital status, race, level of education, number of years on welfare, physical health, or social support?

In this research question, levels of depression is the criterion (dependent variable) and age, marital status, race, level of education, number of years on welfare, physical health, and social support are the factors (independent variables). By using multiple regression analysis, the researcher's aim is to find out which set of these factors best predicts the levels of depression among welfare recipients. This would help social work practitioners to plan early intervention and prevention strategies for welfare recipients who are likely to experience higher levels of depression.

Regression Equation

The results of multiple regression analysis are expressed in a regression equation that represents a combination of the best factors predicting the criterion. This equation simply follows the equation of a straight line. It can be either unstandardized scores (raw scores) or standardized scores (z score). They are expressed in the following formulas:

> Unstandardized Regression Equation:
>
> $$Y = a + b_1X_1 + b_2X_2 + b_3X_3 + \ldots + b_iX_i$$
>
> Y = criterion (dependent variable)
> a = Y intercept (the value of Y when all X values are zero)
> b = unstandardized regression coefficient
> X = factors (independent variables)
>
> Standardized Regression Equation:
>
> $$Z_Y = \beta_1 Z_{X_1} + \beta_2 Z_{X_2} + \beta_3 Z_{X_3} + \ldots + \beta_i Z_{X_i}$$
>
> Z_Y = z score for criterion (dependent variable)
> β (beta) = standardized regression coefficient
> Z_X = z score for each factor (independent variable)

In the previous example, levels of depression could be expressed as follows:

1. Unstandardized Scores:

$$\text{Depression} = a + (b_1 \times \text{age}) + (b_2 \times \text{marital status}) + (b_3 \times \text{race})$$
$$+ (b_4 \times \text{education}) + (b_3 \times \text{years on welfare})$$
$$+ (b_6 \times \text{physical health}) + (b_7 \times \text{social support})$$

2. Standardized Scores:

$$Z_{\text{depression}} = (\beta_1 \times Z_{\text{age}}) + (\beta_2 \times Z_{\text{marital status}}) + (\beta_3 \times Z_{\text{race}}) + (\beta_4 \times Z_{\text{education}})$$
$$+ (\beta_5 \times Z_{\text{years on welfare}}) + (\beta_6 \times Z_{\text{physical health}}) + (\beta_7 \times Z_{\text{social support}})$$

The purpose of a multiple regression analysis is to find out which set of the seven factors best predicts depression and what their regression coefficients are.

Main Coefficients Produced by Multiple Regression Analysis

Multiple regression analysis generates coefficients that provide valuable information about the relationship between the dependent and independent variables. These include the following:

1. *Unstandardized Regression Coefficient:* This represents the regression coefficient between the criterion and one factor. It is the slope of the regression line. It represents the proportion of change in the criterion (Y) for each unit of change in the corresponding factor (X_i). It is computed based on the actual raw scores in all variables entered in the regression analysis. It is symbolized by a lowercase b.

2. *Standardized Regression Coefficient (Partial Correlation):* This represents a linear correlation coefficient between the criterion and one factor while controlling for the effect of all other factors in the analysis. It is symbolized by the Greek letter β (beta).

    Standardized regression coefficients are more desirable than the unstandardized regression coefficient (b) because they are based on transforming the raw scores of all variables to z scores, causing all variables to have the same units of measure and therefore more comparable.

    Like the Pearson correlation coefficient, beta ranges from −1.00 (perfect negative correlation) to +1.00 (perfect positive correlation). A zero coefficient indicates no correlation between the criterion and the corresponding factor.

3. *Regression Constant:* This represents the y axis intercept. It is the value of the criterion (Y) when the values of all factors (Xs) are zero (X = 0). It is symbolized by the lowercase a.

4. *Multiple Correlation Coefficient:* This represents the correlation coefficient between the criterion (Y) and *all* factors (X) entered in the regression equation. It ranges between 0 (no linear relationship) to 1 (perfect linear relationship).

It is symbolized by a capital letter R, to distinguish it from the lowercase simple correlation r.

To find the size and direction of the relationship between the criterion and each factor, simply look at the size and the sign (plus or minus) of the standardized regression coefficient (beta).

5. *Multiple R Square* (R^2): This is similar to the coefficient of determination in the Pearson correlation coefficient (r^2). It represents the proportion of the variance in the criterion (dependent variable) that is explained by the multiple factors in the regression equation. The complement of R^2, that is, $(1 - R^2)$ represents the proportion of the unexplained variance in the criterion.

Assumptions

Because multiple regression analysis is an extension of the Pearson correlation coefficient, it requires the same basic assumptions of the Pearson r.

1. The sample must represent the population from which it is selected and to which generalization will be made.

2. The criterion (dependent variable) must be continuous data and measured at the interval level of measurement or higher.

3. The shape of the distribution of the criterion must approximate the shape of a normal curve.

In addition, multiple regression analysis requires the following six assumptions:

4. *Factors (independent variables):* While the criterion must be measured at the interval level of measurement or higher, factors may be measured at any level of measurement (nominal, ordinal, interval, or ratio). However, if a nominal variable (categorical) is used in multiple regression analysis, it must be recoded to dummy variables prior to entering it in the analysis.

    A dummy variable is a dichotomous variable that is coded as 0 or 1. It is simply expressed in terms of X or Not X. For example, if gender is coded as 1 for male and 2 for female, you may recode 2 into 0 (not male) and leave 1 as is. You may also recode 1 into 0 (male) and 2 into 1 (not male) prior to entering gender in the regression analysis.

    A nominal variable with three or more levels must be recoded into one or more dummy variables. For example, if race is classified as 1 = White, 2 = African American, 3 = Asian American, and 4 = Hispanic, then you may create up to four dummy variables as follows: 1 = White and 0 = Not White; 0 = African American and 1 = Not African American; 0 = Asian and 1 = Not Asian; 0 = Hispanic and 1 = Not Hispanic.

5. *Linearity:* The relationship between the criterion and all factors is assumed to be a linear relationship.

Practically, it is almost impossible to confirm this assumption. However, it is recommended to examine linearity by creating a scatterplot for each factor with the criterion and then eyeballing each scatterplot. Minor deviation from linearity does not greatly affect the results of multiple regression analysis. If a curvilinear relationship exists in one or more scatterplots, consider transforming the data to a square root, logarithm, or other methods of transformation (see chapter 5).

6. *Normality:* The shape of the distribution of the residuals must approach the shape of a normal curve. Residuals refer to the differences between the observed (actual) scores and the predicted scores. If the analysis is perfect, the differences between the observed scores and predicted scores will be zero.

   To examine the assumption of normality, create a histogram with a normal curve for the residual scores. This procedure is available in most statistical software. In SPSS, you can request a histogram with a normal curve for the residuals (see figure 12.3) simultaneously along with the results of the multiple regression analysis. If a distribution is severely skewed, consider transforming the data to the square root, logarithm, or other methods of transformation (see chapter 5).

7. *Homoscedasticity:* For each value of the independent variables (factors), the dependent variable (criterion) should be normally distributed (have equal variance). In other words, the variance around the regression line should be the same for all values of the independent variables.

   To examine the assumption of homoscedasticity, plot the residuals against the predicted values. This plot can also be generated simultaneously along with the results of multiple regression analysis. If the distribution is normally distributed (homoscedastic), the data will form a straight diagonal line (see figure 12.4).

8. *Multicollinearity:* Multicollinearity occurs when two independent variables (factors) are highly correlated. When this occurs, both variables measure essentially the same thing.

   a. Detecting multicollinearity: To check data for multicollinearity, you may use one of the following two options:

      i. Run and examine the Pearson correlation coefficient for each pair of independent variables (factors). A correlation coefficient that is greater than .85 ($r > .85$) indicates a multicollinearity problem.

      ii. Check the variance inflation factor (VIF). This is the reciprocal of tolerance: the proportion of variance in one independent variable that is unexplained by the other independent variables ($1 - R^2$). It can be computed along with the multiple regression coefficients in SPSS or any other statistical program. A VIF value that is greater than 4 usually indicates a multicollinearity problem.

    b. Solving the problem: When two variables appear to be highly correlated, you may consider one of the following two methods:

      i.   Remove one variable: If you believe that one of the two highly correlated variables isn't necessary for the regression analysis, consider removing it. For example, if physical health and mental health are being used to predict life satisfaction among the elderly and both are highly correlated, you may consider removing the one that you believe is less important for life satisfaction and enter the second one in the regression analysis.

      ii. Create composite variables: If feasible, consider creating a new variable that combines the scores of both variables. In the above example, you may merge the scores of physical health and mental health to create a new variable (e.g., health in general). However, if the two variables have different units of measures (e.g., 1 to 10 for physical health and 10 to 50 for mental health), then transform their raw scores to standard scores (z scores) before creating the new variable.

9. *Sample Size:* There is no clear agreement among researchers on the optimum sample size for multiple regression analysis. Researchers have used anywhere from 10 to 50 cases per each predictor. Ideally, the larger the sample size, the better the generalizability of the results to the population from which the sample was drawn. This is especially important if the data are not normally distributed. As a rule of thumb, a sample size of at least $50 + 8m$ ($N \geq 50 + 8m$, where m = number of factors) is needed to utilize multiple regression analysis. For example, to examine the relationship between one criterion and six factors, you need at least 98 subjects; that is, $N \geq 50 + 8 \times 6 \geq 50 + 48 \geq 98$.

Selecting Appropriate Factors for Regression

The purpose of multiple regression analysis is to produce the most significant set of factors that predicts a criterion. Therefore, each factor entered in the regression analysis should have a significant bivariate relationship with the criterion. If the two do not have a significant relationship to begin with, it is unlikely that one will predict the other.

By selecting only variables that are significantly correlated with the criterion, the number of variables is decreased and so, in turn, are the required number of cases. Thus, prior to entering factors in the regression analysis, it is recommended to examine the bivariate relationship between each factor and the criterion. First, determine the appropriate bivariate statistical test (see chapters 7 to 11) and then run the test. Factors that show significant relationships with the criterion should be entered in the regression analysis while factors that do not should not be entered.

Methods of Regression

While some researchers may decide to enter all independent variables at once, others may decide to enter them based on specific criteria. There are a number of ways to enter independent variables in a regression analysis. The most common three methods are the following:

1. *Forward Method:* At the beginning of the regression analysis, bivariate correlation coefficients are computed for each factor (independent variable) with the criterion (dependent variable). Then the factor with the largest correlation coefficient is entered. The next factor entered in the equation will have the second largest correlation coefficient. Using this method, once a factor is entered in the regression equation, it remains. This procedure continues until no more factors contribute significantly to the variance in the criterion.

2. *Backward Method:* This method begins by entering all factors at once in the regression equation. Then multiple R square (R^2) and partial correlation coefficients (beta) are computed. In the next step, the factor that has the smallest partial correlation coefficient with the criterion is removed from the regression equation. Then the factor that has the second smallest partial correlation coefficient is removed. This procedure stops when the variance in the criterion significantly drops.

3. *Stepwise Method:* This is perhaps the most used method of regression analysis. It combines both the forward and backward methods and thus overcomes the problems of these two methods. As with the forward method, here, factors are entered based on the size of their partial correlation coefficients: the one with the largest correlation coefficient is entered first in the regression equation, followed by the second factor with the largest correlation coefficient. Unlike the forward method, after a new variable is entered, the contribution of factors already in the equation is reassessed. As with the backward method, factors that no longer contribute significantly to the variance in the criterion are removed from the regression equation. The procedure stops when no more factors contribute significantly. This chapter uses the stepwise method.

PRACTICAL EXAMPLE

Predicting Job Satisfaction among Social Workers

Use the SPSS *Job Satisfaction* data file (appendix A) to predict levels of job satisfaction among social workers based on a number of factors. Examine the following research question:

> Which set of factors best predicts levels of job satisfaction among professional social workers: gender, ethnicity, level of education, region of employment, working with colleagues, quality of supervision, promotion, or role conflict?

Step 1: State the research question.

Unlike with bivariate statistics, in multiple regression analysis it is unnecessary to state a null and alternative hypothesis. This is because here the researcher's aim is not to verify or falsify a research hypothesis, but rather to produce a regression model that best predicts a criterion. Thus, in multiple regression analysis simply state the research question. In this case, the research question is as follows:

Which set of the following factors best predicts levels of job satisfaction (**SATISFAC**) among professional social workers: gender (**D1**), ethnicity (**D6**), level of education (**EDUCAT**), region of employment (**D8**), working with colleagues (**COLLEAG**), quality of supervision (**SUPERVIS**), promotion (**PROMOT**), and role conflict (**ROLECONF**)?

Step 2: Choose alpha.

Set alpha at .05 ($\alpha = .05$). Results will be significant only if $p \leq .05$.

Step 3: Select the appropriate statistical test.

Because the purpose is to examine which factors best predict job satisfaction among social workers, the most appropriate test is multiple regression analysis. However, before starting, this analysis evaluate the data to determine whether they meet the assumptions.

a. The dependent variable must be measured at the interval or higher level of measurement. In this research question, job satisfaction is the criterion (dependent variable), which is measured at the interval level.

b. The shape of the distribution of the dependent variable must approach the shape of a normal curve. To evaluate this assumption, look at the histogram with a normal curve for job satisfaction. Figure 12.1 describes the distribution for job satisfaction, where the shape of the distribution is not severely skewed.[1] It appears to approach the shape of a normal curve.

c. Factors entered in the regression analysis can be measured at any level of measurement (nominal, ordinal, interval, or ratio). However, if nominal variables (categorical) are used, they must be recoded to dummy variables before they are entered.

The factors (independent variables) in this research question are gender, ethnicity, level of education, region of employment, working with colleagues, quality of supervision, promotion, and role conflict. Working with colleagues, quality of supervision, promotion, and role conflict are continuous variables, measured at the interval level. Gender, ethnicity, level of education, and region of employment are categorical variables, and must be coded as 0 and 1. Looking at the SPSS data file, gender, ethnicity, and level of education are coded as 0 and 1. Region of employment is coded as 1 = North, 2 = Center,

---

[1] If the distribution is severely skewed, consider transforming job satisfaction to the square root or other methods of transformation (see chapter 5).

Figure 12.1:   Histogram of Job Satisfaction

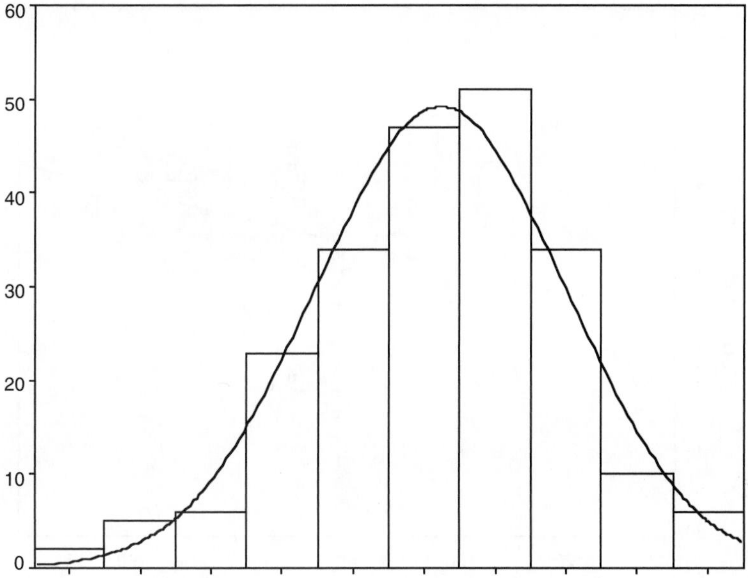

and 3 = South. In this case, it must be recoded to three dummy variables as follows: North (1 = North; 0 = Others); Center (1 = Center; 0 = Others); South (1 = South; 0 = Others).

SPSS syntax for recoding **D8** to three new variables:

RECODE D8 (SYSMIS=SYSMIS) (1=1) (2=0) (3=0) INTO NORTH.
EXECUTE.

RECODE D8 (SYSMIS=SYSMIS) (1=0) (2=1) (3=0) INTO CENTER.
EXECUTE.

RECODE D8 (SYSMIS=SYSMIS) (1=0) (2=0) (3=1) INTO SOUTH.
EXECUTE.

---

d.   The relationship between the criterion and the factors is assumed to be linear. This assumption is evaluated by looking at the scatterplot for each factor with the criterion. As you may recall from chapter 7, a scatterplot is only appropriate when both the dependent variables (criterion) and independent variables (factor) are continuous. In this case, we have four continuous factors: working with colleagues, quality of supervision, promotion, and workload. Thus, use SPSS to create four scatterplots (see chapter 7). Figure 12.2 presents a scatterplot for job satisfaction and working with colleagues (A), quality of

Figure 12.2.A: Scatterplot for Working with Colleagues and Job Satisfaction

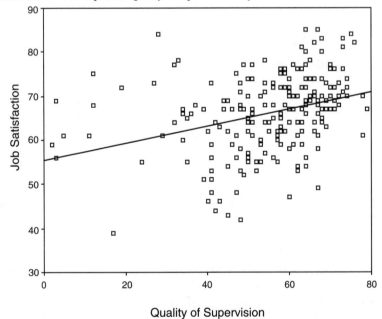

Figure 12.2.B: Scatterplot for Quality of Supervision and Job Satisfaction

Figure 12.2.C: Scatterplot for Promotion and Job Satisfaction

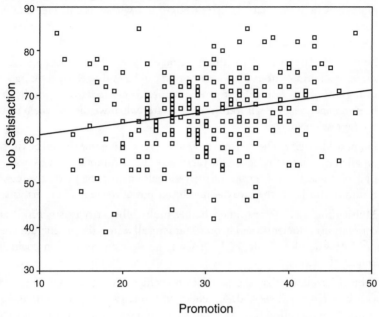

Figure 12.2.D: Scatterplot for Workload and Job Satisfaction

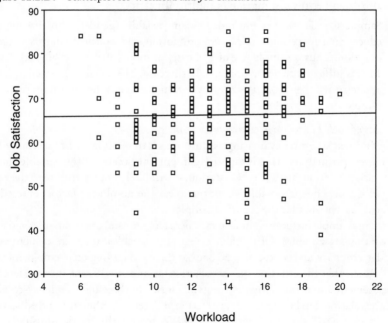

supervision (B), promotion (C), and workload (D). Eyeballing these scatter-plots shows a linear relationship (a straight line with dots clustered around it) between job satisfaction and each factor, with minor deviation (a few dots appear far from the line).

e. Normality: The shape of the distribution of the residuals must approach the shape of a normal curve. This assumption can be evaluated by looking at the histogram of the residuals. It can be requested along with the multiple re-gression analysis. We will return to this later when we discuss the output of the regression analysis.

f. Homoscedasticity: The variance around the regression line should be the same for all values of the independent variables. This assumption can be evaluated by looking at the scatterplot of the residuals against the predict values. We return to this later when we discuss the output of the regression analysis.

g. Multicollinearity: To examine whether multicollinearity exists, run Pearson correlation coefficients (see chapter 7) among all factors (do not include the de-pendent variable). Table 12.1 displays the Pearson correlation coefficients among all factors.

Table 12.1 shows that the correlation coefficients among the independent variables range between .014 (gender and quality of supervision) and .449 (working with colleagues and promotion). No correlation coefficient exceeds .85, thus indicating that no multicollinearity exists among the factors.

We revisit this issue when we look at the variance inflation factor (VIF), which also examines the assumption of multicollinearity.

h. Sample size: There are eight independent variables (gender, ethnicity, region, education, supervision, colleagues, promotion, and workload) in this research question. Thus, a sample size of 114 cases or more $[50 + 8m = 50 + (8 \times 8) = 114]$ is sufficient to do the analysis. In this case, 218 social workers completed and returned the *Job Satisfaction* survey, which exceeds the minimum required sample size.

Step 4: Select factors to be entered in analysis.
The next step after evaluating assumptions is to select factors to be entered in the regression analysis. This is especially important because if the variable shows no bivariate relationship with the criterion, it will likely not contribute to the vari-ance in the dependent variable. Also, the lower the number of factors entered in the analysis, the smaller the required sample size.

Our example includes eight factors, where four are categorical variables and four are continuous variables. Of the four categorical variables, three are dichotomous (gender, ethnicity, and education) and one has three groups (region of employment).

Recall that the criterion (job satisfaction) is measured at the interval level of measurement and is normally distributed. Thus, run three independent t-tests to test the relationship between job satisfaction and gender, ethnicity, and education (see chapter 8). Then run a one-way ANOVA to test the relationship between

Table 12.1: Pearson Correlation Coefficients

		D1 (Gender)	D6 (Ethnicity)	D8 (Region)	EDUCAT	COLLEAG	SUPERVIS	PROMOT	LOAD
D1 (Gender)	Pearson correlation	1	-.475**	-.006	-.053	.133*	.014	-.146*	.174**
	Sig. (1-tailed)	.	.000	.467	.216	.025	.418	.015	.005
	N	218	217	217	218	218	214	218	218
D6 (Ethnicity)	Pearson correlation	-.475**	1	-.388**	-.053	-.232**	-.165**	-.042	-.123*
	Sig. (1-tailed)	.000	.	.000	.218	.000	.008	.271	.035
	N	217	217	217	217	217	213	217	217
D8 (Region)	Pearson correlation	-.006	-.388**	1	.033	.082	.065	.215**	.043
	Sig. (1-tailed)	.467	.000	.	.314	.116	.172	.001	.263
	N	217	217	217	217	217	213	217	217
EDUCAT	Pearson correlation	-.053	-.053	.033	1	-.092	-.109	-.122*	.041
	Sig. (1-tailed)	.216	.218	.314	.	.089	.056	.036	.274
	N	218	217	217	218	218	214	218	218
COLLEAG	Pearson correlation	.133*	-.232**	.082	-.092	1	.431**	.449**	-.045
	Sig. (1-tailed)	.025	.000	.116	.089	.	.000	.000	.254
	N	218	217	218	218	218	214	218	218
SUPERVIS	Pearson correlation	.014	-.165**	.065	-.109	.431**	1	.296**	-.057
	Sig. (1-tailed)	.418	.008	.172	.056	.000	.	.000	.204
	N	214	213	213	214	214	214	214	214
PROMOT	Pearson correlation	-.146*	-.042	.215**	-.122*	.449**	.296**	1	-.060
	Sig. (1-tailed)	.015	.271	.001	.036	.000	.000	.	.191
	N	218	217	217	214	214	214	218	218
LOAD	Pearson correlation	.174**	-.123*	.043	.041	-.045	-.057	-.060	1
	Sig. (1-tailed)	.005	.035	.263	.274	.254	.204	.191	.
	N	218	217	217	218	218	214	218	218

*Correlation is significant at the 0.05 level (1-tailed).
**Correlation is significant at the 0.01 level (1-tailed).

Table 12.2.A: Descriptive Statistics—Job Satisfaction by Gender

			Group Statistics		
	D1 (Gender)	N	Mean	Std. deviation	Std. error mean
SATISFAC	.00 Male	36	64.6944	8.78252	1.46375
	1.00 Female	182	66.4505	8.82896	.65445

Table 12.2.B: Independent *t*-Test—Job Satisfaction by Gender

		Levene's test for equality of variances		t-test for Equality of Means						
									95% confidence interval of the difference	
		F	Sig.	*t*	df	Sig. (2-tailed)	Mean difference	Std. error difference	Lower	Upper
SATISFAC	Equal variances assumed	.036	.849	−1.091	216	.276	−1.7561	1.60909	−4.9276	1.4154
	Equal variances not assumed			−1.095	50.01	.279	−1.7561	1.60339	−4.9766	1.4644

region and job satisfaction (see chapter 9). The results of the three independent *t*-tests and ANOVA are presented in tables 12.2 through 12.5.

Table 12.2.B shows no significant difference (Sig. = .276, $p > .05$) between male and female social workers with regard to their levels of job satisfaction. Both males and females have similar mean scores in job satisfaction, 64.69 and 66.45 (table 12.2.A). Therefore, this variable may not be included in the regression analysis.

Table 12.3.B shows a significant difference (Sig. = .000, $p < .05$) between Arab and Jewish social workers with regard to their levels of job satisfaction. Table 12.3.A shows that Jewish social workers have higher levels of job satisfaction (mean = 67.69) than Arab social workers (mean = 63.03). Therefore, this variable will be included in the regression analysis.

Table 12.4.B shows a significant difference (Sig. = .088/2 = .044, $p < .05$)[2] between undergraduate and graduate social workers with regard to their levels of job satisfaction. Table 12.4.A shows that graduate social workers have higher levels of job satisfaction (mean = 68.58) than undergraduate social workers (mean = 65.73). This variable will also be included in the regression analysis.

Table 12.5.A shows a significant overall difference (Sig. = .000) among the three regions of employment (North, Center, and South) with regard to levels of job satisfaction. The post hoc Bonferroni test (table 12.5.B) shows that there is no significant difference between North and Center regions with regard to job satisfaction (first line, first row, fourth column; Sig. = .652). On the other hand, there

---

[2]Divide the *p* value by 2 if you have a one-tailed hypothesis. In this case, we hypothesize that graduate social workers will have higher job satisfaction than undergraduate social workers.

Table 12.3.A: Descriptive Statistics—Job Satisfaction by Ethnicity

		Group Statistics			
	D6 (Ethnicity)	N	Mean	Std. deviation	Std. error mean
SATISFAC	.00 Jews	145	67.6897	8.15605	.67732
	1.00 Arabs	72	63.0278	9.39129	1.10677

Table 12.3.B: Independent t-Test—Job Satisfaction by Ethnicity

		Levene's test for equality of variances							95% confidence interval of the difference	
									t-test for Equality of Means	
		F	Sig.	t	df	Sig. (2-tailed)	Mean difference	Std. error difference	Lower	Upper
SATISFAC	Equal variances assumed	2.292	.132	3.8	215	.000	4.6619	1.23752	2.223	7.101
	Equal variances not assumed			3.6	125	.000	4.6619	1.29758	2.094	7.230

Table 12.4.A: Descriptive Statistics—Job Satisfaction by Education

		Group Statistics			
	EDUCAT (Level of Education)	N	Mean	Std. deviation	Std. error mean
SATISFAC	.00 Undergraduate	185	65.7297	8.79800	.64684
	1.00 Graduate	33	68.5758	8.71791	1.51759

Table 12.4.B: Independent t-Test—Job Satisfaction by Education

		Levene's test for equality of variances							95% confidence interval of the difference	
									t-test for Equality of Means	
		F	Sig.	t	df	Sig. (2-tailed)	Mean difference	Std. error difference	Lower	Upper
SATISFAC	Equal variances assumed	.198	.657	−2	216	.088	−2.8460	1.66030	−6.118	.42643
	Equal variances not assumed			−2	44	.091	−2.8460	1.64969	−6.170	.47781

is a significant difference between North and South (second line, first row, fourth column; Sig. = .000). The second row shows a significant difference between Center and South regions (second line, fourth column; Sig. = .021). These findings suggest that social workers from the South region are significantly different than social workers from the other two regions.

Table 12.5.A: One-Way ANOVA—Job Satisfaction by Region

			SATISFAC		
	Sum of squares	df	Mean square	F	Sig.
Between groups	1294.728	2	647.364	8.885	.000
Within groups	15591.843	214	72.859		
Total	16886.571	216			

Table 12.5.B: Post Hoc Bonferroni—Job Satisfaction by Region

			Multiple Comparisons				
			Dependent Variable: **SATISFAC**				
						95% confidence interval	
		Mean					
(I) **D8** (Region)	(J) **D8** (Region)	difference (I–J)	Std. error	Sig.		Lower bound	Upper bound
1.00 North	2.00 Center	−1.9927	1.61107	.652		−5.8802	1.8947
	3.00 South	−5.7500*	1.44973	.000		−9.2481	−2.2519
2.00 Center	1.00 North	1.9927	1.61107	.652		−1.8947	5.8802
	3.00 South	−3.7573*	1.37658	.021		−7.0789	−.4356
3.00 South	1.00 North	5.7500*	1.44973	.000		2.2519	9.2481
	2.00 Center	3.7573*	1.37658	.021		.4356	7.0789

*The mean difference is significant at the .05 level.

As you may recall, a categorical variable with three or more levels must be re-coded to one or more dummy variables prior to entering it in the regression analysis. In this case, because the one-way ANOVA and the post hoc test show that South is significantly different than the other two regions, it is recommended to create a new dummy variable using South as one group (coded as 1) and All Others as the second group (coded as 0). Recall that we already created three new dummy variables. However, we will only enter South in the regression analysis.

The next step is to select which continuous factors will be entered in the analysis. To select these factors, run a Pearson correlation between job satisfaction (criterion) and each factor (supervision, colleagues, promotion, and workload). Table 12.6 presents the Pearson correlation coefficients generated by SPSS.

Table 12.6 shows that job satisfaction has a significant correlation with working with colleagues ($r = .283$; $p < .05$), quality of supervision ($r = .324$; $p < .05$), and promotion ($r = .213$; $p < .05$). On the other hand, no significant correlation is found between job satisfaction and workload ($r = .016$; $p > .05$). Thus, workload may not be entered in the regression analysis.

To conclude, the variables ethnicity, education, south, colleagues, supervision, and promotion have significant bivariate relationships with job satisfaction, and will

Table 12.6:   Correlation between Job Satisfaction and Factors

		SATISFAC	COLLEG	SUPERVIS	PROMOT	LOAD
SATISFAC	Pearson correlation	1	.283**	.324**	.213**	.016
	Sig. (1-tailed)	.	.000	.000	.001	.407
	N	218	218	214	218	218
COLLEAG	Pearson correlation	.283**	1	.431**	.449**	−.045
	Sig. (1-tailed)	.000	.	.000	.000	.254
	N	218	218	214	218	218
SUPERVIS	Pearson correlation	.324**	.431**	1	.296**	−.057
	Sig. (1-tailed)	.000	.000	.	.000	.204
	N	214	214	214	214	214
PROMOT	Pearson correlation	.213**	.449**	.296**	1	−.060
	Sig. (1-tailed)	.001	.000	.000	.	.191
	N	218	218	214	218	218
LOAD	Pearson correlation	.016	−.045	−.057	−.060	1
	Sig. (1-tailed)	.407	.254	.204	.191	.
	N	218	218	214	218	218

**Correlation is significant at the 0.01 level (1-tailed).

be entered in the regression analysis. The variables gender and workload have no significant relationships with job satisfaction and will be excluded from the analysis.[3]

Step 5: Run multiple regression analysis (Use SPSS).

The multiple regression procedures in SPSS enable you to select and compute many statistics and coefficients and create various plots that provide valuable information. For the purpose here, request only the statistics and coefficients that we have discussed and create a histogram with a normal curve for the residual scores.

How to Compute Multiple Regression Coefficients in SPSS.   In our research question, the dependent variable is job satisfaction (**SATISFAC**) and the independent variables are ethnicity (**D6**), education (**EDUCAT**), region (**SOUTH**), supervision (**SUPERVIS**), colleagues (**COLLEAG**), and promotion (**PROMOT**).

To run a multiple regression analysis in SPSS, follow these steps:

a.   Open the SPSS *Job Satisfaction* data file.

b.   Click on *Analyze* in the SPSS main toolbar.

c.   Scroll down, click on *Regression,* and click on *Linear* (screen 12.1).

d.   A dialog box called *Linear Regression* will open (screen 12.2.A).

e.   Scroll down in the variables list, click on **SATISFAC,** and click on the upper arrow button to move it in the *Dependent* box.

[3]Because these variables will not be entered in the regression analysis, the minimum required sample size decreases from 114 to 98. Decreasing the number of factors decreases the required sample size.

Screen 12.1:   SPSS *Linear Multiple Regression* Main Toolbar

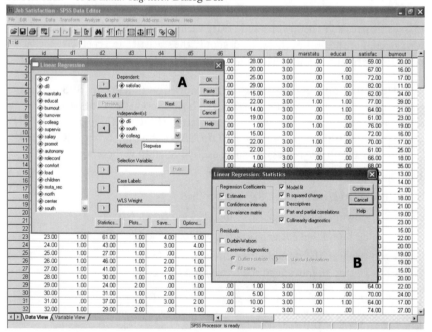

Screen 12.2:   SPSS *Linear Regression* Dialog Box

f. Scroll down in the variables list, click on **D6** (ethnicity), and click on the arrow button associated with *Independent(s)* to move it in the *Independent(s)* box. Repeat this step to move **SOUTH, EDUCAT, SUPERVIS, COLLEAG,** and **PROMOT** in the *Independent(s)* box.

g. Click on the drop-down arrow button associated with *Method* to select the method of data entry in the regression (Forward, Stepwise, Backward). In this case select *Stepwise*.

h. Click on *Statistics* in the bottom of the *Linear Regression* dialog box. A new dialog box called *Linear Regression: Statistics* will open (screen 12.2.B).

i. Make sure that the box of *Estimates* under *Regression Coefficients* is checked (SPSS default). If not, check it. This computes the standardized (β) and unstandardized (b) regression coefficients, their levels of significance (t and p values), and the regression constant (a).

j. Make sure that the box of *Model Fit* is checked (SPSS default). This computes the multiple correlation coefficient (R), R square, and adjusted R square. It also computes an ANOVA table and the level of significance for the overall model.

k. Check the box *R Squared Change*. This command computes the change in proportion to the variance in the criterion and whether the change is significant.

l. Check the box *Collinearity Diagnostics*. This command computes the *Tolerance* and the *Variance Inflation Factor* (VIF). You need this only to check if a multicollinearity problem exists.

m. Click on *Continue* to return to the *Linear Regression* dialog box (screen 12.2.A).

n. Click on *Plots*. A new dialog box called *Linear Regression: Plots* will open (screen 12.3.B).

o. Under *Standardized Residual Plots,* check the boxes of *Histogram* and *Normal Probability Plot*. You need these plots to check the assumption of normality. The *Histogram* command creates a histogram with a normal curve and the *Normal Probability Plot* command creates a normal probability plot for the residuals.

p. Click on *Continue* and click on *OK*.

SPSS syntax for stepwise multiple regression analysis:

```
REGRESSION
/STATISTICS COEFF OUTS R ANOVA COLLIN TOL CHANGE
/NOORIGIN
/DEPENDENT SATISFAC
/STEPWISE D6 SOUTH EDUCAT COLLEAG SUPERVIS
PROMOT
/RESIDUALS HIST (ZRESID) NORM (ZRESID).
```

To select a different regression method, change Stepwise (fifth line) with Backward or Forward.

Screen 12.3:   SPSS *Linear Regression: Plots* Dialog Box

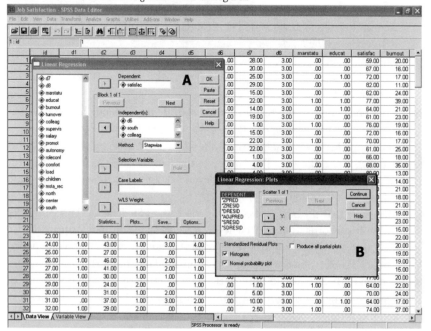

Interpreting the Output   The following output presents the results of multiple regression procedures. These results include four tables (12.7 to 12.10) and two graphs (figures 12.3 and 12.4). Other tables produced by SPSS were omitted because they are not necessary for our purposes at this level.

Table 12.7 displays the number, order, and regression method for how variables are entered and removed from the regression equation. It has four columns:

1. *Model:* This column shows the number of steps the regression method utilized to produce the best regression model for predicting the dependent variable (criterion). Table 12.7 shows (under *Model*) that the regression method utilized four steps to produce a final regression model (equation).

2. *Variables Entered:* The second column in table 12.7 shows the order in which the independent variables were entered in the regression equation. In the stepwise method, the variable that has the largest correlation coefficient with the dependent variable will be entered first followed by the second, the third, and so on. The process stops when no more independent variables contribute significantly to the variance in the dependent variable.

   Table 12.7 (second column, Variables Entered) shows that quality of supervision (**SUPERVIS**) was entered first, followed by region (**SOUTH**), level of education (**EDUCAT**), then working with colleagues (**COLLEAG**).

   Notice that no other variables were entered after **COLLEAG**. This is because

Table 12.7:   Results of Multiple Regression Analysis—Methods of Variable Entry

		Variables Entered/Removed[a]	
Model	Variables Entered	Variables Removed	Method
1	SUPERVIS	.	Stepwise (Criteria: Probability-of-F-to-enter <= .050, Probability-of-F-to-remove >= .100).
2	SOUTH	.	Stepwise (Criteria: Probability-of-F-to-enter <= .050, Probability-of-F-to-remove >= .100).
3	EDUCAT (Level of Education)	.	Stepwise (Criteria: Probability-of-F-to-enter <= .050, Probability-of-F-to-remove >= .100).
4	COLLEAG	.	Stepwise (Criteria: Probability-of-F-to-enter <= .050, Probability-of-F-to-remove >= .100).

[a]Dependent Variable: SATISFAC

neither ethnicity nor promotion (recall that six variables were entered in the regression analysis) was entered in the regression equation simply because neither contributed significantly to the variance in job satisfaction.

This column thus displays the number and order of the variables that best predict job satisfaction. In this example, four variables are shown: supervision, region, education, and colleagues.

3. *Variables Removed:* This column summarizes the variables that no longer contribute significantly to the variance in job satisfaction after a new variable is entered in the regression equation. In this example, the list is empty because all variables entered in the regression equation remain significant after each entry (e.g., supervision remained significant after south was entered; supervision and south remained significant after education was entered, etc.).

4. *Method:* This column describes the regression method in which variables are entered in the regression equation (stepwise, forward, backward, etc.). In this case, variables were entered based on the stepwise method. The column also shows that variables are entered only if their correlation with the criterion is significant at alpha of .05 or less.

Table 12.8 has 10 columns, of which only 5 are appropriate for our discussion at this level:

1. Model (first column) conveys the number and order of the best variables entered in the regression equation.

2. R (second column) conveys the correlation coefficient between the criterion and the factor(s) at each step.

3. The R Square (third column) conveys the proportion of the variance in the criterion that is accounted for by all factors entered in the equation at each step.

Table 12.8:   Results of Multiple Regression Analysis—Model Summary

| | | | | | | Change Statistics | | | |
Model	R	R Square	Adjusted R Square	Std. error of the estimate	R square change	F change	df1	df2	Sig. F change
1	.324[a]	.105	.101	8.34527	.105	24.693	1	211	.000
2	.399[b]	.160	.152	8.10521	.055	13.684	1	210	.000
3	.430[c]	.185	.173	8.00289	.025	6.404	1	209	.012
4	.454[d]	.206	.191	7.91535	.022	5.648	1	208	.018

Model Summary[a]

[a]Predictors: (Constant), **SUPERVIS**
[b]Predictors (Constant), **SUPERVIS, SOUTH**
[c]Predictors: (Constant), **SUPERVIS, SOUTH, EDUCAT** (Level of Education)
[d]Predictors: (Constant), **SUPERVIS, SOUTH, EDUCAT** (Level of Education), **COLLEAG**
[e]Dependent Variable: **SATISFAC**

4. The R Square Change (sixth column) conveys the change in the proportion of the variance in the criterion as a result of entering a new factor. When only one factor is entered, R Square and R Square Change are identical.

5. Sig. F Change (tenth column) conveys the level of significance for the R Square Change. A Sig. value of .05 or less indicates a significant change in the R square.

Table 12.8 shows four steps where variables were entered in the regression equation:

Model 1: Quality of supervision (**SUPERVIS**) was entered at the first step. The first row, second column (R = .324) show that the correlation between supervision and job satisfaction is .324. The R Square column shows that supervision contributes 10.5% to the variance in job satisfaction (first row, third column; R^2 = .105). The sixth column (R Square Change) shows that supervision added 10.5% to the variance in job satisfaction. Since this is the first step in the analysis, the R Square and R Square Change are the same (only one variable is in the regression equation, supervision). The tenth column shows that this proportion (R Square Change) is significant at alpha of .05 (first row, tenth column; Sig. F Change = .000).

Model 2: Region of employment (**SOUTH**) was entered at the second step. The table shows that the multiple correlation among all variables in the equation at Model 2 (step 2) and job satisfaction is .399 (second row, second column; R = .399). These variables are supervision (entered at step 1) and region of employment (entered at step 2). The two variables together accounted for 16% of the variance in job satisfaction (second row, third column; R Square = .160). The second variable (region of employment) added 5.5% to the variance in job satisfaction (second row, sixth column; R Square Change = .055).[4] This R Square Change is still significant at alpha of .05 (second row, tenth column; Sig. F Change = .000).

Model 3: Level of education (**EDUCAT**) was entered at the third step. Table 12.8 shows that the multiple correlation among all variables in the equation and job satisfaction is .430 (third row, second column; R = .430). These variables are supervision (entered at step 1), region of employment (entered at step 2), and level of education (entered at step 3). The three variables accounted for 18.5% of the variance in job satisfaction (third row, third column; R Square = .185). The third variable (level of education) added 2.5% to the variance in job satisfaction (third row, sixth column; R Square Change = .025). This R Square Change is still significant at alpha of .05 (third row, tenth column; Sig. F Change = .012).

Model 4: Working with colleagues (**COLLEAG**) was entered at the fourth step. The table shows that the correlation among all variables in the equation and job satisfaction is .454 (fourth row, second column; R = .454). These variables are supervision (entered at step 1), region of employment (entered at step 2), level of education (entered at step 3), and working with colleagues. The four variables accounted for 20.6% of the variance in job satisfaction (fourth row, third column; R Square = .206). The fourth variable (**COLLEAG**) added 2.2% to the variance in job satisfaction (fourth row, sixth column; R Square Change = .022). This R Square Change is still significant at alpha of .05 (fourth row, tenth column; Sig. F Change = .018).

The Model Summary table is followed by footnotes. The first four footnotes list the variables in each step (a = **SUPERVIS**, b = **SUPERVIS, SOUTH**, etc.). The last footnote shows the dependent variable (**SATISFAC**). This table shows that quality of supervision is the best predictor of job satisfaction, followed by region of employment, level of education, and working with colleagues.

Table 12.9 displays the results of the one-way ANOVA. Multiple regression analysis uses one-way ANOVA (chapter 9) to examine the overall level of significance for each regression model. There will be one ANOVA test for each model.

Table 12.9 lists the order of the models at the first column (Model) and then provides the sum of squares (second column), degrees of freedom (third column), mean square (fourth column), the ANOVA F ratio (fifth column), and the overall level of significance (sixth column). The last two columns are to be reported.

Model 1: The first row shows the results of ANOVA for the first model (supervision). With only one factor in, the model is a significant predictor of job satisfaction (first row, last two columns; F= 24.69, Sig. = .000).

Model 2: The second row shows the results of ANOVA for the second model (supervision and region). With these two factors in, the model is also a

[4]You may compute the variance that each variable contributes simply by subtracting the R Square at the previous step from the R Square at the current step.

Table 12.9:   Results of Multiple Regression Analysis—ANOVA

				ANOVA[a]		
Model		Sum of squares	df	Mean square	F	Sig.
1	Regression	1719.685	1	1719.685	24.693	.000[a]
	Residual	14694.794	211	69.644		
	Total	16414.479	212			
2	Regression	2618.650	2	1309.325	19.931	.000[b]
	Residual	13795.829	210	65.694		
	Total	16414.479	212			
3	Regression	3028.818	3	1009.606	15.764	.000[c]
	Residual	13385.661	209	64.046		
	Total	16414.479	212			
4	Regression	3382.702	4	845.675	13.498	.000[d]
	Residual	13031.777	208	62.653		
	Total	16414.479	212			

[a]Predictors: (Constant), **SUPERVIS**
[b]Predictors: (Constant), **SUPERVIS, SOUTH**
[c]Predictors: (Constant), **SUPERVIS, SOUTH, EDUCAT** (Level of Education)
[d]Predictors: (Constant), **SUPERVIS, SOUTH, EDUCAT** (Level of Education), **COLLEAG**
[e]Dependent Variable: **SATISFAC**

significant predictor of job satisfaction (second row, last two columns; $F = 19.93$, Sig. = .000).

Model 3: The third row shows the results of ANOVA for the third model (supervision, region, and education). With these three factors in, the model is a significant predictor of job satisfaction (third row, last two columns; $F = 15.76$, Sig. = .000).

Model 4: The fourth row shows the results of ANOVA for the fourth model (supervision, region, education, and colleagues). With these four factors in, the model is still a significant predictor of job satisfaction (second row, last two columns; $F = 13.50$, Sig. = .000).[5]

To sum up, the results of ANOVA show that the four-factor model significantly predicts job satisfaction ($F = 13.50; p < .05$).

Table 12.10 displays the unstandardized and standardized coefficients, their levels of significance, and the collinearity statistics. It has eight columns:

The first column (Model) conveys the number and order of the models and lists the variables entered in the regression equation in each step.

The second and third columns (B and Std. Error) convey the unstandardized regression coefficients (o) and their standard errors.

---

[5]The more variables entered into the regression equation, the smaller the F value.

Table 12.10:   Results of Multiple Regression Analysis—Variables In

Model		Unstandardized Coefficients		Standardized Coefficients			Collinearity Statistics	
		B	Std. error	Beta	t	Sig.	Tolerance	VIF
1	(Constant)	55.533	2.199		25.253	.000		
	SUPERVIS	.193	.039	.324	4.969	.000	1.000	1.000
2	(Constant)	54.072	2.172		24.895	.000		
	SUPERVIS	.184	.038	.308	4.857	.000	.996	1.005
	SOUTH	4.122	1.114	.235	3.699	.000	.996	1.005
3	(Constant)	52.898	2.194		24.108	.000		
	SUPERVIS	.194	.038	.325	5.159	.000	.984	1.016
	SOUTH	4.199	1.101	.239	3.815	.000	.995	1.005
	EDUCAT	3.908	1.544	.159	2.531	.012	.988	1.013
	(Level of Education)							
4	(Constant)	46.905	3.327		14.099	.000		
	SUPERVIS	.152	.041	.256	3.718	.000	.808	1.238
	SOUTH	4.058	1.090	.231	3.722	.000	.992	1.008
	EDUCAT	4.098	1.530	.167	2.679	.008	.985	1.015
	(Level of Education)							
	COLLEAG	.169	.071	.163	2.377	.018	.808	1.237

Coefficients[a]

[a]Dependent Variable: SATISFAC

The fourth column (Beta) conveys the standardized regression coefficients (β). This reports the size and direction of the partial correlation between each factor and the criterion (in this case, job satisfaction).

The fifth and sixth columns (t and Sig.) convey the t value and the level of significance (p) for each regression coefficient. This examines whether the correlation between the criterion and the corresponding factor is significant.

The seventh and the eighth columns (Tolerance and VIF) convey the collinearity measures, which evaluate the assumption of collinearity. For this purpose, only examine the VIF column. Remember that SPSS does not compute these measures if you do not request them.

These coefficients and statistics are reported for each factor entered in the regression equation and reassessed once a new variable is entered. We will only need the last row which displays coefficients for all variables that best contribute to the variance in the criterion (job satisfaction); that is, Model 4.

1.   The first line in Model 4 (**CONSTANT**) conveys the regression constant (the *a* value in the unstandardized regression equation). The second column shows that the constant for this model is 46.91 (first line, fourth row, second column; B = 46.905) with a standard error of 3.33 (first line, fourth row, third column; Std. Error = 3.327).

Table 12.10 does not report the standardized coefficient for the constant (first line, fourth row, fourth column; beta =). This is because, as you may recall from the formula of the regression equation, the constant (a) for a standardized regression equation is zero.

The table shows that this regression constant is significant (first line in Model 4, fifth and sixth columns; $t = 14.099$, Sig. $= .000$).

2. The second line in Model 4 reports the coefficients and statistics for the strongest variable in the equation, supervision. The unstandardized regression coefficient for supervision is .15 with a standard error of .041 ($b_{SUPERVIS} = .15$).

    The table shows that the partial correlation (beta) between supervision and job satisfaction is .256 ($\beta_{SUPERVIS} = .26$). This indicates a positive partial correlation between supervision and job satisfaction; the better the supervision, the higher the levels of job satisfaction. This correlation is significant (second line in Model 4, fifth and sixth columns; $t = 3.718$, Sig. $= .000$).

    The Variance Inflation Factor (VIF) for supervision (second line in Model 4, eighth column) is 1.238. A VIF greater than 4 usually indicates a problem of multicollinearity. A VIF of 1.238 shows that no multicollinearity exists between supervision and any other factor.

3. The third line in Model 4 reports the coefficients and statistics for the second strongest variable in the equation, region of employment (**SOUTH**). The unstandardized regression coefficient is 4.058 with a standard error of 1.09 ($b_{SOUTH} = 4.06$).

    The partial correlation (beta) between region of employment and job satisfaction is .231 ($\beta_{SOUTH} = .23$) which indicates that social workers from the south (coded as 1) tend to be more satisfied than social workers from other regions (coded as 0). This correlation is significant (third line in Model 4, fifth and sixth columns; $t = 3.722$, Sig. $= .000$).

    The VIF of region of employment (third line in Model 4, eighth column) is 1.008. This is smaller than the cutoff score of 4, which indicates no multicollinearity problem between region of employment and any other factor entered in the regression analysis.

4. The fourth line in Model 4 reports the coefficients and statistics for the third strongest variable in the equation, level of education (**EDUCAT**). The unstandardized regression coefficient is 4.098, with a standard error of 1.53 ($b_{EDUCAT} = 4.098$).

    The partial correlation (beta) between level of education and job satisfaction is .167 ($\beta_{EDUCAT} = .17$), which indicates that graduate social workers (coded as 1) tend to be more satisfied than undergraduate social workers (coded as 0). This correlation is significant (fourth line in Model 4, fifth and sixth columns; $t = 2.679$, Sig. $= .008$).

    The VIF of level of education (fourth line in Model 4, eighth column) is 1.015.

Again, this value is smaller than the cutoff score of 4, which indicates no multicollinearity problem between level of education and any other factor entered in the regression analysis.

5. The fifth line in Model 4 reports the coefficients and statistics for the least strongest variable in the equation, working with colleagues (**COLLEAG**). The unstandardized regression coefficient for working with colleagues is .169, with a standard error of .071 ($b_{COLLEAG}$ = .17).

The table shows that the partial correlation (beta) between working with colleagues and job satisfaction is .163 ($\beta_{COLLEAG}$ = .16). This indicates a positive partial correlation between working with colleagues and job satisfaction; the better the collegial relationship, the higher the levels of job satisfaction. This correlation coefficient is significant (fifth line in Model 4, fifth and sixth columns; t = 2.377, Sig. = .018).

The VIF for working with colleagues (fifth line in Model 4, eighth column) is 1.237, which is also smaller than the cutoff score of 4. This indicates no multicollinearity problem between level of education and any other factor entered in the regression analysis.

Figure 12.3 displays a histogram with a normal curve for the distribution of the standardized regression residuals. The shape of the distribution of the residuals

Figure 12.3:   Histogram of Residual Scores—Job Satisfaction

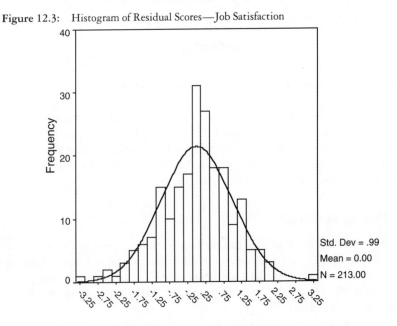

Regression Standardized Residual

Figure 12.4:   Normal Probability Plot of Standardized Residuals—Job Satisfaction

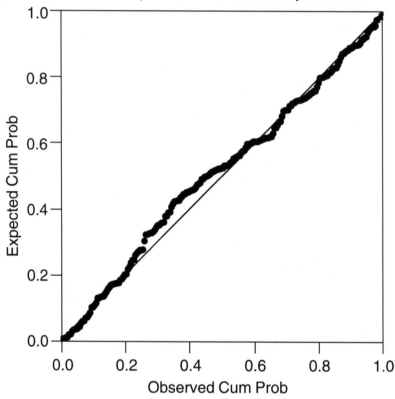

approaches the shape of a normal curve, which indicates that the assumption of normality is met.

To assess the assumption of homoscedasticity, look at the normal probability scatterplot for the standardized residuals. The y axis represents the predicted scores and the x axis represents the observed scores. If the distribution is normal, the points form a straight diagonal line. Figure 12.4 shows a diagonal line, with minor deviations. This indicates that the assumption of homoscedasticity is met.

Writing the Results

When writing the results of the regression analysis, present the number of factors that best predict the criterion, their order from most significant to least significant, the proportion of variance each contributes to the criterion, each partial correlation coefficient, and its level of significance. In our example, the results can be summarized as follows:

A stepwise multiple regression analysis was conducted to estimate a model that best predicts levels of job satisfaction among social workers. The results of the stepwise analysis revealed that four of the six factors emerged as significant predictors of job satisfaction ($F = 13.50$; $p < .05$). With a beta of .26 ($p < .05$), quality of supervision emerged as the strongest predictor of job satisfaction, accounting for 10.5% of the variance in job satisfaction. The second strongest factor was region of employment ($\beta = .23$; $p < .05$) accounting for an additional 5.5% of the variance in job satisfaction. The third strongest factor was level of education ($\beta = .17$; $p < .05$) followed by working with colleagues ($\beta = .16$; $p < .05$). Each factor accounted for only 2.5% and 2.2%, of the variance in job satisfaction.

These results indicate that higher job satisfaction is a function of better quality of supervision, being employed in the south region, higher levels of education, and better colleagial relationships. Overall, the model explains almost 21% of the variance in job satisfaction ($R = .45$). On the other hand, almost 80% of the variance in job satisfaction is unaccounted for by this model.

Writing the Regression Equation.   Once a regression model has been estimated and all coefficients have been computed, write the regression equation. This will help compute the level of job satisfaction for an individual social worker. Recall that job satisfaction was found to be a function of quality of supervision, region of employment, level of education, and working with colleagues. The unstandardized regression equation for job satisfaction is as follows:

$$Y = a + b_1X_1 + b_2X_2 + b_3X_3 + \ldots + b_iX_i$$
$$Job\ Satisfaction = 46.91 + (.15 \times supervision) + (4.06 \times south)$$
$$+ (4.10 \times education) + (.17 \times colleagues)$$

For example, if John (a social worker) was from the south (a score of 1), had a BSW (a score of 0), a score of 60 on the supervision scale, and a score of 50 on the working with colleagues scale, then we could predict John's score on *Job Satisfaction* as follows:

$$Job\ Satisfaction = 46.91 + (.15 \times 60) + (4.06 \times 1) + (4.10 \times 0) + (.17 \times 50)$$
$$= 46.91 + 9.0 + 4.06 + 0 + 8.5 = 68.47$$

Presentation of Results in a Summary Table

When presenting the results of multiple regression analysis in a summary table, report the multiple correlation coefficient and R Square for each factor (from the Model Summary Table), the partial correlation coefficient, the t value, level of significance for each factor (from the coefficients table), the overall F ratio, and level of significance for each model (from the ANOVA table). The table should be part of the results section. Factors should be presented based on their partial correlation, from the largest to the smallest beta. Table 12.11 presents the results of the multiple regression analysis for job satisfaction.

In this table, the first two columns (R and R^2) are from the Model Summary Table (table 12.8), the second three columns (β, t, and p) are from the Coefficients

Table 12.11:   Results of Multiple Regression Analysis—Predictors of Job Satisfaction

Factor	R	R^2	β	t	p	F	p
Supervision	.32	.11	.26	3.72	.000	24.69	.000
Region	.40	.16	.23	3.72	.000	19.93	.000
Education	.43	.19	.17	2.68	.000	15.76	.000
Colleagues	.45	.21	.16	2.38	.018	13.50	.000

table (table 12.10), and the last two columns (F and p) are from the ANOVA table (table 12.9).

SUMMARY

Multiple regression analysis is perhaps the most-used multivariate statistical technique in social work research. It allows social work researchers and practitioners to predict a specific outcome (criterion) based on several observed factors (independent variables). For example, by predicting which clients are more likely to be drug addicts, clinically depressed, or to experience anxiety, social work practitioners can plan early intervention techniques that will reduce or prevent such problems to occur.

This chapter began with a discussion of the purpose of multiple regression analysis and the regression equation. Two equations were introduced: unstandardized and standardized regression equations. The unstandardized regression equation is based on actual raw scores while the standardized regression equation is based on transformation of the scores of all variables in the equation to standard scores (z scores).

The chapter introduced and discussed major coefficients produced by the regression analysis, including the unstandardized regression coefficient (b), standardized regression coefficient (beta), multiple correlation coefficient (R), multiple R square (R^2), and the regression constant (a).

The chapter also presented and discussed the assumptions underlying multiple regression analysis, including level of measurement of the dependent variable, normality of distribution, linearity of the relationship between the criterion and factors, multicollinearity, and the assumption of the sample size required to undertake multiple regression analysis. The chapter also discussed methods for evaluating each assumption.

Because multiple regression analysis examines multiple independent variables to predict one dependent variable, the chapter discussed how to select and enter only the independent variables most likely to contribute to the variance in the dependent variable. This section was followed by a discussion of forward, stepwise, and backward regression methods. The chapter presented a practical example illustrating the use of multiple regression analysis in social work. Finally, how to use SPSS to analyze the data and how to interpret the output and write and present the results of multiple regression analysis were presented.

PRACTICAL EXERCISES

I. Access the SPSS *Depression-Elderly* data file (appendix A).

1. State a research question predicting the relationship between self-esteem (**ESTEEM**) and gender (**GENDER**), age (**AGE**), race (**RACE**), sick (**SICK**), economic resources (**ER**), emotional balance (**EB**), physical health (**PH**), trusting others (**TRO**), mobility (**MOB**), cognitive status (**CS**), social support (**SS**), and negative recent life events (**NRLEV**).

2. What are the assumptions of multiple regression analysis?

3. Do your data meet these assumptions? Justify your answer.

4. What variables will you enter in the regression analysis? Why?

5. Use SPSS to run a stepwise multiple regression analysis.

6. Discuss and present your findings in a summary table.

7. What is the regression equation for self-esteem?

8. Jim (an 87-year-old white male) participated in the *Depression-Elderly* survey. Jim considered himself as a sick person. Jim's scores were the following: economic resources = 18; emotional balance = 14; physical health = 13; trusting others = 22; mobility = 15; cognitive status = 21; social support = 23; negative recent life events = 6. Use the equation in question 7 to predict Jim's score on self-esteem.

II. Access the SPSS *Depression-Welfare* data file (appendix A).

1. State a research question predicting the relationship between depression (**CES_D**) and age (**AGE**), marital status (**MST_REC**), levels of education (**EDUCAT**), physical health (**PH**), social support (**SUPPORT**), time off welfare (**JOB1**), currently employed (**JOB2**), and job training (**JOB3**).

2. What variables will you enter in the regression analysis? Why?

3. Use SPSS to run a stepwise regression analysis.

4. Discuss and present your findings in a summary table.

5. What is the regression equation for depression?

Appendix A: SPSS Data Files

DATA FILE 1: DEPRESSION-ELDERLY (N = 99)

This file contains data collected from a random sample of 99 people ages 60 years and older. Participants indicated their age, gender, race, education, marital status, and whether they perceived themselves as sick or not. They also completed the Center for Epidemiologic Studies Depression Scale (CES-D) (Radloff, 1977), the Rosenberg Self-Esteem Scale (Royse, 1999), the Life Satisfaction Index (Wood, Wylie, & Sheafor, 1969), the Iowa Self-Assessment Inventory (Morris & Buckwalter, 1988), and the Geriatric Scale of Recent Life Events (Kiyak, Liang, & Kahana, 1976). Table 1 describes the *Depression-Elderly* variables list.

Table 1:   SPSS *Depression-Elderly* Variables List

Variable Name	Variable Label	Range	Value labels
AGE		60–101	Actual age
GENDER		0–1	0 = Female 1 = Male
RACE		0–1	0 = Not White 1 = White
EDUCAT	Level of education	1–4	1 = Less than high school 2 = High school 3 = Some business/college
MSTATUS	Marital status	1–3	1 = Widowed 2 = Married 3 = Divorced/Separated
SICK	Consider self sick	0–1	0 = No 1 = Yes
ER	Economic resources	5–32	Scale (from low to high)[1]
EB	Emotional balance	10–32	Scale (from low to high)
PH	Physical health	7–26	Scale (from low to high)
TRO	Trusting others	13–32	Scale (from low to high)
MOB	Mobility	5–30	Scale (from low to high)
CS	Cognitive status	8–32	Scale (from low to high)
SS	Social support	10–32	Scale (from low to high)
ESTEEM	Level of self-esteem	18–40	Scale (from low to high)
SATISFAC	Life satisfaction	3–14	Scale (from low to high)
CES_D	Level of depression	0–47	Scale (from low to high)
NRLEV	Negative life events	0–11	Number of events
REV_SS	Reverse of SS	1–23	Scale (from high to low)[2]
LG10_SS	Log10 for SS	0–1.36	Scale (from high to low)
ZER	z Score for ER	−2.9 – 1.58	Scale (from low to high)
DEPRESS	Depression	0–1	0 = Not depressed 1 = Depressed

[1]Low scores indicate lower value of the corresponding scale. (The lower the scores in economic resources, the less the economic resources; the lower the scores in depression, the lower the levels of depression.)
[2]Low scores indicate higher value of the corresponding scale.

DATA FILE 2: DEPRESSION-WELFARE (N = 107)

This file contains data collected from a random sample of 107 former welfare recipients in Prince George's County, MD. Participants completed a number of demographic, health, and job-related questions. They also completed the Rosenberg Self-Esteem Scale (Royse, 1999), the Center for Epidemiologic Studies Depression Scale (CES-D) (Radloff, 1977), and a 19-item social support scale (Barusch, Taylor, and Abu-Bader, 1999). Table 2 describes the *Depression-Elderly* variables list.

Table 2:   SPSS *Depression-Welfare* Variables List

Variable Name	Variable Label	Range	Value labels
AGE		21–61	Actual age
GENDER		0–1	0 = Male 1 = Female
RACE		1–6	1 = African American 2 = Asian or Pacific Islander 3 = Hispanic 4 = Native American 5 = White 6 = Mix or Multiracial
MSTATUS	Marital status	1–6	1 = Married 2 = Single, never married 3 = Divorced 4 = Widowed 5 = Separated 6 = Living together unmarried
HOUSE	Any government assistance for housing	0–1	0 = No 1 = Yes
PH	Physical health	1–5	1 = Poor 2 = Fair 3 = Good 4 = Very good 5 = Excellent
HEALTH	Health in general	1–5	1 = Much worse 2 = Somewhat worse 3 = About the same 4 = Somewhat better 5 = Much better
JOB1	Time off welfare		Number of months
JOB2	Employment status	0–1	0 = No 1 = Yes
JOB3	Participated in job training	0–1	0 = No 1 = Yes
S_ESTEEM	Level of self-esteem	22–40	Scale (from low to high)
CES_D	Level of depression	0–47	Scale (from low to high)
SUPPORT	Social support	0–11	Scale (from low to high)
RACE_REC	Race (Recoded)	0–1	0 = Other 1 = African American
MST_REC	Recoded MSTATUS	0–1	0 = Other 1 = Single, never married
EDUCAT	Level of education	0–1	0 = Less than high school 1 = High school or higher
DEPRESS	Depression	0–1	0 = Not depressed 1 = Depressed

DATA FILE 3: GROUP DESIGN (N = 50)

This file contains hypothetical data collected from a sample of 50 subjects who were severely depressed. Participants were randomly assigned to four groups (Experiment 1 = 15, Control 1 = 15, Experiment 2 = 10, Control 2 = 10). Participants in the first experiment and control groups completed a depression scale before the therapy was administered (**DEPRESS1**) and then after it was completed (**DEPRESS2**). The second experiment and control groups completed the depression scale only after the therapy was completed (**DEPRESS2**). Table 3 describes the Group Design variables list.

Table 3:   SPSS *Group Design* Variables List

Variable Name	Variable Label	Range	Value labels
GENDER		0–1	0 = Male 1 = Female
GROUP	Treatment group	1–4	1 = Experiment 1 2 = Control 1 3 = Experiment 2 4 = Control 2
DEPRESS1	Pretest depression	17–29	Scale (from low to high)
DEPRESS2	Posttest depression	9–27	Scale (from low to high)

DATA FILE 4: JOB SATISFACTION (N = 218)

This file contains data collected from a random sample of 218 Arab and Jewish social workers in Israel. Social workers answered questions related to their gender, age, marital status, number of children, education, ethnicity, time at current job, and region of employment. They also completed the Index of Job Satisfaction (Brayfield & Rothe, 1951) and Correlates of Work Satisfaction (Abu-Bader, 1998). In addition, social workers completed a number of items related to autonomy and role conflict (Quinn & Staines, 1979), comfort (Quinn & Shepard, 1974), and workload (Caplan, Cobb, French, Harrison, & Pinneau, 1975). Table 4 describes the *Job Satisfaction* variables list.

Table 4:   SPSS *Job Satisfaction* Variables List

Variable Name	Variable Label	Range	Value labels
D1	Gender	0–1	0 = Male 1 = Female
D2	Age	22–62	Actual age
D3	Marital status	1–5	1 = Married 2 = Single 3 = Divorced
D4	Number of children	0–8	Actual number
D5	Level of education	1–4	1 = BSW/BA 2 = MSW 3 = PhD 4 = Other
D6	Ethnicity	0–1	0 = Jews 1 = Arabs
D7	Years at job	1–35	Number of years
D8	Region	1–3	1 = North 2 = Center 3 = South
MARSTATU	Marital status (Recoded)	0–1	0 = Married 1 = Never married
EDUCAT	Education (Recoded)	0–1	0 = Undergraduate 1 = Graduate
SATISFAC	Level of job satisfaction	39–85	Scale (from low to high)
BURNOUT	Level of burnout	8–49	Scale (from low to high)
TURNOVER	Level of turnover	2–34	Scale (from low to high)
COLLEAG	Satisfaction with colleagues	13–65	Scale (from low to high)
SUPERVIS	Satisfaction with supervisor	2–79	Scale (from low to high)
SALARY	Satisfaction with salary	4–35	Scale (from low to high)
PROMOT	Satisfaction with promotion	12–48	Scale (from low to high)
AUTONOMY	Autonomy at work	6–22	Scale (from high to low)[3]
ROLECONF	Role conflict	2–15	Scale (from low to high)
COMFORT	Comfort at work	7–25	Scale (from high to low)[4]
LOAD	Load at work	6–20	Scale (from low to high)

[3]Higher scores in autonomy indicate lower levels of autonomy at work.
[4]Higher scores in comfort indicate lower levels of comfort at work.

DATA FILE 5: PRETEST-POSTTEST (N = 30)

This file contains hypothetical data collected from a sample of 30 subjects who were severely depressed. Participants were randomly assigned to two groups (Experiment = 15 and Control = 15). All participants completed a depression scale before the therapy was administered (CESD1) and then after it was completed (CESD2). Participants in the control group received no therapy. Table 5 describes the *Pretest-Posttest* variables list.

Table 5:   *Pretest-Posttest* Variables List

Variable Name	Variable Label	Range	Value labels
GENDER		0–1	0 = Male
			1 = Female
GROUP	Treatment group	1–2	1 = Experiment
			2 = Control
CESD1	Pretest depression	18–28	Scale (from low to high)
CESD2	Posttest depression	12–28	Scale (from low to high)

DATA FILE 6: RESEARCH FINAL (N = 30)

This file contains the final grades in a Research Methods course of 30 graduate social work students who took the course using the old teaching technique. The file also contains the final grades of 30 graduate students who took the course under the new teaching technique. Table 6 describes the *Research Final* variables list.

Table 6:   *Research Final* Variables List

Variable Name	Variable Label	Range	Value Labels
PREVIOUS	Previous grades	40–88	Actual final score
CURRENT	Current grades	55–95	Actual final score

Appendix B: Welfare Survey

WELFARE SURVEY

ID #: _____

When were you born?

___/___/___

What is your gender?
- ❑ Male
- ❑ Female

What race are you?
- ❑ African American
- ❑ Asian or Pacific Islander
- ❑ Hispanic
- ❑ Native American (American Indian)
- ❑ White
- ❑ Mix or Multiracial: please specify: _____
- ❑ Other: please specify: _____.

How many years of education do you have?

_____ years

Do you receive government assistance to help pay for your housing?
- ❑ No
- ❑ Yes

> a. IF YES, What type of housing assistance?
> - ❑ Section 8
> - ❑ Public housing
> - ❑ Other: please specify: _____

How would you describe your physical health?

- ❑ Excellent
- ❑ Very good
- ❑ Good
- ❑ Fair
- ❑ Poor

Please circle the number for each statement that best describes how often you felt or behaved this way during the past week. (*This is the CES-D Scale.*)

0 = Rarely or none of the time (Less than 1 day)
1 = Some or a little of the time (1–2 days)
2 = Occasionally or a moderate amount of time (3–4 days)
3 = Most or all of the time (5–7 days)

1.	I was bothered by things that usually don't bother me.	0 1 2 3
2.	I did not feel like eating; my appetite was poor.	0 1 2 3
3.	I felt that I could not shake off the blues even with help from my family or friends.	0 1 2 3
4.	I felt that I was just as good as other people.	0 1 2 3
5.	I had trouble keeping my mind on what I was doing.	0 1 2 3
6.	I felt depressed.	0 1 2 3
7.	I felt that everything I did was an effort.	0 1 2 3
8.	I felt hopeful about the future.	0 1 2 3
9.	I thought my life had been a failure.	0 1 2 3
10.	I felt fearful.	0 1 2 3
11.	My sleep was restless.	0 1 2 3
12.	I was happy.	0 1 2 3
13.	I talked less than usual.	0 1 2 3
14.	I felt lonely.	0 1 2 3
15.	People were unfriendly.	0 1 2 3
16.	I enjoyed life.	0 1 2 3
17.	I had crying spells.	0 1 2 3
18.	I felt sad.	0 1 2 3
19.	I felt that people disliked me.	0 1 2 3
20.	I could not get "going."	0 1 2 3

Appendix C: Rosenberg Self-Esteem Scale

ROSENBERG SELF-ESTEEM SCALE

Below is a list of statements dealing with your general feelings about yourself.

If you STRONGLY AGREE with the statement, circle SA.
If you AGREE with the statement, circle A.
If you DISAGREE with the statement, circle D.
If you STRONGLY DISAGREE with the statement, circle SD.

1.	On the whole, I am satisfied with myself.	SA A D SD
2.	At times I think I am no good at all.	SA A D SD
3.	I feel that I have a number of good qualities.	SA A D SD
4.	I am able to do things as well as most other people.	SA A D SD
5.	I feel I do not have much to be proud of.	SA A D SD
6.	I certainly feel useless at times.	SA A D SD
7.	I feel that I am a person of worth, at least on an equal plane with others.	SA A D SD
8.	I wish I could have more respect for myself.	SA A D SD
9.	All in all, I am inclined to feel that I am a failure.	SA A D SD
10.	I take a positive attitude towards myself.	SA A D SD

Appendix D: *z* Scores

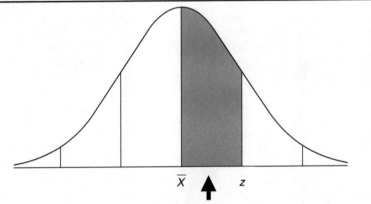

Area between the mean and *z*

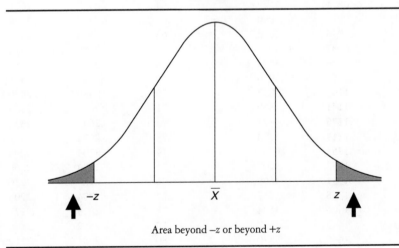

Area beyond −*z* or beyond +*z*

z Table

z (+ or −)	Area between $\overline{X}$ and z	Area beyond z	z (+ or −)	Area between $\overline{X}$ and z	Area beyond z
.00	.0000	.5000	.42	.1628	.3372
.01	.0040	.4960	.43	.1664	.3336
.02	.0080	.4920	.44	.1700	.3300
.03	.0120	.4880	.45	.1736	.3264
.04	.0160	.4840	.46	.1772	.3228
.05	.0199	.4801	.47	.1808	.3192
.06	.0239	.4761	.48	.1844	.3156
.07	.0279	.4721	.49	.1879	.3121
.08	.0319	.4681	.50	.1915	.3085
.09	.0359	.4641	.51	.1950	.3050
.10	.0398	.4602	.52	.1985	.3015
.11	.0438	.4562	.53	.2019	.2981
.12	.0478	.4522	.54	.2054	.2946
.13	.0517	.4483	.55	.2088	.2912
.14	.0557	.4443	.56	.2123	.2877
.15	.0596	.4404	.57	.2157	.2843
.16	.0636	.4364	.58	.2190	.2810
.17	.0675	.4325	.59	.2224	.2776
.18	.0714	.4286	.60	.2257	.2743
.19	.0753	.4247	.61	.2291	.2709
.20	.0793	.4207	.62	.2324	.2676
.21	.0832	.4168	.63	.2357	.2643
.22	.0871	.4129	.64	.2389	.2611
.23	.0910	.4090	.65	.2422	.2578
.24	.0948	.4052	.66	.2454	.2546
.25	.0987	.4013	.67	.2486	.2514
.26	.1026	.3974	.68	.2517	.2483
.27	.1064	.3936	.69	.2549	.2451
.28	.1103	.3897	.70	.2580	.2420
.29	.1141	.3859	.71	.2611	.2389
.30	.1179	.3821	.72	.2642	.2358
.31	.1217	.3783	.73	.2673	.2327
.32	.1255	.3745	.74	.2704	.2296
.33	.1293	.3707	.75	.2734	.2266
.34	.1331	.3669	.76	.2764	.2236
.35	.1368	.3632	.77	.2794	.2206
.36	.1406	.3594	.78	.2823	.2177
.37	.1443	.3557	.79	.2852	.2148
.38	.1480	.3520	.80	.2881	.2119
.39	.1517	.3483	.81	.2910	.2090
.40	.1554	.3446	.82	.2939	.2061
.41	.1591	.3409	.83	.2967	.2033

z Table (continued)

z (+ or −)	Area between $\overline{X}$ and z	Area beyond z	z (+ or −)	Area between $\overline{X}$ and z	Area beyond z
.84	.2995	.2005	1.26	.3962	.1038
.85	.3023	.1977	1.27	.3980	.1020
.86	.3051	.1949	1.28	.3997	.1003
.87	.3078	.1922	1.29	.4015	.0985
.88	.3106	.1894	1.30	.4032	.0968
.89	.3133	.1867	1.31	.4049	.0951
.90	.3159	.1841	1.32	.4066	.0934
.91	.3186	.1814	1.33	.4082	.0918
.92	.3212	.1788	1.34	.4099	.0901
.93	.3238	.1762	1.35	.4115	.0885
.94	.3264	.1736	1.36	.4131	.0869
.95	.3289	.1711	1.37	.4147	.0853
.96	.3315	.1685	1.38	.4162	.0838
.97	.3340	.1660	1.39	.4177	.0823
.98	.3365	.1635	1.40	.4192	.0808
.99	.3389	.1611	1.41	.4207	.0793
1.00	.3413	.1587	1.42	.4222	.0778
1.01	.3438	.1562	1.43	.4236	.0764
1.02	.3461	.1539	1.44	.4251	.0749
1.03	.3485	.1515	1.45	.4265	.0735
1.04	.3508	.1492	1.46	.4279	.0721
1.05	.3531	.1469	1.47	.4292	.0708
1.06	.3554	.1446	1.48	.4306	.0694
1.07	.3577	.1423	1.49	.4319	.0681
1.08	.3599	.1401	1.50	.4332	.0668
1.09	.3621	.1379	1.51	.4345	.0655
1.10	.3643	.1357	1.52	.4357	.0643
1.11	.3665	.1335	1.53	.4370	.0630
1.12	.3686	.1314	1.54	.4382	.0618
1.13	.3708	.1292	1.55	.4394	.0606
1.14	.3729	.1271	1.56	.4406	.0594
1.15	.3749	.1251	1.57	.4418	.0582
1.16	.3770	.1230	1.58	.4429	.0571
1.17	.3790	.1210	1.59	.4441	.0559
1.18	.3810	.1190	1.60	.4452	.0548
1.19	.3830	.1170	1.61	.4463	.0537
1.20	.3849	.1151	1.62	.4474	.0526
1.21	.3869	.1131	1.63	.4484	.0516
1.22	.3888	.1112	1.64	.4495	.0505
1.23	.3907	.1093	1.65	.4505	.0495
1.24	.3925	.1075	1.66	.4515	.0485
1.25	.3944	.1056	1.67	.4525	.0475

(Table continued)

z Table (continued)

z (+ or −)	Area between $\overline{X}$ and z	Area beyond z	z (+ or −)	Area between $\overline{X}$ and z	Area beyond z
1.68	.4535	.0465	2.10	.4821	.0179
1.69	.4545	.0455	2.11	.4826	.0174
1.70	.4554	.0446	2.12	.4830	.0170
1.71	.4564	.0436	2.13	.4834	.0166
1.72	.4573	.0427	2.14	.4838	.0162
1.73	.4582	.0418	2.15	.4842	.0158
1.74	.4592	.0409	2.16	.4846	.0154
1.75	.4599	.0401	2.17	.4850	.0150
1.76	.4608	.0392	2.18	.4854	.0146
1.77	.4616	.0384	2.19	.4857	.0143
1.78	.4625	.0375	2.20	.4861	.0139
1.79	.4633	.0367	2.21	.4864	.0136
1.80	.4641	.0359	2.22	.4868	.0132
1.81	.4649	.0351	2.23	.4871	.0129
1.82	.4656	.0344	2.24	.4875	.0125
1.83	.4664	.0336	2.25	.4878	.0122
1.84	.4671	.0329	2.26	.4881	.0119
1.85	.4678	.0322	2.27	.4884	.0116
1.86	.4686	.0314	2.28	.4887	.0113
1.87	.4693	.0307	2.29	.4890	.0110
1.88	.4699	.0301	2.30	.4893	.0107
1.89	.4706	.0294	2.31	.4896	.0104
1.90	.4713	.0287	2.32	.4898	.0102
1.91	.4719	.0281	2.33	.4901	.0099
1.92	.4726	.0274	2.34	.4904	.0096
1.93	.4732	.0268	2.35	.4906	.0094
1.94	.4738	.0262	2.36	.4909	.0091
1.95	.4744	.0256	2.37	.4911	.0089
1.96	.4750	.0250	2.38	.4913	.0087
1.97	.4756	.0244	2.39	.4916	.0084
1.98	.4761	.0239	2.40	.4918	.0082
1.99	.4767	.0233	2.41	.4920	.0080
2.00	.4772	.0228	2.42	.4922	.0078
2.01	.4778	.0222	2.43	.4925	.0075
2.02	.4783	.0217	2.44	.4927	.0073
2.03	.4788	.0212	2.45	.4929	.0071
2.04	.4793	.0207	2.46	.4931	.0069
2.05	.4798	.0202	2.47	.4932	.0068
2.06	.4803	.0197	2.48	.4934	.0066
2.07	.4808	.0192	2.49	.4936	.0064
2.08	.4812	.0188	2.50	.4938	.0062
2.09	.4817	.0183	2.51	.4940	.0060

z Table (continued)

z (+ or −)	Area between $\overline{X}$ and z	Area beyond z	z (+ or −)	Area between $\overline{X}$ and z	Area beyond z
2.52	.4941	.0059	2.94	.4984	.0016
2.53	.4943	.0057	2.95	.4984	.0016
2.54	.4945	.0055	2.96	.4985	.0015
2.55	.4946	.0054	2.97	.4985	.0015
2.56	.4948	.0052	2.98	.4986	.0014
2.57	.4949	.0051	2.99	.4986	.0014
2.58	.4951	.0049	3.00	.4987	.9993
2.59	.4952	.0048	3.01	.4987	.9993
2.60	.4953	.0047	3.02	.4987	.9992
2.61	.4955	.0045	3.03	.4988	.9992
2.62	.4956	.0044	3.04	.4988	.9992
2.63	.4957	.0043	3.05	.4989	.9992
2.64	.4959	.0041	3.06	.4989	.9991
2.65	.4960	.0040	3.07	.4989	.9991
2.66	.4961	.0039	3.08	.4990	.9991
2.67	.4962	.0038	3.09	.4990	.9990
2.68	.4963	.0037	3.10	.4990	.0010
2.69	.4964	.0036	3.11	.4991	.0009
2.70	.4965	.0035	3.12	.4991	.0009
2.71	.4966	.0034	3.13	.4991	.0009
2.72	.4967	.0033	3.14	.4992	.0008
2.73	.4968	.0032	3.15	.4992	.0008
2.74	.4969	.0031	3.16	.4992	.0008
2.75	.4970	.0030	3.17	.4992	.0008
2.76	.4971	.0029	3.18	.4993	.0007
2.77	.4972	.0028	3.19	.4993	.0007
2.78	.4973	.0027	3.20	.4993	.0007
2.79	.4974	.0026	3.21	.4993	.0007
2.80	.4974	.0026	3.22	.4994	.0006
2.81	.4975	.0025	3.23	.4994	.0006
2.82	.4976	.0024	3.24	.4994	.0006
2.83	.4977	.0023	3.25	.4994	.0006
2.84	.4977	.0023	3.26	.4994	.0006
2.85	.4978	.0022	3.27	.4995	.0005
2.86	.4979	.0021	3.28	.4995	.0005
2.87	.4979	.0021	3.29	.4995	.0005
2.88	.4980	.0020	3.30	.4995	.0005
2.89	.4981	.0019	3.31	.4995	.0005
2.90	.4981	.0019	3.32	.4995	.0005
2.91	.4982	.0018	3.33	.4996	.0004
2.92	.4982	.0018	3.34	.4996	.0004
2.93	.4983	.0017	3.35	.4996	.0004

(Table continued)

z Table (continued)

z (+ or −)	Area between $\overline{X}$ and z	Area beyond z	z (+ or −)	Area between $\overline{X}$ and z	Area beyond z
3.36	.4996	.0004	3.44	.4997	.0003
3.37	.4996	.0004	3.45	.4997	.0003
3.38	.4996	.0004	3.46	.4997	.0003
3.39	.4997	.0003	3.47	.4997	.0003
3.40	.4997	.0003	3.48	.4997	.0003
3.41	.4997	.0003	3.49	.4998	.0002
3.42	.4997	.0003	3.50	.4998	.0002
3.43	.4997	.0003			

References

Abu-Bader, S. H. (1998). *Predictors of work satisfaction between Arab and Jewish social workers in Israel.* Unpublished doctoral dissertation, University of Utah, Salt Lake City.

Barusch, A., Taylor, M. J., & Abu-Bader, S. H. (1999). *Understanding families with multiple barriers to self-sufficiency.* Salt Lake City, UT: Social Research Institute, University of Utah.

Bloom, M., Fischer, J., & Orme, J. G. (2003). *Evaluating practice: Guidelines for the accountable professional* (4th ed.). Boston: Allyn and Bacon.

Brayfield, A. H., & Rothe, H. F. (1951). An index of job satisfaction. *Journal of Applied Psychology, 35*(5), 307–311.

Caplan, R., Cobb, S., French, J. R. P., Harrison, R. V., & Pinneau, S. R. (1975). *Job demands and workers health.* Washington, DC: U.S. Department of Health, Education, and Welfare.

Carlberg, C. (2004). *Managing data with Microsoft Excel.* Indianapolis, IN: Que Publishing.

Craft, J. L. (1985). *Statistics and data analysis for social workers.* Itasca, IL: F. E. Peacock Publishers, Inc.

Crocker, L., & Algina, J. (1986). *Introduction to classical and modern test theory.* Fort Worth, TX: Harcourt Brace Jovanovich College Publishers.

Cronk, B. C. (2004). *How to use SPSS: A step-by-step guide to analysis and interpretation* (3rd ed.). Glendale, CA: Pyrczak Publishing.

Cuzzort, R. P., & Vrettos, J. S. (1996). *The elementary forms of statistical reason.* New York: St. Martin's Press.

Delwiche, L. D., & Slaughter, S. J. (1998). *The little SAS book: A primer* (2nd ed.). Cary, NC: SAS Publishing.

Edwards, A. L. (1979). *Multiple regression and the analysis of variance and covariance* (2nd ed.). New York: W. H. Freeman and Company.

Elifson, K., Runyon, R. P., & Haber, A. (1998). *Fundamentals of social statistics* (3rd ed.). New York: McGraw-Hill.

Fisher, R. A. (1915). Frequency distributions of values of the correlation coefficient in samples of an infinitely large population. *Biometrika, 10,* 507–521.

Fortune, A. E., & Reid, W. J. (1999). *Research in social work* (3rd ed.). New York: Columbia University Press.

Fox, W. (1998). *Doing statistics using MicroCase* (3rd ed.). Bellevue, WA: MicroCase Corporation.

Fox, W. (1998). *Social statistics* (3rd ed.). Bellevue, WA: MicroCase Corporation.

Gilmore, J. (2004). *Painless Windows: A handbook for SAS users* (3rd ed.). Cary, NC: SAS Publishing.

Glicken, M. D. (2003). *Social research: A simple guide.* Boston: Allyn and Bacon.

Hardyck, C. D., & Petrinovich, L. F. (1969). *Introduction to statistics for the behavioral sciences.* Philadelphia: W. B. Saunders.

Heppner, P. P., Kivlighan, D. M., & Wampold, B. E. (1992). *Research design in counseling.* Pacific Grove, CA: Brooks/Cole.

Hinkle, D. E., Wiersma, W., & Jurs, S. G. (1994). *Applied statistics for the behavioral sciences* (3rd ed.). Boston: Houghton Mifflin.

Howell, D. C. (2002). *Statistical methods for psychology* (5th ed.). Belmont, CA: Wadsworth.

Kanji, G. K. (1999). *100 statistical tests.* London: Sage.

Kiyak, A., Liang, J., & Kahana, E. (1976). A methodological inquiry into the schedule of recent life events. In D. J. Mangen & W. A. Peterson (Eds.), *Research instruments in social gerontology, Vol. 1: Clinical and social psychology.* Minneapolis: University of Minnesota Press.

McClave, J. T. (1991). *Statistics* (5th ed.). San Francisco: Dellen.

Mertler, C. A., & Vannatta, R. A. (2002). *Advanced and multivariate statistical methods: Practical application and interpretation.* Los Angeles: Pyrczal.

Minium, E. W. (1978). *Statistical reasoning in psychology and education* (2nd ed.). Canada: Wiley.

Montcalm, D., & Royse, D. (2002). *Data analysis for social workers.* Boston: Allyn and Bacon.

Morris, W. W., & Buckwalter, K. C. (1988). Functional assessment of the elderly: The Iowa self-assessment inventory. In C. F. Waltz & O. L. Stricklan (Eds.), *Measurement of nursing outcomes, Volume 1: Measuring client outcomes* (328–351).

Munro, B. H. (2005). *Statistical methods for health care research* (5th ed.). Philadelphia: Lippincott.

Quinn, R. P., & Shepard, L. J. (1974). *The 1972–73 quality of employment survey.* Ann Arbor: Institute for Social Research.

Quinn, R. P., Staines, G. L. (1979). *The 1977 quality of employment survey.* Ann Arbor: Institute for Social Research.

Radloff, L. S. (1977). The CES-D Scale: A self-report depression scale for research in the general population. *Applied Psychological Measurement, 1*(3), 385–401.

Roscoe, J. T. (1975). *Fundamental research statistics for the behavioral sciences* (2nd ed.). New York: Holt, Rinehart, and Winston.

Rosenthal, J. A. (2001). *Statistics and data interpretation.* Belmont, CA: Wadsworth.

Rowntree, D. (1981). *Statistics without tears: A primer for non-mathematicians.* New York: Charles Scribner's Sons.

Royse, D. (1999). *Research methods in social work* (3rd ed.). Chicago: Nelson-Hall.

Rubin, A., & Babbie, E. (2005). *Research methods for social work* (5th ed.). Pacific Grove, CA: Brooks/Cole.

Runyon, P. R., & Haber, A. (1976). *Fundamentals of behavioral statistics* (3rd ed.). Reading, MA: Addison-Wesley.

SAS Publishing. (2001a). *SAS learning edition 1.0.* Cary, NC: Author.

SAS Publishing. (2001b). *Step-by-step programming with base SAS software.* Cary, NC: Author.

Siegel, S., & Castellan, N. J. (1988). *Nonparametric statistics for the behavioral sciences* (2nd ed.). New York: McGraw-Hill.

SPSS Inc. (1999). *Intermediate topics: SPSS for Windows 10.0.* Chicago: Author.

SPSS Inc. (2001). *Advanced techniques: ANOVA.* Chicago: Author.

SPSS Inc. (2001). *Advanced techniques: Regression.* Chicago: Author.

SPSS Inc. (2001). *Statistical analysis using SPSS.* Chicago: Author.

SPSS Inc. (2002). *Syntax I: Introduction to syntax.* Chicago: Author.

Stinson, C., & Dodge, M. (2004). *Microsoft Excel 2003 inside out.* Redmond, WA: Microsoft Press.

Tabachnick, B. G., & Fidell, L. S. (2001). *Using multivariate statistics* (4th ed.). Boston: Allyn and Bacon.

Walkenbach, J. (2003). *Microsoft Office Excel 2003 bible.* Indianapolis: Wiley.

Weinbach, R. W., & Grinnell, R. M. (2004). *Statistics for social workers* (6th ed.). Boston: Allyn and Bacon.

Wood, V., Wylie, M. L., & Sheafor, B. (1969). An analysis of a short self-report measure of life satisfaction: Correlation with rater judgments. *Journal of Gerontology, 24,* 465–469.

Index